NILO Ha Tien

A Novel of Naval Intelligence in Cambodia

HL Serra

*For Ron —
Hope you like the story.
All the Same Navy. Cheers, Larry*

NILO Ha Tien
A Novel of Naval Intelligence in Cambodia
HL Serra

AuthorHouse™
1663 Liberty Drive
Bloomington, IN 47403
www.authorhouse.com
Phone: 1-800-839-8640

© 2009 HL Serra. All rights reserved.
No part of this book may be reproduced, stored in a retrieval system, or transmitted by any means without the written permission of the author.
First published by AuthorHouse 6/3/2009
ISBN: 978-1-4389-8754-5 (sc)
ISBN: 978-1-4389-8755-2 (e)
Printed in the United States of America
Bloomington, Indiana
This book is printed on acid-free paper.

DEDICATION

For all the men and women who served in Vietnam, to let them know what we were doing behind the scenes.

And especially for those who gave their lives in Naval Intelligence operations—Jack Graf, Ken Tapscott, Al Hollowell, and R. O. Williams, and thereafter—Jack Herriott, Giles Whitcomb, and Lee Entas.

And for Chris Serra, who relived these experiences many times with his father.

ACKNOWLEDGMENTS

For many reasons this novel took nearly 40 years to research and write. The list of those who contributed and influenced its content and style is probably infinite, but the following individuals deserve special mention:

Father Vin Haggin, Navy Catholic Chaplain at Khe Sanh, for the suggestion to write it all down; Josephine Serra, my aunt and family matriarch, to stick with it to completion; Irving Dilliard, 33-year editor at the *St. Louis Post Dispatch*, and novelist Joan Oppenheimer, for their guidance in the development of style; Philip Babb, my predecessor as NILO Ha Tien, for encouragement and for his superb photographs of the Ha Tien area; Captains John Rains, U.S. Army Cambodia veteran, and Patricia Miller Rains, for post-Vietnam adventures, for production, photographic, editing and publication assistance, and especially for their friendship through thick and thin; Crane Davis, U.S. Marine Corps Vietnam veteran, for his encouragement and construction of maps and the book's covers; Benjamin A. G. Fuller, CIA director of I Corps in Vietnam 1967-1968, for introducing me to the intelligence world; Captain L. W. "Bill" Morgan, N-2 Force Intelligence Officer, for having confidence to send a 24-year-old Navy lieutenant on sensitive missions into Cambodia; Frank Brown, of the U.S. Army's 525 Military Intelligence Group, for his comradeship and instruction in intelligence tradecraft; VADM Earl F. "Rex" Rectanus (Ret.), former Director of Naval Intelligence, for his comradeship and support; Buck Lanier, 20-year military affairs editor of Knight-Ridder newspapers, for his critical assistance and support; Wey Semmes, and Gary Blinn, experienced Swift boat commanders and authors, for their sharp eye for details; Professors Ben Kiernan of Yale and Larry Berman of UC Davis for their friendship, support and sharp eye for details; CDR Pete Decker (Ret.), former NILO Duc Hoa, CAPT John Vinson (Ret.), former NILO Tra Cu, and JR Reddig, editor of NIPQ, for their friendship and assistance; Ralph Christopher, fellow brown-water sailor and author of *River Rats* and other Navy in Vietnam books, for his encouragement to publish and tell a story unknown to most brown-water sailors.

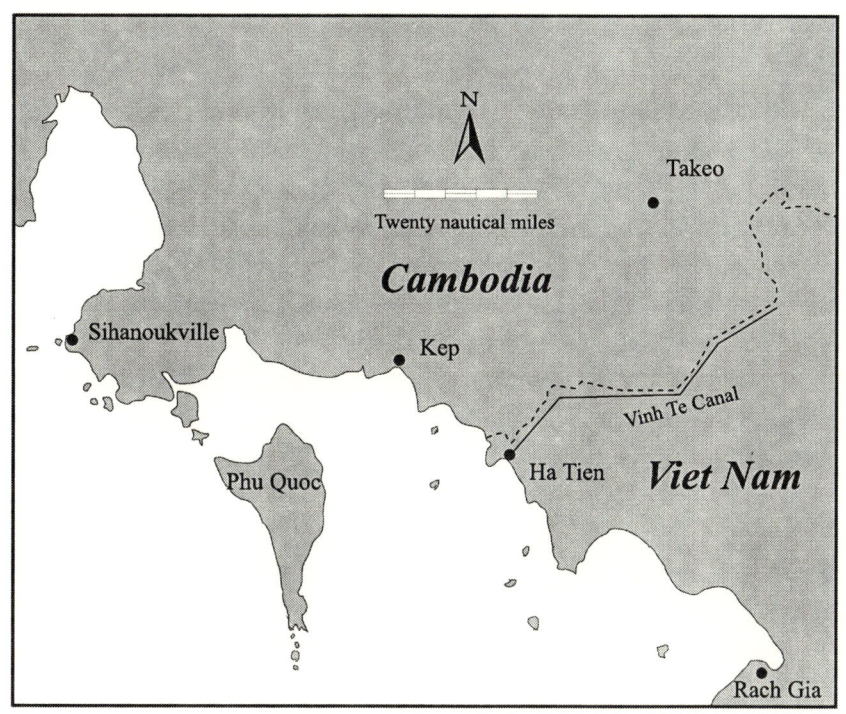

Sihanoukville, Cambodia, to Rach Gia, Vietnam

Introduction

The author was fortunate to be in the right place at the right time in volunteering for duty with Naval Intelligence on the Cambodian border in 1970 during the Vietnam War. This story is told as fiction for a number of reasons: To inject a textural and sensory feel for the places, people and events; to protect the innocent and the guilty; to allow the author a flight of fancy in undertaking the prosecution of a naval officer for his intelligence activities.

Virtually all of the events described herein actually happened, and the author leaves the reader to guess which did not. He will probably guess wrong, truth being stranger than fiction.

HL Serra
San Diego, California,
July 4, 2009

Three-headed palm tree at Ha Tien

1

Greenhorn

Frank Brown knew it was a Hook before he pulled himself from his bed to the window. The big Chinook helicopter, "Hook" to foot soldiers, circled Phao Dai twice. The wide blades PAP-PAP-PAPed as the Hook slowed and hovered above the big white H on the concrete pad.

Frank guessed the chopper was heavily laden because dust and debris flew 30 feet up the hill. The wide fuselage settled like the haunches of a fat man on a rickety chair. The rotor slowed and the rear ramp slammed to the ground. Two pallets of beer skidded into the dust, rocked on edge, then landed flat. The ramp retracted, the turbines whined and the big blades took huge bites of air, lifting the fuselage into a low hover.

Frank turned away from the window and pulled on his shorts. He glanced back when the blades abruptly changed pitch and the Hook dropped onto the pad again. The side door swung open and two overstuffed sea bags careened onto the dirt. After them came a youth in spanking new jungle fatigues and a black beret which trailed a black ribbon.

The helo lifted again before the door closed. The beret flew off the youth's head and bounced away in a cloud of dust like a leaf before an autumn storm. The youngster looked bewildered by the flying dust. He dropped his rifle, put his back to the maelstrom of the rotor wash and hunkered, hands over his ears.

"Greenhorn," Frank shouted, then laughed, as he watched the new guy brush himself off and drag his gear to the path that led up the hill.

Frank met him halfway. The young man had a dark but untanned complexion, wiry limbs, and a thin frame. He wore a short GI haircut and he had the blackest hair Frank had seen on an American in Vietnam. It differed from oriental hair only in the way it glinted reddish instead of blue under the tropic sun. Frank looked at the boyish face and surmised the newbie was an enlisted technician for the Army microwave station. Then, to his surprise, he noticed combat black lieutenant's bars on a fatigue uniform with tags that read "MEDICI" and "U.S. NAVY." A baby full lieutenant, Frank thought.

Frank studied the newcomer and guessed he was 15 years older than the kid, who was no more than 22. The lieutenant's brown eyes searched Frank's face with precise mechanical movements like a hawk's, taking in everything, resting finally on the oval of eyes, nose and chin, as if memorizing his features. The cold intensity of those eyes left Frank strangely uncomfortable.

"I'm Thomas Medici, Naval Intelligence Liaison Officer for Ha Tien," he said to Frank, and he held out his hand.

"Frank Brown, 525 Army Intelligence." Frank smiled and shook Medici's hand. "So we finally got a new NILO. Welcome aboard, as you Navy guys say. Let me help you with these." He grabbed a dusty sea bag.

They walked up the parched hill together. As they rounded the curve near the top, Medici started. A king cobra stood in their path, a 5-foot question mark balanced on its coil. Medici dropped the bag and chambered a round in his M-16, but the cobra darted with astonishing speed into the dry brush as he aimed.

Frank laid his hand on Medici's rifle and deflected it toward the ground. "Don't shoot into the hill. It's peppered with claymore mines. They'll blow in our direction if you hit one. Or a round might ricochet up into the team house."

"But the snake!" Medici said.

"It's okay. It's the cobra. He doesn't hurt anybody. He's very old and curious. He keeps a lot of Viet Cong away because they've heard about him and they're afraid."

Looking unconvinced, Medici ejected the bullet from the rifle and continued up the hill.

Frank said nothing the rest of the way. Medici unsettled him. The previous NILO had informed Frank that in a last-minute change Medici, a staff intelligence officer, had been ordered as his replacement. That didn't augur well. Staffers screwed up in the field. And Medici's quick trigger finger pleased Frank even less. He hoped the initial phase of John Wayne-itis would pass swiftly. He decided to keep an eye on Medici until he learned the survivor's creed: The less shooting the better.

If Medici were to grow as an intelligence officer, Frank thought, he would come to rely on his powers of observation and his sixth sense. He would discover the human brain's superb capability to catalog and store a mosaic of thousands of seemingly unrelated facts from which an intelligence professional detected subtle trends. But Medici had a lot to learn before he reached that point. Things like leaving the shooting to line soldiers. For the first weeks Frank would try to steer him away from the novelty and fascination of ordnance. Then they'd work on subtlety.

Frank Brown,
U.S. Army,
525 Military
Intelligence Group,
NILO's mentor.

NILO Ha Tien.

2

Welcome Aboard, NILO

When he reached the top of the hill, Medici put down the sea bag and looked around. He had a commanding view of the Ha Tien peninsula and Cambodia. Ha Tien, Vietnam. The end of the line. The last outpost before Cambodia.

For a moment he felt thrilled by the awareness that what he did here in these early months of 1970 could change the course of the war and affect the power and prestige of his country. The realization more than the climb left him breathless. Then, embarrassed by his grandiose thoughts, he inhaled, cleared his mind and got to work imprinting the panoramic view in his memory a sector at a time.

From the base of the hill, dusty brown flats rolled the five kilometers to the Cambodian border. Now late January, the dry season, he knew that by mid-April these same flats would flood with monsoon rains, leaving the thin dike roads, rivers and Gulf the only ways to travel.

The brown Giang Thanh River flowed by the foot of the hill and mixed with the jade water of the Gulf of Thailand like the first dollop of cream in a cup of coffee. The Navy patrol boat base floated along the riverbank, a flotsam of plywood, steel and dark green fiberglass. Upriver he could see ancient white stucco buildings with moss-stained orange roofs, a legacy of French colonial architecture which marked the center of Ha Tien town. Even at this distance from the village he smelled the rotting bales of fish whose drippings made nuoc mam, the spicy Vietnamese fish sauce.

Medici looked north. On the horizon he glimpsed the Cambodian Pirate Islands, placid blue patches that breached the green surface of the Gulf like giant whales. He looked along the coast from this hill, called Phao Dai by the villagers, and saw the Mui Nai peninsula, a single brown bluff dotted with green squares of banana grove which cut cleanly into the tropic water.

Then his gaze was drawn involuntarily across the dry flats to Nui Dai Dung (called "Nooey Die Young" by the river rats) Mountain, a forbidding gray limestone plug. The very sight of it caused a fear twitch in his gut. The mountain redirected the borderline between Cambodia and Vietnam. From it, behind the veil of Cambodia's neutrality, he knew the North Vietnamese brazenly trucked tons of Communist weapons in plain view of the Americans, to taunt them. Across the border beyond the mountain, in what must have been a trick of vision, Cambodia mesmerized him with a kaleidoscope of fertile colors from forest green to key lime, as if its neutrality magically kept out the dry season as well as the war.

He could hardly believe he was staring into Cambodia, Prince Sihanouk's gentle kingdom which tottered between North Vietnam and the United States in this chapter of the Indochina War. Cambodia—the target of his spy network, his reason to be here. His mission was to discover information to disrupt North Vietnamese weapons infiltration through Cambodia, without violating the country's neutrality. In Saigon the staff officers winked or snickered when they dutifully added the neutrality part. In his heart, Medici knew he must push Cambodia off the tightwire, whichever way it fell.

"NILO, this is Trung, your net handler," Frank Brown said. He gestured to a short slip of a Vietnamese with a face completely pocked from some childhood disease. "I'll leave you alone. Part of our spook protocol, I guess you'd call it." He got in his Jeep and left.

Medici led Trung to the team room and got out his map. "How did you know I was here?" he asked.

Trung smiled.

"Cambodia, Trung. I want agents in Cambodia. All the way to Phnom Penh. Up the coast to Sihanoukville. I want to know how, when, and where the Russian and Chinese weapons are shipped in, trucked down the coast, and infiltrated across the border. I want agents in Cambodia as soon as you can recruit them."

Trung said nothing, but nodded. He steepled his hands in a wai, the Buddhist gesture of peace, and left. Medici watched him putt down the hill on his battered Vespa.

Well, you wanted it and now you have it, the real thing, Medici thought. He sat in a folding chair and stared at Cambodia through the screen door. He leaned back and his mind drifted, recalling the improbable events which brought him to Ha Tien.

Fishing boats line the waterfront of Ha Tien district town.

Phao Dai, home base of NILO Ha Tien.

3

Staff Duty

Commander Carheart opened the slatted door with the blue plastic sign "Watermine Warfare" and strode into the workroom of his section of the Naval Intelligence staff in Saigon. LTjg Medici sat cross legged on the floor, staring alternately at the black-faced watch in his hand and the pencil-size brass cylinder on the floor at the far end of the room. To Carheart he looked as if he were deep in a yoga exercise.

"What's going on, Tom?" the thin, gray-haired commander asked.

"Just timing this Russian detonator. The North Vietnamese swimmers use it for mines up near the DMZ. We've had intelligence reports that the fuse times are unreliable, sometimes as short as eight instead of 15 minutes…"

"YOU MEAN IT'S TICKING?" Carheart screamed.

"Yes, 12 minutes so far."

Carheart leapt over Medici for the door.

"Commander, I removed the blasting cap and primer. There's only the spring plunger, acid vial and copper wire left. No chance of explosion," Medici explained cheerfully.

Carheart cautiously reentered, still puzzled, and stood next to Medici. The cylinder bucked and made a SPROING noise. The tiny steel plunger flew across the room and its sharp point lodged in the welt of Carheart's brown shoe. He gaped at Medici who calmly marked the elapsed time on a sheet of paper.

"Twelve minutes 48 seconds. Off, but not enough to scare swimmers from using them." He shook his head, then looked up and saw Carheart's bewildered expression.

Carheart bent and twirled the plunger from his shoe. "Are you still booked to go to the DMZ next week?" he asked. He handed the plunger to Medici.

"Yessir. They've captured documents from the 9th North Vietnamese Naval Swimmer Battalion. I'd like to review them myself before they're mauled by joint intelligence. If they contain any advance operation stuff, we can get the SEALs to interdict and throw 'em off balance." He paused, then cleared his throat. "There is something I'd like to speak to you about if you have a minute."

Carheart pointed to his tiny private office with a plain wooden chair placed next to the desk like a confessional. They entered and sat, Carheart in the tilting chair, Medici next to the desk. Carheart noticed that Medici looked pensive.

"Commander, I enjoy working for you and the staff. But there's something missing. I don't mind the long hours and the briefings and getting up at 4 A.M. to write the *Daily Bugle* intelligence briefing for the admiral. But I'm champing at the bit. It's hard to read intelligence reports from the field and not be able to get out there and take the risks and collect Cambodian intelligence by myself."

Carheart smiled. "Don't get upset. It's 'staff syndrome.' You young bucks are so revved up, you can't believe you're serving the Navy well by performing staff functions." He winced when he realized 'staff functions' sounded like a euphemism for bowel movements the way he said it. He added quickly, "You're one of the best watermine warfare officers we've had yet. You should take pride in that."

"What I want is to transfer to field operations, take over the Ha Tien agent post on the Cambodian border. I want to be a Naval Intelligence Liaison Officer. I know quite a bit about Cambodia, because I've read all the messages from the border and I speak French fluently. I'm a natural for the post."

Carheart frowned. He knew Medici wanted off the staff and he wasn't surprised. The jaygee had already spent a year on the gunline on the cruiser *Tulsa* and had gone in-country Vietnam as Tulsa's boat officer just for sport. As an adventure, watermine warfare paled by comparison to the border post. But didn't he realize that staff duty was SAFE? Little chance to get shot here.

"Commander, it's nice living in a hotel in the embassy section of Saigon, and playing tennis at the Cercle Sportif. But eating good steak dinners and drinking wine every night and going to bars is not

17

my idea of a year in the war zone."

"Tom, listen to me. You're needed here. Remember, you've only now gotten up to speed after your break-in period. I can't get anyone new in time to replace you. I don't see what…"

"I've already thought about that. Lee Menteer in logistics would love this job. He's already learned all I know about mine warfare out of his own curiosity. Give it to him. Then Commander Kease can order me out to Ha Tien. The jaygee with orders for the post is on his way. I bet he can be persuaded to take Lee's nice safe slot in logistics rather than head straight to the Cambodian border."

"No, Tom, I'm sorry. End of discussion." He turned from Medici and opened a file in front of him.

Medici walked back to his office, disappointed. He fiddled with papers for a minute, then thought, the hell with Carheart. He left the office to continue lobbying Commander Kease for appointment to the Ha Tien NILO post. Tricky stuff, this staff business.

Paul Kease appraised the young jaygee coldly, then scratched the wiry fringe of red hair that edged his bald head. LTjg Medici exuded enthusiasm for Cambodia and the NILO post at Ha Tien. But there would be a big brouhaha on the staff if he were pulled from the watermine warfare division. Kease didn't need any more enemies.

Since only Kease's division of the intelligence staff ever *did* anything, a jealous prejudice had developed against him and his NILOs. Admiral Zumwalt made it clear that his boat drivers and the NILOs in the hairy locations were to be given first priority for supplies, weapons and food. That irritated the staff officers who lobbied for special favors for their paper-pushing administrative personnel, who in turn would blackmail their commanders by failing to do assigned work properly if they didn't get what they wanted.

"Tom, I've got a meeting now. Let's continue this discussion over dinner tonight at the Meyercord. We can get a steak." Kease rose. "But I hear ya. You seem to have worked out a solution that'll keep the staff machinery working with Lee's transfer to your job. Let me think about it." He opened the door and stepped into the hall.

NILO HA TIEN

Medici followed Kease into the hall as Commander Carheart came out of his office. Carheart exchanged icy glances with them, then turned and walked down the hall to the bathroom.

Kease looked at Medici. "You may have created your own war zone right here on staff. I'll make you NILO Saigon!" Medici laughed, but Kease knew he'd made his point.

4

Got Job

Medici ordered a Scotch as the waiter seated him. The Army mess, a restaurant for officers atop the Meyercord Hotel, had the air of an 1890s San Francisco bordello. The garish red of tablecloths, napkins, and flocked wallpaper assaulted his eye. He mellowed with the peaty Scotch, pleased with his luck in getting as far as this meeting in his quest for Ha Tien, gateway to Cambodia.

"Earth to Medici!" Paul Kease barked and startled him out of his reverie of jungles and Khmer temples. Kease beckoned to the Vietnamese maitre d'.

"Got any Mateus?"

"*Da, Trung-ta,*" the smiling waiter answered.

Kease's ready smile, fringe of red hair and freckled face made him look like a jaunty teenager. Everyone likes this guy, Medici thought. The waiter returned quickly with a chilled bottle.

"How about a steak, Tom? Comes with baked potato and the works. Best deal on the menu. That's what I'll have. They do it up right here despite the whorehouse decor."

"Sounds good to me. Make it two. I've been eating at the crummy Army mess across the street from my hotel to save a few bucks. I'm tired of uni-gravy and mystery meat."

"You know, you won't eat well if you go to Ha Tien," Kease said. His brow furrowed. "Officially it's a small advisory team. You'll live with ground pounders and eat their miserable field rations." Kease watched Medici.

To see if I squirm, Medici thought. He didn't.

"Commander, I didn't come to Vietnam to eat well." He took a gulp of wine. Time to make his pitch. He drew himself up and looked Kease in the eye.

"Commander, I don't know what you know about me, but I think I should tell you a few things. First, I volunteered for duty with Naval Intelligence, although I admit the draft was on my tail.

Naval Intelligence has been in the back of my noggin for a long time.

"There's a family grudge involved. My father was a lawyer when Pearl Harbor was attacked. He joined the Navy and volunteered for Naval Intelligence. He was all set to go when Washington cancelled his orders, because they'd discovered that his father was born in Italy, and Italy was part of the Axis. So it's a question of family honor." He drank more wine.

"After I volunteered, I was surprised when I got orders to staff in Saigon. I kind'a hoped for embassy duty in London, but here I am."

"Fortunes of war," Kease said.

"I'm disappointed how boring staff duty is, even though it's important. I sit there in the attic every morning reviewing intelligence reports for the *Daily Bugle* and go nuts reading about the romance and danger of what goes on in the field. Especially at the places along the Cambodian border. Exotic names like Vinh Te Canal, Vinh Gia, Chau Doc and Ha Tien." Medici's eyes glazed.

Uh-oh, Cambodia-itis, Kease thought.

"I've painted a vivid mental picture of makeshift hooches ringed with sand bags and concertina wire and lapped by steaming green jungle. I feel it when Vinh Gia's overrun or a boat is ambushed on the canal. I can't help it." He shrugged and stared at his wine glass.

Kease stared at Medici, then his face cracked with a smile. "You had me going there. I thought you were serious. You've read too much Andre Malraux." He poured them more wine.

"I am serious. And you're right. *The Royal Way* looms in my mind when I think of Cambodia: mysterious jungle paths and crumbling, vine-covered temples built by Cambodia's ancient people. The idea of testing myself in that kind of environment excites me." He tossed down half a glass of wine. The fantasy stuff's working, he thought. Kease is buying all of it.

"Commander, I'm an honors graduate of Princeton. I speak French fluently and get by in Vietnamese. I was a fleet-qualified officer of the deck on the cruiser Tulsa before I came here. My C/O, Captain Hanford, asked me to be his flag lieutenant if he made admiral. If he hadn't died of a brain tumor...."

Kease knocked over his wine glass. The spreading stain turned the red tablecloth blood dark. "Hanford? Ed Hanford?" His good humor evaporated.

"Yes. Did you know him?"

"Know him! He was my mentor. We served on the Cyrus Vance mission to Cyprus. We put together a cease fire between the Turks and the Greeks, due to Ed's careful work. Best damn naval officer I've ever known. He died of a tumor? When?"

"Two months ago, before I came to staff. He had these bad headaches while we were under way. Went in for some tests when I was on leave. They found an inoperable tumor the size of an orange. Nothing they could do. I went to see him at Balboa Naval Hospital before flying to Saigon. He smiled and looked peaceful, but he didn't recognize me."

Kease stared. Medici guessed he was off somewhere in Cyprus with Hanford. His own emotions embarrassed him. On one hand, he felt bad recounting the morbid details. On the other, he was pleased that the Hanford connection was helping.

The sound of small-arms fire on the street below brought Kease back. The waiter looked down through the wire bomb screens and said it was okay, just some militiamen fooling around.

Kease stared at Medici, still unnerved. "He asked you to be his flag lieutenant?" he said quietly.

"Yessir. Told me I had my stuff together. I was looking forward to serving with him."

Kease tapped his fingers on the wet red cloth, then stopped. He said, "Okay. If you're a Hanford-trained man, you've got the job. You're my new NILO Ha Tien. I'll talk to Commander Holland tonight. We'll have a little mediation tomorrow to mollify your boss. You're my man."

Commander Holland slouched in his office chair and listened solemnly to the competing views, his hangdog face impassive. Carheart explained why he thought Medici should remain on his staff to permit continuity within his division.

Kease came out abrupt and blunt. He said Medici was the best trained officer to come through staff, he spoke French and

NILO Ha Tien

Vietnamese and really wanted the Ha Tien NILO post. He left out the Andre Malraux stuff. He said 1970 would probably be the "Year of Cambodia." He needed an exceptionally good and careful man out at the border.

Holland sat quiet for a long time. He called in his yeoman to verify that the ordered-in NILO could be switched to Lee Menteer's logistics job and Menteer to Medici's. Holland sat silent another two minutes with his hands steepled while the three men shifted in their seats.

Then he looked at Carheart and said, "Bill, I'm fully sympathetic with your desire for continuity within your division. God knows with officers here for only a year, the turnover problem's disastrous."

He turned to Kease. "But I think Paul's right. We need a handpicked man for Ha Tien with all that's going on in Cambodia. The intelligence from that post will be very important to the Navy."

He glanced at Medici, who sat between the two bosses. "I have to say I'm impressed with this young man. We don't get many volunteers for Naval Intelligence, fewer for duty in Vietnam. When one of our best wants to go out to the field to do his part, I think we should let him go if we want to retain him as a career officer. Young men need to fight wars, and this is the only war we've got." He looked over his glasses at the two commanders beside Medici. "And I don't see any of us volunteering for the post."

He folded his glasses, laid them on his desk and sat up to full height. "Tom will be transferred today to Paul's division specifically to relieve NILO Ha Tien. Lee Menteer will take Tom's spot in watermine warfare, and the young man ordered to Ha Tien will go to logistics to fill Lee's job."

The commanders nodded. Medici smiled, relieved that the staff politics were over. Somewhere in his gut a small knot tightened. They all stood. Carheart shook hands with everyone and excused himself.

"One more thing," Holland said. Medici and Kease turned. Holland reached into his top desk drawer and pulled out a small plastic envelope. From it he drew two sets of shiny silver railroad tracks, full lieutenant bars.

"Tom, you won't get to wear silver in the field, so I thought we'd frock you right now." He handed the bars to Kease, who removed Medici's collar bars and replaced them with the tracks.

"Congratulations," Holland said. "Far as I can tell from the officer register, you're the youngest lieutenant in the Navy. Good luck and smooth sailing!"

"Go over to see LTjg Kenck at the Cambodian Shop tomorrow," Kease said as they walked down the hall. "He'll brief you on the Cambodian situation and your mission." He paused. "Go easy with him. He also wanted the Ha Tien NILO post, but I thought you'd do better in the field. He already knows I've chosen you."

Medici barely heard him. He felt buoyant, as if shiny new lieutenant bars lifted him with each step. He'd done it. He was NILO Ha Tien, the Navy's spy on the border and, perhaps, into Cambodia. And a full lieutenant. He had known the promotion came with the job. For reasons of protocol the Navy gave NILOs rank equivalent to their Vietnamese counterparts. He hadn't known it would feel this good to jump ahead of the thousands of jaygees in the Navy. Maybe this year wouldn't be so bad after all.

Medici smiled at the French woman entering the gates of the embassy compound. She smiled back flirtatiously. He read AMBASSADE DE LA REPUBLIQUE FRANCAISE on the brass sign of the gate and walked further down the street. At the end of the embassy fence, he saw a shabby two-story colonial building. Its sign reported the names "ACME SALT CO., S.A." and "ABC MARINE," definitely cover companies for the Navy's Cambodian Shop. The shop had been installed here to keep its activities and visitors away from naval staff, as part of the charade that the U.S. Navy was not involved in Cambodian intelligence gathering. Every military and civilian intelligence service had an interest in Cambodia, and each adopted the convention of an isolated, disavowed "Cambodia Shop."

He walked up the tiled stairs to the door on the second floor marked ABC MARINE and rapped hard on the black enameled steel.

NILO HA TIEN

The peephole slid open and a watery, bloodshot eye assessed him. "Yes?" said a voice.

"I'm Tom Medici. I'm supposed to see LTjg Kenck. Commander Kease sent me."

The steel bolt slid noisily back, and the door groaned open. "Come in," the voice said.

Medici entered. Before him on a huge rosewood conference table lay a large Indochina map and a fat file. The door clanked shut. He turned to see a plump, pasty-faced jaygee in wash khakis.

The man had a nervous, jerky demeanor. His eyes darted with horror to Medici's flashing new lieutenant bars, then to Medici's face.

"I'm Kenck. I run N-207."

"207? We don't have an N-207 division," Medici said.

"Of course we do. It's the Cambodian Shop. We just don't broadcast it to every jerk on the staff," Kenck laughed.

Medici looked around. A small alcove near the door held a desk and, behind it, a padlocked armoire. Medici looked up and couldn't believe his eyes. Wedged between the top of the armoire and the ceiling he saw a life-size, inflatable pink plastic female lying face up, knees bent, thighs suggestively apart. Kenck's desk was covered with stacks of Danish pornography magazines. Medici looked at the man nervously, but could not find appropriate words.

"Let's get started," Kenck said, gesturing to a seat at the rosewood table. Long, blackboard-size map frames covered the walls. Kenck had draped them with blue cloth, so nothing could be seen but bits of map corners where the cloth didn't reach.

The guy really trusts me, Medici thought.

Kenck stood at parade rest in front of the table where Medici sat. "Lieutenant,"—he almost choked on the word, "you've been chosen to fill the most important field collection post in Indochina. I hope you appreciate the gravity of the assignment."

Medici nodded acknowledgment.

Kenck lifted the blue cloth and pointed on the map in front of him to the west end of the border between Vietnam and Cambodia. The name Ha Tien appeared where the border entered the Gulf of Thailand.

"A crappy little fishing village called Ha Tien is the peephole into Cambodia for our watchers."

Probably an NVA peephole into Vietnam, too, Medici thought.

"We have our own NILO there. Among other things he runs Collection Team 5, our spies for that part of Indochina. The Army has a detachment from the 525 Military Intelligence Group, guy named Frank Brown, with his own agents. Special Forces have *their* own intelligence officer with his spies. Finally, the CIA has its agents, not very well placed I might add, who are run by its people at embassy house in Rach Gia, the province capital. And God knows what agents the North Vietnamese have in place." Kenck walked around the table. "The place is crawling with spies," he said, pronouncing each word with emphasis. "Try not to trip over each other." He laughed derisively.

"Operationally, you'll report directly to the Chief of Staff for Intelligence here at naval headquarters, but your administrative boss is LCDR Plover, Fourth Coastal Zone Intelligence Officer in Rach Gia. They call him the Walrus, 'cause he's so fat, but don't let him hear it. Go through him for any support items you need.

"Your primary mission as NILO is to provide intelligence of a character useful to the Navy rather than other services. We have a river division at Ha Tien. The boats patrol the border along the canal and river during the day, then set ambushes at night." Medici leaned over the map and studied the serpentine border.

"Why? Because Ha Tien sits smack on the west end of North Vietnam's Military Region 3, the sector charged with infiltrating weapons and ammunition into the Mekong Delta from Cambodia.

"That's a lot of stuff. It usually comes into Sihanoukville, here, in northwest Cambodia." With a plump white finger he pointed to the map. "On Soviet and Chinese ships. The munitions are unloaded and split 50-50 with certain Cambodian military commanders, then the NVA's half is trucked down to the border for infiltration into Vietnam in small quantities. The smugglers have to travel by water along the Gulf coast or across the canal and river. That's where our boats interdict them. The tactical intelligence from your network will be important to the boat drivers. Try to tell them where and when the likely intercepts will be, as your agents report. Also tell them when enemy sharpshooters are in the area, so they can take the necessary precautions." Kenck lit a menthol Salem. Medici waved the smoke away.

"There's a detachment of Navy gunship helicopters, Seawolves, on an LST anchored off Ha Tien. The ship will provide your coded radio link to us. You won't have that luxury in Ha Tien, just Army telephone and voice radio. The Seawolves will provide you with visual reconnaissance flights when they can, but their main mission is to provide air cover for the boats. They're on 24-hour scramble. You'll probably have to brownnose them a bit and fly combat patrols if you want any help from them." Kenck drew on the Salem. Smoke oozed from his open mouth, up over his lip, and he inhaled it again into his nose.

"But the real reason I'm sending you out to Ha Tien"—Medici puzzled at the 'I'—"is because I think big things are about to happen in Cambodia. You probably know that Prince Sihanouk has adamantly asserted neutrality throughout the war, keeping us out and letting the North Vietnamese in. We've heard rumblings of dissatisfaction with Sihanouk among the populace, and anything can happen." He poked a pinky finger in his ear and vibrated it rapidly.

"From now on, we want more political intelligence from Cambodia, and you have authority to direct your agents deeper into Cambodia to get it. The North Vietnamese have used Cambodia throughout the war, thanks to Snooky looking the other way. Now, we want to know how to hit 'em where it hurts. You tell us where." He grinned, displaying yellow teeth.

"How am I supposed to find this stuff out?" Medici asked. "I thought we weren't supposed to go into Cambodia because of its neutrality and the Rules of Engagement."

"Right. The Rules of Engagement keep us out of Cambodia, except under hot pursuit circumstances." He leaned closer to Medici. "You'll never get a direct order from the staff, but it's up to you to do what you must to get information. That's what your post is about, Lieutenant. You are not to discuss it with anyone." He smiled. "You're gonna' *do* Cambodia, pal."

Medici squirmed. He didn't like a LTjg making suggestions like this, a back channel. But what could he do? Kease had sent him here specifically to be briefed on his Cambodian mission. And Kenck was right that it was up to the field guys to decide how to do their jobs. The little knot in his gut wound a notch tighter.

"You'll want to read all the present NILO's message traffic for the past year. It's in here." Kenck slid the fat file across the table to Medici. "You have to remember the emphasis was different when he went out a year ago. He's stayed on our side of the border. Mostly. Any questions?"

Medici shook his head.

"By the way, the team house at Ha Tien was attacked by mortar fire last week." Kenck smiled. "Only one Vietnamese killed. The NILO was unhurt. He's already in his 14th month of a 12-month tour, so I've called him in. He's on his way to Saigon now."

Medici coughed.

"So your turnover will be a little more difficult." Kenck laughed.

"Then give me some quiet so I can learn the file. I'll leave early tomorrow."

Kenck nodded. Medici started reading. He had a flight to catch.

The screen door of the team room slammed and Frank Brown stood over Medici. "Come on, NILO, let's get you moved in. Plenty of time to snooze later."

Embarrassed for being caught daydreaming, Medici jumped to his feet and followed Frank to his new quarters.

5

Morning

Medici threw off the thin blanket and sat up. He could feel the sun's heat radiating through the corrugated metal roof that sloped across the corner of his room.

He grabbed his shaving kit and towel, slipped into thongs and scuffed down the hall. The smell of coffee enveloped him as he passed through the team room. Three soldiers sat quietly eating breakfast, but he did not speak to them. The only route to the bathroom led through the team room, and he had quickly discerned that the team's unwritten code of etiquette forbade communication between those in transit and those at table. After he washed and dressed for breakfast, he would sit and greet his teammates. Now he merely passed through the room, invisible.

He exited through the red-leaded team room door, turned right across the porch, thongs flapping down the three steps to the bathroom. He could see heat waves shimmering from the flat tin roof. As he entered, the pleasing aroma of coffee gave way to the smell of human excrement. He braced.

Belden, the Army electrician, sat on the first commode like a sculpture meditating. His bowels let go in loose wet spasms. Medici placed his shaving kit on the sink and in the mirror saw Belden clean himself with rough rice paper and deposit it into a battered tin lard can. There wasn't enough water for the luxury of flushing the paper.

Belden walked to the enormous earthen cistern in which they saved their shaving water. He took a battered aluminum pan from the stack, dipped it deeply, filled it, then carried it back to the commode. There he flipped up the seat with his foot and from as high as he could reach, dumped the pan of gray water. The force drove his droppings up and over the trap to the cesspool.

"Bum voyage!" Belden said with panache.

Medici stripped off his olive drab skivvies and hung them on a nail over his green towel. The color already sickened him, olive this, olive that. Army stuff, not crisp Navy colors. He stepped into the small shower room with a bar of soap in hand and turned on the faucet. After a few seconds a small stream of water trickled from the fixture as if the rain god were urinating into the pipe.

For a moment, Medici thought of the cool, green tile bathroom in his former billet at the Le Qui Don Hotel in Saigon. Private shower, commode, even a bidet. It had once seemed inadequate by American standards. Now it seemed luxurious.

Medici shook his head, pursed his lips and leapt into the tiny stream of water. His scrotum contracted in a spasm from the cold water and goose bumps erupted across his back. He wet down, shut the spigot and soaped himself. They took minimal showers in Ha Tien because water was so scarce, and no one cheated. He braced to rinse off, tingling with cold despite the steamy day, then dried himself vigorously and headed for the sinks.

Frank Brown stepped through the door. "NILO, Trung brought some reports. I put them in your room in a sealed manila envelope."

Medici looked around to make sure the bathroom was empty. Frank's openness about the net handler delivering agent reports irritated him. "Thanks," he said. "I'll get them later."

Medici took an aluminum pan from the stack next to the cistern and placed it in the sink. A pitiful stream trickled into the pan from the single faucet, floating the residue of the previous shaver. He wondered if anyone was leafing through his reports. When an inch and a half had collected in the pan, he cupped his hands, splashed the cold water on his beard and rubbed energetically. The bristles rose stiffly in the cold water. He applied shaving cream, stroked down with his razor and felt each hard, cold bristle pull from the follicle as the razor caught and severed it.

He rinsed, refoamed and shaved up, then rinsed again and examined his work in the broken mirror nailed above the sink. His untanned cheeks looked blue, but smoothly shaven. Bluebeard the pirate, Bluebeard the NILO. He smiled. The Ha Tien cold water shave, he thought. You avoided scraping the skin of your face at the price of a high cut on the whiskers.

Displeased but resigned, Medici lifted the bowl of shaving dregs, carried it to the cistern and dumped it into the gray pool of water, foam and stubble. He tossed the aluminum pan back on the stack and walked back to his room where, after locking the reports in the armoire, he put on Bermuda shorts and an olive tee shirt. Adequately groomed, he walked back to the team room, smiled, greeted several teammates and ate breakfast.

6

NILO Routine

Medici sipped at his third glass of coffee. He sat at the table closest to the team house door, a vantage point from which he could see part of Cambodia across the border.

His net handler Trung had brought a sheaf of agent reports, identified only by the agents' code numbers. The stack lay before him, flimsy rice paper sheets next to his yellow legal pad and a ballpoint pen. The neat geometric forms on the red and white checked tablecloth pleased him, even though it meant a paperwork day.

He sat in the steel folding chair and bumped it forward to the table. The table's high top nudged him mid-pectorals. He rested his bare arms on each side of the reports. It was midmorning but already his moist forearms clung to the plastic surface. He picked up the first report, written in Trung's fine, lycée-taught, feminine script. He used "No." for number and a cross bar on the sevens. The report was unusually long.

> "Collection Team 5
> Report No. 70-34
> Agente 5512/Rpt No. 16
> 1200H 31 Jan, 1970

"1. On 28 Jan. '70 a Soviet ship, the *Minsk*, tied up inside the quay wall at Sihanoukville (Kompong Som), Cambodia and unloaded one-hundred sixty (160) tons of weapons and ammunition including AK-47 assault rifles, SKS carbines, B-40 rocket-propelled grenade launchers, 107mm recoilless rifles and 122mm long-range rockets.

"2. Cambodian Army personnel supervised and inventoried the unloading. The weapons crates were clearly marked in Russian and French, and were divided equally by the Cambodians into two separate go-downs. Numerous trucks bearing the sign "HAK LY TRUCK CO." were at the freight loading doors of the pier warehouses. (Hak Ly is a Cambodian businessman of Chinese ethnicity, a respected member of the overseas Chinese community in Phnom Penh, CB, and reported to be a colonel in the Viet Cong.)

"3. On 29 Jan '70 at 11 A.M. approximately 80 tons of weapons and ammo (six large truckloads) were transshipped via Cambodian Route 4 in Hak Ly trucks to Phnum Koki, Cambodia, then by local road to a North Vietnamese Army (NVA) staging area in a mountain with limestone caves near Phnum Sre Cham where a small river estuary enters the Gulf of Thailand. The remaining one-half of the weapons were shipped on Cambodian Army trucks to Phnom Penh via Cambodian Route 4. Other large stores of weapons remained in the warehouses.

"4. From Phnum Sre Cham the weapons were carried by cart and pickup truck to a Chinese Communist trawler, the *Hundred Flowers*, which had beached at high tide in the estuary. The Chinese name and markings were painted over and a Thai name and flag were installed. The trawler was loaded then dragged itself off the beach at the next high tide with a kedge anchor. It sailed south along the CB coast to Phnum Angkoul, Cambodia, in Kep District approx 5 kms north of the Vietnam border, where the trawler beached and was unloaded by approximately 50 Khmer Rouge (Cambodian Communist) soldiers. The cargo was broken down to small parcels which were placed in 30-50 Vietnamese fishing junks for night transport to Nui Sai Voi, Vietnam, where Viet Cong (VC) transportation units hand carried it to staging areas in caves around Hon Chong Mountain for use by VC units operating in western Mekong Delta and Kien Luong province.

"5. The transit from Phnum Angkoul, CB to Hon Chong, Vietnam occurs only when the transport junks receive an all-clear light signal from VC cadre stationed at the Vietnamese Regional Force outpost at Xom Cui hill (coords VS 480435). From the vantage point of the hill, VC observers are able to see north for 10 km, which includes the coastline from Ha Tien to Cambodian border. The all-clear signal (2 long flashes) in response to interrogation signal from junks (2 sets of 2 quick flashes) is given only if no patrol boats are maneuvering in vicinity of Ha Tien Bay and peninsula.

"6. Agent obtained this information from Cambodian port captain at Sihanoukville with whom he drinks frequently. The story was reported to agent to underscore futility of US/VN night boat patrols on the Rach Giang Thanh River and Vinh Te Canal. Port captain, who makes money reselling pilfered Cambodian weapons to VC/NVA, said the end run around Ha Tien along the coast was safest, large weapons infiltration to date. End of report."

Medici read the report twice. The detail alone lent credibility. The agent was a French-educated Cambodian businessman who imported foreign foodstuffs and spent his time in the port of Sihanoukville and the capital, Phnom Penh.

Medici himself had seen the light flashes the agent reported, and with a compass had triangulated their location to the top of Xom Cui hill, a Vietnamese Regional Force outpost. With night binoculars he had tracked the junk that sent the interrogating signals, then dispatched a high-speed river patrol boat to search and bring the junk to the town pier.

The boat was improbably empty after six hours of fishing. The blinking light came from a poor electrical connection, the owner said. Medici inspected and found a wire loop, painstakingly spliced to appear jury-rigged, which served easily as a signaling key, but which could plausibly be explained away otherwise, as the owner did now.

The bilges of the boat had been recently banged and scuffed by heavy objects with sharp edges, very likely the corners of new wooden cases of Russian weapons. The Vietnamese chief of police wanted to put the old man who owned the junk into "special interrogation," a euphemism for torture. Having seen its gruesome results, Medici decided they could not detain the junk and its crew any longer and ordered it released. To his amazement, the investigation of the Xom Cui Regional Force outpost by the Vietnamese command showed "no possible VC infiltration of the outpost."

Medici transmitted the agent report verbatim with a summary of his investigation of the lights. He concluded:

"8. NILO Evaluation/Comment: B-2. This agent has reported accurately with verifiable detail during the last six months. This report is consistent with previous information on the Sihanoukville connection and confirms personal observations of NILO. It suggests that the night boat ambushes on canal and river are effective to the extent that they cause VC to try end runs by sea, as in the report, or through the gap in night patrol boat coverage on the Vinh Te Canal."

Medici quickly read through the other reports. He found one on the local presence of an NVA boat ambush team, which he would tell the boat captains about in the afternoon briefing. Another reported that the North Vietnamese Red Star Transportation Battalion knew of the unpatrolled gap on the Vinh Te Canal, and were already setting up to move weapons through it to avoid contact with patrol boats.

Medici made notes on these, then walked down the hall to his tiny office. He seldom worked in the office anymore, since it reeked horribly when the midday sun cooked the tin roof it shared with the bathroom. The stench and heat kept him out except to get supplies and to plot enemy units on the large wall map.

He went to the wall map, demurely covered with a royal blue cloth, as if that provided any real security, and lifted it to write on the clear plastic sheets that overlaid the large-scale aerial map of the border. He carefully plotted in black the information about the Red Star Battalion working through the gap, and drew red arcs for the new coastal infiltration route from Sihanoukville.

With his foot he felt under the plywood desk and brought out a scorched coffee can. Carefully, he burned the original rice paper agent reports with a stick match, stirring the ashes with a fork. The burn did not comply with intelligence procedures, but he told Saigon burning reports was better than having them read or stolen by their Vietnamese allies with whom they shared the compound.

Medici picked up the message he had written to the intelligence staff in Saigon, walked across the patio, and leapt over the wall onto the dusty path to the river boat base at the foot of the hill. The squadron sent a daily courier boat to the offshore Navy ship, an LST, which provided the only secure teletype link to Saigon. He reached the bottom of the hill, crossed the clearing and helo pad. He entered the squadron's office, a plywood enclosure 10 feet square, with copper screening from waist level to tin roof. Red O'Brien, the squadron commander, stood cleaning wax from his ears with the tip of an M-16 bullet while he looked out over the river estuary.

"Hey, Red. Got some traffic for the 'T.' Is there a boat going today?"

"Jesus Christ, NILO, what d'ya think I'm running here, a taxi service? Already sent a boat today. You'll have to wait 'til tomorrow morning." Red turned and looked back out over the river.

Medici paused to compose himself before he answered. "No, I don't think you're running a taxi service. But I'm under orders to transmit my traffic via the ship using your boats as couriers." He spoke precisely. "I don't like the arrangement any more than you do." You red-headed cocksucker, he thought.

Red was much older, but only a lieutenant, so Medici tried to keep things civil between them, because he had to rely on the squadron for much of his transportation. He told Red the item about the Transportation Battalion moving into the gap in the patrol line.

Red laughed. He said, "No shit, Sherlock. Were you surprised they'd found the gap in the patrol barrier?"

"No, but two days is pretty fast to discover the hole and move the Red Star Transportation units, unless they have the straight skinny that relocation of those boats is permanent." Medici paused. "You gonna' run any boats along the gap on random patrol? You know, at least to keep them guessing?"

"No way, NILO. You know the arrangement: No boats move at night unless under fire. Keeps our cover better and it sure helps the morale of the guys on the river. We play our little game of 'You don't bother me, Charlie, and I don't bother you.' Maybe I'll send you out alone in a PBR to run back and forth along those 30 unpatrolled kilometers of the canal," he laughed. "They'd riddle your ass like a duck in a shooting gallery. I can't do that to *my* guys."

"You know they're gonna' come through the hole, Red," Medici said, spreading his hands.

NILO Ha Tien

"Let 'em come, NILO. It's not my problem. If Saigon thinks it's best to move a river squadron away from the border to protect a new base they built, that's their business. I have no intention of stretching my guys thin on the chance they can fill the gap. I don't want any more Bronze or Silver Stars here. Or worse. You dig, NILO?"

"I dig," said Medici, eyes on the horizon, absorbed in thought. A fly crawled languidly through his line of vision on the copper screening. "So there's nothing we can do about the hole?"

"Maybe." Red paused. "I've already requested a squadron of four river minesweepers to assist us. They won't cover the entire gap, but they'll help."

"Okay. See you at the briefing." Medici walked toward the screen door.

"Hey, NILO. Don't you have anything a little less obvious and a little more useful for my guys on the river?" Red spat through the screen.

Medici turned. "Yeah. There's a special North Vietnamese ambush unit in the area, commanded by a Captain Thanh. He's a sharpshooter who's sent around to train ambush squads and raise morale by knocking off a boat or two as OJT. He's supposed to be training guys in Cambodia right now in the vicinity of the Horsehead. He likes the bends in the river there, gives him greater surprise and escape cover. The fucker even wears little black silhouettes of PBRs on his uniform—one for each boat where he's made a kill. I intend to brief the boat captains on him this afternoon before they go out for night patrol."

"Is that all? Don't fuckin' bother about the briefing, I'll tell them myself. They paying you for this shit?"

"Yeah. They promised me just as soon as I take a round in the head, I'll qualify as a river squadron commander." Medici kicked open the screen door on the way out. "And I'm coming to the briefing!" he yelled.

Medici got his pistol and shot 50 rounds into empty cans he floated off the point. The assault of the explosions eased his anger.

7

Interrogation I

Medici jerked the Jeep to a halt in front of the National Police headquarters, leaped out and bolted up the steps into the open room. Old French maps covered one wall; disorganized sheaves of thin white paper covered with Vietnamese memoranda on procedures covered another. Capt. Thach, chief of Ha Tien's detachment of White Mice, the National Police, sat at one of two desks in the room. Across the room in a harsh wooden chair, his ankles bound to its legs, sat a tiny, apathetic Cambodian.

"The detainee?" Medici gestured toward the chair with his thumb and fist.

"Oui, Lieutenant. They caught him crossing the Vinh Te Canal last night and brought him here. We kept him up most of the night in an effort to find out what he knows. I believe he pissed his pants!" Captain Thach laughed.

Medici noticed the floor was wet under the detainee's chair. The odor of urine wafted to him as a hot breeze blew through the window behind the detainee.

"He is Cambode. Look at his skin."

Medici saw that the man's fine nose flared wide at the end. His skin was much darker than Thach's.

"What have you learned from him?" Medici asked in a whisper so the Cambode could not hear.

"He worked in Secret Zone III in Cambodia as part of the Red Star Transportation Battalion. The workers unloaded weapons and ammunition from trucks and hid them in a cave and bunker system the VC constructed there. He was helping move a shipment of AK-47s from the Zone down the small streambed near Ton Hon. They loaded six tiny sampans and pushed them across the canal between your patrol boats. The seventh overturned in midcanal as it glided to the south bank. Your LT. Bonavito heard the splash and started firing at the bank.

"They killed the platoon leader and found our boy here, Nuoc, cowering in the tram, shaking like a leaf. He's thirty-six. Hasn't had a very good life, and is too weak to be a soldier. The VC conscripted him out of the rice paddies at a nearby hamlet when they started to man Secret Zone III several years ago. Have a go at him, Lieutenant!" Thach urged. His tone said he knew his men had done a superb job in the nightlong interrogation.

Medici smiled formally at him. The son of a bitch did his job well and knew it. He had delayed summoning Medici when the detainee was brought in, to insure that the National Police had first chance to sweat him and would be first to report, an intelligence coup in a continuing game of one upmanship. Medici knew he would have to persuade Red to give him first shot at detainees.

Medici cranked the field telephone and called his interpreter Anh Duc who arrived on a bicycle minutes later. Medici asked Thach to leave, then shut all the windows so the room was hot, stifling, and dark. They switched on a bright lamp surrounded by an aluminum reflector, set it on the floor next to Nuoc, and aimed it directly at his sweating face. They carried one of the desks across the room and set it in front of Nuoc. Medici went to his Jeep and returned with a two foot length of inch-thick, hard rubber hose. He slapped it in his palm a couple of times and laid it on the desk, withdrew his .45 from his waistband, chambered a round, then laid the cocked pistol on the desk. Duc stood to his left within the circle of light, his eyes fixed on Nuoc. Nuoc stared beyond the cone of light to the darkness where he doubtless sensed Medici's icy glare.

Duc began the interrogation on Medici's command. Control was crucial in the social dynamics of interrogation. Duc asked Nuoc's name, place of birth, age, and his location before being captured. Nuoc responded very slowly, his voice heavy with fatigue, then with irritation at being asked the same questions for the fiftieth time.

Medici caught the tone of Nuoc's response, seized the rubber hose and slammed it hard against the thin front panel of the desk.

Nuoc lurched at the sharp crack. Medici burst into the circle of light and pushed Duc aside. He swung the rubber hose in a wide roundhouse at Nuoc's head. Nuoc ducked and the hose smacked against the wall.

"Answer more quickly!" Medici shouted in Vietnamese.

He stayed menacingly close to Nuoc and began barking questions at him which Duc translated rapidly and loudly from behind:

"How many men in your Transportation Battalion?"

"Almost three hundred."

"What's the biggest weapon you've seen?"

"Big mortar."

"How big? Show me."

"About the size of a big mooncake...."

"A 106 mm," Duc said.

"What size are the storage rooms of the Zone?"

"I don't remember—there were so many...."

Medici reached for the pistol on the desk and grabbed it by the grip. From outside the circle of light he whipped the pistol in an arc. Nuoc ducked hard, rocking himself and the chair onto the floor. The pistol barrel missed him. Duc stood the chair and Nuoc back up. Nuoc maintained an impassive expression, but huge tears of incomprehension filled his eyes.

Medici trembled with feigned rage and held the pistol high, poised to swing again, then stopped himself when he realized he was using the same "enemy" interrogation tactics the interrogators had used on him in Navy SERE School at Warner Springs. There, the "enemy" interrogators had used physical contact, sharp noises, waterboarding, black box and other techniques to break him to no avail. In fact, he had escaped and gotten a glass of milk and a Wonder Bread and Velveeta sandwich as a reward. He liked that thought.

Medici collected himself for a minute, then opened the windows to let in light and a cool breeze. He turned off the interrogation lamp, moved it away, and instructed Duc to bring the prisoner a cold Coke. When Duc handed him the Coke, Nuoc looked really puzzled, as if wondering whether it were poisoned. Medic gently took the Coke from Nuoc, took a slug himself, and handed it back. Nuoc smiled and drank. Medic walked slowly around the room, then returned, taciturn, watching Nuoc drink his Coke. Nuoc smiled weakly at Medici and nodded.

NILO HA TIEN

After a few more minutes of silence, Medici quietly asked "How big were the storage areas?"

Nuoc described the storage rooms, their size and orientation to each other in such detail that Medici guessed he fabricated some of it to please Medici. He described the largest shipments of weapons he had helped move and the quantity and type of weapons stored in the Zone. Finally, he located the Zone's entrances with respect to hills, streambeds, and Buddhist burial stupas on aerial photographs and maps Medici showed him.

Medici wrote quickly in his small notebook. Even if Nuoc's estimates were quartered, it meant that shocking amounts of Soviet weapons and ammunition had been stockpiled, far more than agents had reported. Now Medici had proof of the terminus of the Sihanoukville connection, and of the North Vietnamese's systematic violation of Cambodia's neutrality.

Nuoc slumped with exhaustion when Medici walked quietly out after two and a half hours of interrogation. Thach entered the room, puzzled how Medici had obtained a solid description of the location, contents, and operation of Secret Zone III, which Thach's interrogators had barely scratched.

Outside, Duc said to Medici "Dai-Uy. What's that English expression about catching more bees with honey than vinegar? I guess it's true."

"It's flies, not bees, Duc." Medici smiled. Duc had hit the nail on the head.

8

Hit Bad at The Bend

Medici knew it was bad as he came through the screen door. The acrid smell of nervous perspiration set his nerves on edge even before he noticed the tense silence. He was about to speak when a high-pitched voice crackled from the speaker of the secure radio circuit:

"LANDLOCK, this is PAPA ONE. We been hit bad at The Bend—Oh God!" The voice broke into sobs punctuated by the steady thudding of a big machine gun. "The engineman... Get some gunships!" The circuit lapsed into silence.

Red O'Brien, the river squadron C/O, stood taut against the plywood radio table, gnawing at the nail of his left ring finger. The bleeding quick spotted his upper lip with blood. He turned, eyes vacant, his mind with the sailors on the river, and seemed not to see Medici. The radioman summoned helicopter gunships on another radio.

"We have to postpone your intelligence briefing, NILO. One of the minesweeps just got 'bushed at The Bend in the river."

Medici nodded. He had walked across the dusty compound to the TOC – Tactical Operations Center – to give the daily intelligence briefing to boat captains heading out for night ambushes on the river between Cambodia and Vietnam. The air felt dank and oppressive in the windowless operations center. He went to the laminated map of the river that covered one whole wall. As he walked, the thin plywood floor groaned with each step. Studying The Bend, he tried to envision the firefight. His finger trembled as it traced the horseshoe bow where Cambodia was the left bank of the river, and Vietnam the right.

"Any casualty report?" he asked Red. He noticed his voice was hoarse.

"Not yet, but we heard the boom of a rocket or grenade."

The radio speaker crackled. "LANDLOCK, this is EAGLE

ONE arriving on scene and hosing the bank with suppression fire," reported a boat captain. "Don't see any muzzle flashes on the bank. PAPA ONE's headed your direction under his own power. But it looks bad from here."

"EAGLE, this is LANDLOCK," said Red into the mike. "Does PAPA ONE have any radio left?"

"This is EAGLE. I'll go alongside and tell him to call if he does. Over."

"If not, get me a casualty report on secure."

"Roger, I'll go—SHIT!" The boat captain's voice jumped two octaves. "They're shooting again!" His transmission cut out in a roll of automatic weapons fire.

"Jesus Christ, NILO, a fuckin' lot of good your intelligence briefings did us out there today."

Medici clenched his jaw and glared directly into Red's eyes, stopping him in his tracks. Medici remembered the laughter of Red and the boat captain weeks earlier when he reported that his agents had identified a crack North Vietnamese ambush unit operating in the area. He wanted to remind Red. Instead, he let his breath out slowly and turned back to the map. This was not the time for a shouting contest.

"LANDLOCK, this is PAPA ONE," called a voice on the verge of tears. "I—I have casualty report. I've got one..." he paused, "one killed, three wounded, two of them bad. Request Medevac." He sobbed.

"How does he know he's dead?" Medici said. "Maybe he's just badly wounded."

As if in response to his question, the green loudspeaker BOOPED again, beginning another secure transmission:

"Engineman took a B-40 rocket in the chest. Nothing we can do for him."

After a while Medici and Red walked outside the shack and stood on the edge of the hill. They looked upriver, waiting for the tortoise-like river minesweeper to reach the Naval encampment at the bottom of the hill. A sooty overcast darkened the afternoon. In a few minutes they saw the muddy bow wave of the minesweeper which the manual said provided it with an extra layer of protection from rockets. Red started down the hill to meet the boat. Medici felt as if he were watching a ceremonious Venetian funeral barge coming alongside the base.

Four seasoned sailors jumped aboard and began their grim work. The greenhorns stood around staring at the boat, hands at their sides. The sailors first helped the wounded to the medical evacuation helicopter that had landed on the pad at the other side of the barges.

Medici knew he should go down and examine the boat to see how the attack occurred. He also felt a morbid, almost prurient desire to witness the gruesome details of the death. But nausea and trembling held him to his spot 50 feet uphill of the sweep. He watched as the sailors carried off one, then two body bags, something small slumped in each. When the sweet smell of charred human flesh reached his nostrils, Medici vomited.

He didn't understand why they had dragged a fire hose aboard the craft, since there was no fire. Then a sailor came up to him looking shaken and said, "He just disappeared, NILO, nothing above the belly-button. Couldn't even find his dog tags. They said his name was Richardson. Just made third-class engineman. They've got to hose the boat. Burnt hamburger all over. The rest of the crew is covered with it too."

Medici walked back to the team house. His obligatory examination of the boat to analyze the attack could wait until tomorrow. For now, the events of his first day of casualties were enough. And the bastards had raided from Cambodia. Some neutrality.

The Horsehead and The Bend of the Giang Thanh River.

9

Night Watch on the Vinh Te

Medici opened the olive drab squeeze bottle of DEET insect repellant and squirted some into his hand. He rubbed his hands together and then slapped repellant on his face, forehead, neck and ears, then a second squirt for his forearms to the elbow and the back of his hands. The stuff smelled really strong. Where it grazed his lips it stung like a bite.

He looked out the window of his room and the sun was just setting over Mui Nai hill. Another forty minutes till dusk, so he'd better get going, he thought. He didn't want to delay the PBR's departure. He was their new NILO and didn't want to be late. He had loaded ten clips of M-16 ammo in a cloth belt and cleaned his M-16. Now he put his flak jacket and the bandolier over one shoulder, carried his helmet and 16 in the other, and headed for the path to the floating PBR base.

Tonight was his first night ambush on the treacherous Giang Thanh River and Vinh Te Canal that separated Cambodia from Vietnam for a 50-mile stretch. Each night Vice Admiral Zumwalt's boats left at dusk and set up night ambushes—"waterborne guard posts" in the Navy vernacular—along the river and canal to intercept any troops or munitions infiltrated across the canal from Cambodia into Vietnam by the North Vietnamese and Viet Cong. Only last year, Black Ponies—the Navy's OV-10 tactical aircraft—had caught 473 North Vietnamese soldiers (ironically from the 473rd NVA Regiment) out in the open in the Tram Forest just south of the border, and killed them all with machine guns in an industrial slaughter. The NVA's local guide had been killed by alert PBR sailors as he crossed last with the unit, and with no guide, the hapless troops wandered in circles or hid in the scraggly Tram to no avail.

NILO HA TIEN

Tonight Medici would ride with PBRs of River Division 532's two-boat Bravo Patrol, on LT(jg) Bomarito—"The Bomber's"—boat, along with Bosun's Mate third Watson, the coxswain, Engineman striker Pogue, Gunner's Mate third Tamarovich, and Seaman Angel, and accompanied by a second PBR, their cover boat. As NILO, he wanted to familiarize himself with the PBR's tactical capabilities, to better understand their operations.

Medici ran downhill along the dirt path that led to the ammi barges where the PBRs nested. He looked in the tiny, screened chow hall, but the sailors had finished dinner and must already be aboard the PBRs. He ran to the second float and found the sailors aboard Bomarito's PBR, the diesels idling. He stepped to the gunwale and said "Permission to come aboard, sir". The Bomber turned, laughed, and said, "Get your butt aboard NILO, we're ready to roll." Medici smiled and stepped aboard placing his gear in the corner of the stern.

"Not there, NILO," said gunner's mate Tamarovich. "That's in the stern gunner's sector to cover our tail. Move the gear forward." Medici complied. Angel, the forward gunner, squeezed by Medici carrying cans of ammunition for his twin .50 caliber machine guns, then stopped next to Medici, sniffed dramatically, and said "Jesus, Lieutenant! What are you expecting, an invasion of giant mosquitoes? You know the VC can smell this stuff 30 yards away." The other enlisted sailors laughed and Medici blushed. As they got under way he reached down to grab some river water, which he rubbed all over his face and arms to dilute the DEET smell.

The PBR cruised up Ha Tien Bay toward the mouth of the Giang Thanh River in the fading light. They traveled northeast between the narrow "Fingers," the skinny islands on either side of the river's fairway. Tamarovich grabbed Medici's arm and pointed to the northern most island and a tall Bael tree, the highest point on the island.

"NILO—that's the Hangman's Tree," Tamarovich shouted over the diesel's roar. "Navy guys hung some VC from that tree when we first started patrolling the border."

The PBR planed on its bow wave now at 26 knots and slalomed its way up the long serpentine loops of the Giang Thanh

River, past The Bend, where one sailor had been killed and five wounded the week before when an NVA unit ambushed his river minesweeper in one of the bloodiest events in a year on the border. They all remained silent at The Bend. Watson maneuvered the boat 180 degrees around The Horse Head, a deadly section of water where the boats completed a 270 degree turn, then found themselves at the flat grassy Ton Hon crossing point, where Cambodians and Vietnamese crossed regularly to the Cambodian market at Ton Hon hamlet. Run aground on the Vietnam bank they saw Mike 6, an olive drab Monitor Assault Craft, a Navy LCM landing craft refitted with rebar armor and a 105mm Howitzer turret mounted amidships. The river battle wagon was permanently on station at the crossing point because of the amount of night traffic along those paths.

The fiberglass PBRs slowed where the Giang Thanh River turned to the east and connected to the Vinh Te Canal through the locks at Dam Chit. As they approach the ancient French-built locks, Medici noticed the lock doors had been blown off and that the water level was quite low—it was the dry season—between the 10-foot banks on each side of the canal. Watson slowed then backed down as they reached the locks so Angel in the forward gun tub could toss a concussion grenade in the water. The grenade exploded with a big THWUMMP and pushed a wide muddy geyser eight feet in the air.

The Bomber said, "That's preventative medicine, NILO. The VC place command detonation mines at the locks to blow as we go through. If we throw in a concussion grenade it blows anything they might have in place." They all searched carefully on the banks for telltale wires of command mines, saw none, so proceeded through the locks to the canal. The boats' stations for night ambush were 2 ½ kilometers east of the locks, a kilometer apart, so they sped along the canal with eyes trained on the crests of each bank for signs of ambush. They passed some Vietnamese children fishing with hand lines at Cong Ca hamlet and waved them away shouting, "Di di mau!" *Run away fast!* But the children did not move and simply waved back.

As they approached their night ambush position Watson slowed and they examined the Cambodian bank for a slight indentation in the brush that would hide at least part of the PBR from sight. Watson expertly found a niche and slid the PBR bow into the north bank. He gave the Jacuzzi drives a goose to slide the bow securely into the niche for their night ambush. It was nearly dark now and Medici was feeling a slight unease, inklings of fear, in his solar plexus.

Watson slid over the bow in the last light, climbed up and over the bank to the Cambodia side and installed a motion and proximity sensor, which would transmit an acoustic signal to the earpiece in the boat if anyone approached the boat from that side of the bank. He returned to the boat, turned the unit on and offered the earphone, like that of a transistor radio, for Medici to monitor. Monitoring the low tone of the sensor, Medici vividly imagined a VC sapper inching up the other side of the bank with a satchel charge to throw into the boat and smash them all to meat bits, or to hit them from two sides with B-40 anti-tank rockets.

As darkness fell the night sounds rose. Medici was surprised how noisy the jungle was at night. He noticed that it was not the night sounds that brought the sailors alert, but the periods of complete silence when all the insects and animals would stop. Watson whispered to him that at any strange night movement the insects and animals would quiet, heightening the boat's alert status, since it might be a VC moving on the Cambodian bank.

After an hour or so in the dark the sailors stood their watches comfortably, making no noise. Their companion boat was a kilometer away and could not be seen or heard.

Medici was sleepy but wired, filled with adrenaline. His senses were super-heightened, his imagination running wild. He listened carefully to the low tones of the sensor for any accelerating pitch that would indicate movement on the bank. The feeling was odd, exhaustion urging sleep on him, adrenaline in his nervous system keeping him alert. He felt his eyes closing then jerked his eyelids up in a constant tug-of-war. He was impressed how silent the crew members were, guns manned, dozing but alert at the slightest sound. A frog or turtle plopped in the canal behind the boat and instantly all the crew members brought their guns to bear without a sound. Very efficient, very deadly. These river sailors were real professionals, Medici thought. It was amazing to him how in the combat zone men either got it together quickly or were moved back from "the line." There was always the line in a war, the furthest point out from bloated headquarters staff, the place where the rubber met the road and the probability of death or maiming was highest. And tonight he was there.

He thought of "Z"—Vice Admiral Zumwalt—who had come to the border a few months ago and ridden night ambush on a Swift Boat. Clearly against doctrine and statute—flag officers were not to needlessly expose themselves to harm on the line—Zumwalt did it anyway and boosted morale 1,000 percent among the river sailors patrolling the Cambodian border at Ha Tien. Zumwalt had his hand slapped by MACV and the Secretary of Defense for that caper, but secretly all the staff officers and sailors in the field admired him immensely for having ridden night ambush at the border.

Watson nudged Medici and pointed to the Vietnam canal bank 20 meters behind them. He said nothing but pointed to his ear, then back at the bank. Medici's heart pounded. Watson slowly lifted his M-14 7.62-millimeter rifle—its rounds penetrated the bush better than the M-16s—and slowly tracked movement Medici could not see, while the Bomber covered the bank with the night vision scope. Watson trained his rifle left at something moving away from the PBR toward the east, then stood quietly for a minute before lowering the weapon. He shrugged his shoulders at Medici and sat down again on the engine cover. Medici's heart slowed and he eased back to a slouch, repositioned the earphone, got comfortable and, without realizing it, dozed off.

He thought his obnoxious clock radio alarm was buzzing to awaken him in their home in Imperial Beach for early duty on *Tulsa*. He reached for the snooze alarm but hit the PBR's dozing enginemen. Then adrenaline shot through Medici and his heart pounded when he realized the acoustic sensor was signaling, and he didn't know what to do. He reached over and nudged Watson and pointed to the earphone. "Contact?" he whispered.

Watson took the earphone and listened intently, then rose and nudged everyone to full alert. Each sailor quickly and quietly sat up and took the safety off his weapon. None moved. Medici could feel the tension in the air around him. Watson gestured to Tamarovich for each of them to go over the bow, one each side, to move up the bank to get cross bearings on whatever was tripping the sensor. Medici thought they were crazy: why not just toss a grenade over the bank from the bow?

Watson and Tamarovich slid silently off the bow and edged up the bank 20 feet apart. Medici watched them with the boat's night vision scope, two solid white silhouettes against a grainy green background. Watson got to the top first, lifted his head silently, turned an ear toward the sensor, then lowered himself to the ground. He picked up a rock and tossed it carefully in an arc, and it hit with a thump. The urgent acoustic alarm peaked, then returned to its rest tone.

Watson and Tamarovich returned to the boat, laughing quietly. "Nice monitoring, NILO. You can even sense ferocious canal rats with that thing." The crew snickered quietly, and Medici heard whispered from the bow, "Fuckin' boot, NILO," then the boat settled down again.

The stars moved through the night sky. In a semiconscious state Medici noticed the constellations he first saw in the east were now well down on the western horizon. He looked at his watch. It was 4:00 a.m. and just a hint of false dawn showed in the east. The boat had remained quiet since the canal rat, except for the hourly "Click-click" on the PRC-25 radio, as the cover boat keyed the mic to signal all was well, and Bomber answered back with a second "Click-click."

Watson stood up, M-14 aimed again at the south bank he had scrutinized before. Then, from 50 yards to the east, a shrill human cry rang out, shattering the night. Watson fired eight rounds quickly over a 20-degree sector in the direction of the cry, and the cry ended. The crew was at the ready, guns cocked. Doctrine taught them the enemy would come from the north bank out of Cambodia, but in fact they were more vulnerable to attack from the south bank in Vietnam. The cries did not resume. The secure radio BOOPed, and their cover PBR asked if they were under attack. The Bomber said no, just a recon by fire on human-like cries, possibly VC crossing signals.

51

Dawn came quickly, surely. When it was fully light they retrieved the sensors, broke ambush and backed to the south bank so Watson could recon the area of the cries. With the PBR idling off the bank, following him slowly east, Watson slowly reconned the hidden side of the south bank, then darted down out of sight and emerged with a bloody parrot, the source of last night's cries.

They cruised quickly along the canal to the Ton Hon crossing after grenading the locks, and slowed as they passed Mike 6. The morning quiet was broken by the clear sound of the Beatles singing "Ma Belle Amie." It was a weird, quirky song whose rhythms and lyrics Medici did not recognize but knew he would never forget. The adrenaline of a night on ambush burned the song into his grateful mind.

They went alongside Mike 6 but its sailors waved them off yelling, "Be careful!" and pointing to an unexploded 106-millimeter recoilless rifle round wedged between their rebar armor. It had been a direct hit during a night attack but produced only a thud because the round failed to explode. The Monitor Assault Craft had lost her antennas to small arms fire, so they asked the PBR sailors to call Navy ordinance disposal so the crew could bring Mike 6 downriver to Ha Tien to remove the dud round.

The PBR continued downriver. Watson told Medici that the VC use birdcalls as crossing signals, and the unfortunate bird had a cry too much like a human voice. They passed The Horsehead and The Bend and approached The Fingers, the thin islands on each side of the channel leading to Ha Tien Bay.

"Let's sweep The Fingers and show the NILO the Hangman's Tree," Watson said. "There's always action on The Fingers."

The Bomber agreed and Watson nudged the PBR into the northwest island, only 20 meters wide. It was already hot. Angel stayed with the boat while Medici, Watson, The Bomber and Tamarovich spread out from the bow, M-16s locked and loaded. They swept through the gorse, then into deeper jungle. They could barely see the outer bank from the thick growth they struggled through. Watson said, "There it is," and pushed ahead toward the prominent

Bael tree. He started to tell Medici the story of the VC hanged from the tree in Ha Tien's first days of Navy patrols, but yelled and fell to his knees, slapping his back.

Medici froze. Was it a booby trap or punji stakes? Then he felt hot stinging pains on his lower back and began to gyrate. So did the other sailors. Watson yelled, "Fire ants! Back to the boat!" They ran swatting themselves, jumped on the PBR, stripped off their shirts, and brushed the red and black fire ants off each other, cussing them lustily.

"Guess we should have just gone back to base, huh?" Tamarovich said.

Vinh Te Canal and Cambodian border.

Swift Boat on Vinh Te Canal.

NILO Ha Tien

PBR setting ambush.

10

Interrogation II

BM3 Perle shouted as he came through the team house door. "NILO. We caught us an NVA soldier straight outta' Cambodia! He's a tough little rat. Hasn't said a word to Blume or anybody since we caught him two hours ago. You wanna' put bamboo splinters under his fingernails or whatever you do to make him talk?"

"Where is he, Perle?" Medici said. He reached for his fatigue top and M-16.

"We got him tied up to a post near the CONEX boxes against the side of the hill. Want us to bring him up here?"

"No, leave him there, but let him know 'the interrogator' will be around to see him. Got that?"

"Roger, NILO." Perle left.

Instead of walking down the path, Medici woke Duc to be driven formally down the hill to the Navy base, in a way that the NVA prisoner would notice. As they drove downhill in the dusk, Medici instructed Duc to aim the Jeep's bright headlights at the NVA. Duc obliged. He drove fast, halted six feet in front of the NVA, and temporarily blinded him with the lights. Medici thought he whiffed burnt meat from the MSR ambush.

He stepped out, grabbed his M-16, clattered in a banana clip, dismissed the Navy guard and examined the NVA from a distance behind the headlights' glare. The NVA squatted in a ball, arms wrapped around his knees. His bare feet were horny and gnarled from a life of carrying heavy loads without shoes. He was old for a foot soldier, about twenty-four; the newest draftees from Hanoi were teenagers. His gear lay in front of him, beyond his tethered reach: a bandolero of AK rounds; a long, continuous cloth tube with several pounds of short-grained rice; a small canvas kit with vials of French morphine and Chinese malaria medicine; an enameled tin rice bowl with an M-16 hole through it. A near miss. He was lucky not to have been killed. His AK-47 had already been taken as a souvenir by a sailor, Medici guessed. Medici walked around to the side and noticed nine small black patrol boat silhouettes on the man's uniform sleeve. So Captain Thanh's unit had esprit de corps, after the MSR ambush. Medici grinned and tightened his fist on the grip of the M-16.

"What's your name?" Duc translated.

No response.

"Where did you come from in the north?"

No response. The NVA squinted into the glare of the headlights, tilting his head from side to side at Medici, then Duc.

"You're part of Captain Thanh's ambush unit, aren't you?"

The man's eyes widened, but he remained silent.

"Tell him I will shoot the toes off his right foot one by one if he doesn't answer now," Medici said very softly. As Duc translated, Medici chambered a bullet.

The soldier remained silent. Medici walked between the light and the NVA, covering him with shadow. He stood before him for a moment, then put the tip of the barrel above the little toe of the NVA's right foot. The man remained impassive.

Medici felt anger that the detainee remained cool when faced with the threat of maiming. His heart beat faster. He angled the 16 slightly off the toe and fired one round into the dirt. The NVA blinked, but remained expressionless as rocks and dust dropped around them. The sailors at the base scrambled for their weapons at the sound of the gunshot.

Now Medici actually smelled the charred meat of the MSR ambush. His gut churned. Incensed, he strained for control to stop himself from shooting the first toe. Instead he swung the hot barrel of the M-16 in a roundhouse at the NVA's head and heard it clunk. The man rolled to the ground nearly unconscious.

"That's for the ambush," Medici gritted. "Let's go." A river sailor called a corpsman for the NVA while Medici sat erect in the Jeep, waiting as Duc started the engine and drove him up the hill.

That night Medici awoke from a vivid nightmare. He was interrogating the NVA, but instead of striking him, he slid the barrel over the toe and pulled the trigger. Dust and rocks flew, and the rifle's report gave way to a roaring wail of pain from the soldier. Medici sweated in a frenzy of excitement. He backed away to let the headlights fall on the NVA. The man had curled in a ball on the ground, squeezing his right foot with both hands to stop the bleeding. The toe and two inches of bone, flesh and gristle around it were gone. White sinew and bone protruded from the wounds. Medici looked at the man's watery eyes. They showed agony and pain but no fear.

    Medici awoke awash in sweat, nauseous, and trembling with disgust. He got up and drank a beer, sat on the patio wall and stared for a long time at the black Gulf.

11

Sai Thom

Sai Thom saw Kenck stop at the end of the bar and order the usual, a syrup-sweet mai tai. Even from a distance, his flabby pectorals appeared larger than her breasts and tugged at the buttons of his tailored wash khaki shirt. Every night at eight, he came into the Jade Gate and ordered mai tais, drank until he was numb, then slobbered and fawned over the girls until Sai Thom took him upstairs for a short time. He would pass out until 4 a.m. then drag himself back to the Le Qui Don Hotel, his billet. Months ago the girls had told her he bragged that he was Mr. Cambodia, in charge of Naval Intelligence operations there. He talked about his Cambodian "Shop," an office in an old building near the French Embassy in Saigon.

At first Sai Thom dismissed the talk as drunken prattle. After too many drinks GIs thought themselves important. But she reported the remark dutifully to Vo in Manila, and he followed up with inquiries for her about Kenck. Vo, even then aware of the tenuousness of North Vietnam's free run of Cambodia, sensed a rich opportunity. He ordered Sai Thom to establish herself as Kenck's permanent woman, to encourage his ambivalent feelings about the war, and to play on his ego. Vo expected Sihanouk to be deposed, NVA activities to be curtailed, and weapons shipments to stop in Cambodia. Then, Kenck's American intelligence on Cambodia would be invaluable.

Early on, Sai Thom elicited only smatterings of information from Kenck when he was drunk. Then all at once he grew more alienated from his country's cause, when another naval officer got the field post for which Kenck had volunteered in a fit of bravado.

Sai Thom sensed opportunity in his anger. He dwelled bitterly on the successes of the new field officer, at what rightfully should have been *his* spy post. He concocted unnecessarily dangerous missions for the field man in the hope that he would be killed or captured, giving Kenck another chance at the post. But the plan backfired. The man performed each mission better than the last and secured a reputation as a first-rate field officer.

"Sai Thom, my flower. I've missed your warmth," Kenck said. He stuck his hand in her crotch, then kneaded it through the silk of her ao-dai.

"Aiee! My big Trung Uy. I miss you, too. We go your flat?" She grinned. "I know I make you feel numbah one tonight." His sweet pineapple breath nauseated her.

He pouted. "Only if Jennifer can come, too. I have plenty of love for her and you tonight." He patted his protruding lower abdomen.

Sai Thom moistened her lips with her tongue and nodded. She fought to contain the disgust. Each time he brought the revolting inflatable doll to their couplings, she thought she could take no more. She bridled at providing sex and fawning obedience to this degenerate American. Lying in bed with him and the doll, while he alternately fornicated with it, then her, stretched to the limit her sense of discipline and duty to her people. When he mounted her, she could only grimace and focus her mind's eye on her parents in Haiphong who had proudly watched her receive the order of Ho Chi Minh for her secret activities against Saigon. She smiled at Kenck and tickled his palm with her finger.

He nuzzled her soft neck. "I think sometime I must visit Vo myself," he said. "A trip to Manila would be nice."

Her eyes widened.

12

Navy Fire Team

"Yo! You the new NILO?" A paunchy warrant officer with a huge hooked nose bellowed the greeting.

"Yeah. I'm Tom Medici." He sat up in his bunk. "What do you want?" He blinked his sticky eyes, rubbed them with his fingers and tried to focus. He crawled out from the thin camouflage blanket and sat on the edge of his bunk in skivvies.

"Sorry to bug you so early, NILO, but I just came over from An Thoi. Have to leave as soon as the boat's ready to go. I'm Stan Zablocki. Used to be stationed here until about a month ago, when I decided to transfer myself over to the island. When I arrived here we were mortared on Christmas Eve. When I went to An Thoi they got mortared for the first time ever! Heh heh. They call me trouble with a capital 'T.'"

"Then get the fuck out of here and back to An Thoi. We don't need any mortaring, thanks," Medici said. They laughed. Zablocki's enthusiasm and humor appealed to Medici, despite the man's annoying Philadelphia whine. He began talking a mile a minute from the side of his mouth.

"No, NILO, that's wrong. A little pot stirring is what the VC really need here. They get away with murder on the Ha Tien peninsula. They've killed our guys and infiltrated huge amounts of weapons from inside Cambodia, and we can't touch them. They know we walk on eggshells 'cause they can overrun us so easy, and we can't shoot at them or interfere because of Cambodian neutrality and our Rules of Engagement. I have with me exactly what Ha Tien needs. The right medicine from Doctor Zablocki."

Medici laughed again. Zablocki should be peddling snake oil from the back of a wagon, he thought.

"Why do I feel like I'm about to buy a pig in a poke?" Medici said. He stood, pulled on a pair of Bermudas and followed Stan through the dayroom to see what he had brought.

They walked down the brick steps to Zablocki's Jeep. In the back seat lay a worn 81mm mortar tube, the letters "9th ARVN Div" barely visible where someone had tried to file them off. The heavy baseplate was strapped to the Jeep's hood.

"This is just what we need? Look over there behind the cyclone fence, Stan. That's a 4.2-inch mortar the militiamen use. It nearly blows us off the shitter, it's so goddam big. What do we need this popgun for?"

"Ah, Lieutenant, thought you'd never ask. I worried for a moment that you were mentally slower than your predecessor, but your question shows there's hope." He paused. "Why the mortar? Navy fire team. I say again, Navy fire team!"

"Stan, what do you think our boats are doing on river ambush every night? Camping for merit badges?"

"That's tactical, NILO. I'm talkin' strategic. Remember, the four deuce can only reach the Vietnam side of the bad guys' staging area, Nooey Die Young Mountain. You have flown the back side already, I presume. The flat staging area and caves where they store the good stuff are inaccessible to the 4.2 mortar at this distance. The boats can't get anywhere near the mountain. Hence, the VC do what they damn well please with their supply shipments on the Ha Tien peninsula."

Stan smiled. "Until now. I've talked to some of the Navy guys and they'd like to embarrass our milk toast Army brethren. We'll set up at various places on the peninsula during the day, draw some enemy fire, then use the mortar for suppression fire to hammer the shit out of the VC staging area behind Die Young like they've never been hammered before!"

Medici considered his words. For all his hype, Stan was right. The U.S. forces, such as they were, existed in Ha Tien solely to stop the NVA's shipment of weapons and supplies from Cambodia to Vietnam. But the Navy's interdiction effort had reduced the Army's activity to zero. And the 30-kilometer hole in the Navy's patrol barrier on the Vinh Te Canal was large enough to slip the Queen Mary through without detection. Yet here at the border, hidden behind Die Young Mountain, lay the major staging area for the infiltration of war materials into the Mekong Delta. Chinese and Soviet ships brought enormous loads of weapons and ammo into Sihanoukville, Cambodia's only deepwater port, and Hak Ly, a Chinese with the rank of colonel in the Viet Cong, trucked them down to the border to Nooey Die Young once a week. At night, from the team house patio, Medici watched the headlights of Hak Ly's trucks pull into Die Young.

The Rules of Engagement prohibited artillery and aircraft fire into Cambodia, unless enemy units fired first, and the convoys could not be taken under fire without provocation.

The Army's aircraft were located at Can Tho, the capital of the delta, a useless two-hour flight time away. The Navy Seawolf gunships were under orders to support naval units engaged in firefights on the Vinh Te Canal.

The cunning of the NVA supply operation became irritatingly clear to Medici. As long as no provocation of U.S. forces occurred during the truck shipments, they were home free. Zablocki had figured this out for himself and had conceived a plan to hit them in their staging area at the border. All the fire team had to do was provoke some enemy fire, then mortar the shit out of the Die Young staging area, arguably as suppression fire permitted under the Rules of Engagement.

The plan blossomed in Medici's mind beyond the Navy fire team to potentially larger operations. If they could draw fire when aircraft or a Navy ship was around, they could drop some big stuff into the staging area. The variations were limitless and technically didn't violate the Rules of Engagement if they first received hostile fire each time, even if they provoked it, as long as they didn't fire first into Cambodia. And besides, he thought, they could fudge a little now since the standing truce had been broken when Capt. Thanh had ambushed the MSR from the Cambodian side of the border and killed a sailor. Fair is fair.

Medici smiled slowly. "Stan, you one smart dude. You figured out exactly how to hurt their supply effort from Cambodia. I'm gonna call you the 'Strategic Polack.'"

"As long as I get to go along on these fire team missions, you can call me anything you want." Zablocki grinned.

"Let's hide the mortar before the major asks questions,"

Medici said. He looked to ensure the major was not around, and they carried the heavy baseplate and tube to the generator shed.

The following week Zablocki rode a Mike boat from An Thoi to Ha Tien and brought 20 cases of 81mm mortar ammo, high-explosive, incendiary, and shrapnel rounds. They loaded two cases of each into Medici's Jeep with the big yellow NILO letters on the windscreen and retrieved the mortar and baseplate from the generator shed. Zablocki rounded up two sleepy junk sailors to help him and Medici in their adventure, and LT jaygee Ferrara, from the ATSB.

They drove along Route 8A toward the border and stopped at the Thach Dong militia outpost within shooting distance of Nooey Die Young. Then they humped the ammo, heavy mortar and baseplate the quarter mile along the twisty path to the outpost at the top.

The Spartan outpost surprised them. A three-foot-high wall of gray limestone rock fragments surrounded a six-foot-square hole framed with bamboo logs. Its walls were covered with more gray rock, its roof a single layer of sand bags. The smiling militiamen were happy to see other humans. Ha Tien was end of the line duty for the Vietnamese, and Thach Dong was the last stop in Ha Tien. Medici wondered what these militiamen had done to earn this special duty: slept with the C/O's wife; refused to turn over liberated gold and valuables; or just told the truth about farcical ARVN operations.

The outpost stood squarely at the summit. Craggy limestone slopes dropped away precipitously 30 feet beyond two evil rings of concertina wire, until head-high undergrowth obscured the slopes below. The hill seemed like a mountain. It surveyed vast kilometers of delta paddy, its flatness broken only by Nooey Die Young nestled against the Cambodian border three kilometers away.

Thung, the Vietnamese noncom in charge, spoke three words of English: Shit, goodfuck, VC. After he exhausted this vocabulary, he gestured toward Die Young, miming that sapper commandos had crawled all the way from Die Young up the hill to the concertina wire with big satchel charges last week but failed to get into the compound. The sappers succeeded in tossing two grenades into the perimeter before the .50-caliber tore two of them apart on the wire. Thung smiled broadly and patted the .50, their Protector.

Medici and Zablocki conferred and decided that tossing a few rounds from the .50 into caves visible on the Vietnam side of Die Young would likely draw some fire from the Viet Cong there. They persuaded Thung to let them try the .50, and he nervously agreed.

The big tracers were easy to follow, even in daylight. They flew like golf balls from one mountain to the other, with long orange arcs whose symmetry was disturbed when one entered a cave and ricocheted across the mouth. They didn't have to wait long. After about 20 rounds, feeble green AK tracers struggled vainly to defy gravity and reach the outpost at the top of the hill.

"That's it, hostile fire!" yelled Zablocki to the junkies who had set up the mortar. "Try to drop them just over the crest of Die Young. That way we'll pepper the staging area behind it."

The mortar whumped and whumped. The first rounds landed on the crest of Die Young. They could hear the impact of the adjusted rounds but could not see them because they landed behind the mountain. The Americans shouted with glee when they saw the black smoke of a secondary explosion snake up from behind Die Young. The laughter stopped when they heard the echo of a deeper WHUMP, not their own, and saw a flash from the mouth of one of the caves. They all dove for the small bunker before the first enemy mortar round hit. The Vietnamese looked at the Americans with understanding, which only underscored what jerks the fire team had been. The bunker smelled of nuoc mam and unwashed bodies.

Thung went out to fire the .50 at the mortar site, but Medici pushed him aside, double cocked the machine gun and fired one round before the gun jammed. Perspiring, he recocked the .50 and pulled the trigger. It clicked. Thung grabbed the grips from Medici and violently double cocked the Protector. It wouldn't fire. A mortar round exploded in the underbrush below the summit and they both dived back into the bunker. It reeked of garlicky fear sweat.

Medici looked up at the roof and realized it was only one sand bag thick, useless against a direct hit, which would kill or wound all of them. He felt very stupid. Zablocki still smiled like a lunatic. The man was absolutely nuts, an action freak, Medici concluded.

They remained quiet and tense for 10 minutes after the last mortar shell exploded. Thung ministered to his poor .50 as if trying to bring it back to life by resuscitation. He babbled Vietnamese and gestured wildly to Medici, fear in his black eyes. The message was clear. If the machine gun were not repaired, sapper commandoes from Die Young would retaliate tonight and kill them all while the Americans were safe in their beds at Phao Dai.

Zablocki watched Thung's performance and nodded. "He's right, NILO. We've got to fix the .50. Come on."

The two ran down the hill, exhilarated with the knowledge that they could be mortared any time. In the NILO Jeep they noticed a two-inch shrapnel hole in the right rear panel from an errant round. They sped back to Phao Dai and down to the Mike boat on which Zablocki had arrived. He went aboard and returned with a seven-foot-tall first class gunner's mate named Rothman who carried a tool box and a gunny sack full of heavy parts.

Speeding to Thach Dong, they jumped from the Jeep and ran up the hill, shedding rivulets of sweat in the ferocious afternoon sun. Medici lagged behind. He had liberated a case of Cokes from the bar at Phao Dai and carried them on his head, coolie-style, inching his way to the top.

Rothman dug into his gunny sack, pulled out an entire new receiver mechanism for the .50 and installed it. Thung smiled like a jack-o'-lantern as he watched Rothman repair the Protector, and he gaped when Medici arrived with the case of Cokes. Medici could feel the tension drain from militiamen and Americans when Rothman fired the first rounds from the .50. They all cheered and celebrated with warm Cokes.

On the ride back to Phao Dai, they came upon a wobbly Cambodian truck filled to the rails with round, dark watermelons. The driver's son sat atop the huge pile. In good spirits, Medici kept station behind the truck while the junk sailors crawled onto the hood and caught five melons the laughing boy tossed to the Americans. They ate one and saved the others for their comrades on the hill.

That night, still in a celebratory mood, Zablocki suggested they fire illumination over Moon Eye, the long, wooded peninsula across the water north of Phao Dai, enemy territory after dark.

After a few beers the junk sailors and Medici agreed it

sounded like a good idea, since there had been reports of nighttime VC activity there. They fired two white phosphorous parachute flares which detonated 800 feet above the hillside. They vaguely illuminated some hooches and a steep slope of banana groves, then extinguished 200 feet above ground.

Zablocki, drunk now, lowered the trajectory of the mortar so the flares would ignite closer to the ground for better illumination. He quickly fired two in a row without waiting to see where the first detonated. Both erupted simultaneously, two bright white supernovas 60 feet above the banana grove. They drifted slowly down into the thick leaves, brilliant white glowing eerily through the opaque green, then dropped and burned on the ground.

The Americans watched with fascination as the glowing spots grew into small fires that spread rapidly up the hillside and consumed it in flames. Within minutes the entire grove was aflame, overpowering the full moon that set into the Gulf off Mui Nai. Then they saw two human silhouettes running from a thatched hooch lapped by flames.

Zablocki said, "NILO, is Cambodia burning?"

No one laughed. Instead, they exchanged furtive glances and went to their rooms like naughty boys.

13

3 March 70

Next morning, Medici awoke troubled. The reckless burning of the banana grove and the foolish near-disaster of the Thach Dong mortaring incident left him sheepish. He wondered how he and his cronies could jeopardize the lives of Vietnamese for maverick action and cheap thrills.

He didn't wonder long. When an Army helo approached the pad, he grabbed his flight helmet and ran down to ask for a ride behind Nooey Die Young Mountain where the fire team had mortared the day before.

The young warrant officer pilot—he appeared to be 15—agreed, and they were off as soon as the mailbag was kicked out the door.

The warrant officer asked, "Which way, NILO?"

"That big mountain to the north sticking up like a thumb from the paddies."

"Roger that. Isn't the Cambodian border somewhere around here?"

"No. It's beyond the mountain." Medici didn't say how far, even though it was only a few meters.

"Any hostiles to worry about where we're going?"

"Not usually," he fudged again, leaving out the salient facts of yesterday's return fire. Shit, if he explained the risks and the technicalities of the Rules of Engagement and Cambodian sovereignty each time, nobody would take him. So he fudged.

They flew along Route 8A to the border. Then Medici told the pilot to swing right and dart over Nooey Die Young along the border. They could peer down at the staging area the fire team had mortared yesterday. Medici wanted to see what had caused the secondary explosion.

NILO Ha Tien

They came in at 400 feet. Medici hung out the left door next to the gunner. He spotted an unmanned antiaircraft gun at the junction of trails from the caves down to the dusty staging area. Several wooden cases of AK ammunition stood stacked in three locations near cart paths. A yawning Vietnamese in dirty skivvies was urinating into a pit while scratching his ass. He did a double take as the helo rose from behind Die Young, and when it bore down on him he ran wildly up the slope toward the closest cave. The pilot flew over him, then pulled up into a stall, made a hairpin turn and retraced his course from the opposite direction. This time he came in 50 feet above the back side of Die Young. The big blades popped as he dove and gained speed.

Medici looked over the staging area and into Cambodia where he saw the source of the secondary explosion and black smoke from yesterday's attack. A tiny, charred pedibus lay on its side like a discarded tricycle, the roof and windshield blown off, the tires smoldering oily smoke. He winced.

"What happened to that pedibus, NILO?" said the pilot.

"Must have been a recall. Defective gas tank or something." The door gunner touched his arm. He turned and saw green AK tracers floating next to them, coming from a cave on the slope. The pilot saw them, banked sharply and gained altitude.

"No hostiles, eh, NILO?" He banked around the summit and continued to climb.

Medici was looking down at the caves they shot into yesterday from Thach Dong when angry red .51-caliber tracers accelerated straight at him from the smallest cave. They tore by the helo so close he could study in slow motion the point of burning phosphorous at the tail of each slug. It was wonderful the way time and motion slowed when you were under fire, he thought. The pilot screamed on the intercom, but his voice seemed miles away.

"You motherfucker, NILO! You didn't tell me I was in for this!"

The door gunners did their best to lay suppression fire as the helo banked and turned wildly. The turning prevented the cave gunners from leading the helo into their stream of bullets.

The pilot yelled some more and maneuvered them out of the

range of fire. Then Medici said in a weak voice, "Let's go back to Phao Dai. Sorry about the flak."

The intercom was silent while they flew back to the hill. The pilot barely touched down on the pad to let Medici off. The pilot pulled far too much pitch, went into a power hover, blew dust and grit all over Medici and was gone.

Medici reported to Saigon that for two days in a row Ha Tien had received unprovoked enemy fire from inside Cambodia, and that under the Rules of Engagement suppression fire into Cambodia had been properly returned. Zablocki had predicted correctly how it would come down, Medici reflected. "Unprovoked fire" was technically accurate, even if it didn't explain the context of the two days' adventures.

He told Frank Brown, Tom Roque, and the major about the Thach Dong mortaring and the helo receiving fire. He asked the major, the officer responsible for Ha Tien's security, if he would authorize mortar fire on Die Young from a point closer to the border. It was justified, he said, in that Die Young threatened the area around the mountain and impeded free passage on the highway into Cambodia. The major waffled, then agreed. Medici offered to muster a Navy fire team to respond because the Army was shorthanded.

Next, Medici convinced Frank Brown to drive to the border with him in the afternoon to find a good site for the fire team's mortar, one from which they could strike directly at the staging area behind Die Young. Medici intended to show Frank the staging area and burnt pedibus from the point where the road crossed the border and they could see behind Die Young. Frank didn't care to be shot at after 15 years in the Army, but agreed to go when Medici assured him the risk was minimal.

After lunch Medici and Frank sat and sipped sodas on the terrace in the shade until the sun dropped below the arc of its worst heat. They didn't say much to each other. Around four o'clock Medici went to his room, put his fatigues and boots on, then returned to the patio with his rifle and a radio.

"Shall we head out to the border, Frank?" he asked.

NILO HA TIEN

"Jesus, NILO, rifle and all. I don't know about this," Frank said. They drove in Medici's Jeep through Ha Tien and out Route 8A toward the border.

The town looked calm as they drove through, one of those Asian afternoons that reminded Medici of siesta time in Mexico. The streets were empty and a peace that seemed narcotic hung in the air. The mossy colonial buildings dwindled in number as they drove, and thatched huts appeared in their place in slow motion freeze frames, it seemed to Medici, that allowed him to memorize all the details.

They passed no vehicles on the road to the border. A kilometer out of town they climbed a pimple of a hill next to the road. From the top, using binoculars, they could see beyond Die Young and the border to the small Cambodian hamlets that floated like palm islands in the paddies.

"Krabau's the closest hamlet," he told Frank. "The North Vietnamese Army stays fastidiously away from its villagers. The NVA are under strict orders to observe Cambodian neutrality along the border. That's the main reason Sihanouk tolerates their presence, besides the fact that he can do nothing about it."

Medici drove the Jeep back onto 8A, and it hummed along the macadam surface. The hill of Thach Dong outpost grew larger to their right. Medici's pulse quickened with the memory of the excitement of yesterday's attack. He downshifted and slowed as they came to the turnoff for Thach Dong, wondering if his militia friends were hanging around the bottom of the hill. He searched but saw no one.

He shifted back up, and the engine whined. Then he saw a fluffy gray tree in front of them off the dike road. He studied it carefully, never having noticed it before, and suddenly a second tree erupted in the paddies between the Jeep and the first. The second tree showered water and mud on them. Frank moved violently and tried to shake Medici's arm while he hurled himself into the foot well. He yelled something.

"MORTAR! GODDAMMIT, MORTAR! GET OFF THE ROAD!"

Not again, Medici thought calmly, and stopped. In the quiet

they could hear the WHUMP, WHUMP of a mortar tube firing twice in the distance from the direction of Die Young.

His mental clock ticked off the seconds of trajectory time. His bowels rolled. He looked quickly for some kind of cover. They were sitting ducks on the dike road, elevated above the paddies and silhouetted against the sky. There was nowhere to go. The track to Thach Dong outpost was 500 yards behind them. He couldn't waste time turning around in the same spot with two rounds already launched. Up ahead to the left was the turnoff road to Moon Eye. He jammed the Jeep in first, floored the engine, then power-shifted to second, chirping the tires. They flew.

A first, then a second mortar plume straddled the dike road 50 yards behind them with loud KAHWHUMPS. Medici took the Moon Eye turnoff on two wheels, drove along the smaller dike road 150 yards, then pulled to a stop. Frank was out of the Jeep, over the dike, and into the paddy with his rifle before Medici got out and dragged the radio along with his M-16.

They lay first at water level at the bottom of the dike slope, directly below the Jeep. Medici looked up at it and said, "Shit." He dragged the radio, Frank and the M-16 rapidly along the slope at water level, working his way back to the intersection of dikes supporting the border road and the Moon Eye turnoff. Away from the obvious target the Jeep presented, protected from mortar fire on two sides by the dike walls, they were safe from all but a lucky hit directly behind them.

The North Vietnamese gunners zeroed in on the Jeep with four more rounds, sprayed it with shrapnel, paddy mud and rice roots, but never scored a direct hit. They stopped launching for five minutes, to conserve ammunition, Medici guessed. But when he crawled up the dike to road level, he saw muzzle flashes from the same cave on Die Young which had mortared them yesterday. He located it on his pocket map, then crawled back down as two rounds splashed between them and the Jeep.

"Get down, NILO!" Frank yelled.

Medici called the major at Phao Dai on the radio. The major came on, and Medici told him calmly that they were under mortar fire near Thach Dong. He could not give their exact position because he assumed their transmissions were monitored by a Soviet radio intercept unit, which would relay the information to the mortar team.

The major sounded upset. None of the Americans attached to his small advisory team had been directly fired upon before. Medici requested some suppression fire from the big four-deuce mortar on Phao Dai. Three minutes later, some big rounds landed here and there in the paddy between Thach Dong and Nooey Die Young. Medici requested that they stop, since the rounds were more of a hazard to him and Frank than the North Vietnamese.

The mortars were silent for half an hour. He and Frank thought about crawling back to the Jeep and leaving, but they decided they would wait until twilight.

The radio crackled, and it was the major:

"Barbados, this is Wolfman. In your opinion do you have a TAC E?"

Medici thought. Why did he want to know if it was a tactical emergency? Ah! Air support from Can Tho, the delta capital. Can Tho had never sent aircraft all the way out to Ha Tien. It was understood, sorry gents, that Ha Tien, the end of the line, was on its own.

Not this time, Medici thought. A tactical emergency existed when they were pinned down with mortar fire. Americans in jeopardy from hostile fire….

"Affirmative, Wolfman. We have a TAC E. Can we get some Black Ponies out here?"

"We'll do better than that. Can you hang on for awhile?"

Medici watched the sun touch the peak of Moon Eye. Twilight, then tropic dark would be on them within two hours.

"Roger that. We'll stay for the show."

Frank looked at him and laughed, "What do you mean 'we,' white man?"

"You guys need anything? I can send someone out for a drop," the major said.

"How about a grenade launcher? I'd feel a lot safer," Medici said into the handset.

"Roger. Get this. The Ba is cooking fried chicken. We'll send some out with the launcher. We'll guard this circuit. Yell if anything comes up. Wolfman out."

Nui Dai Dung mountain dominates the Cambodian border.

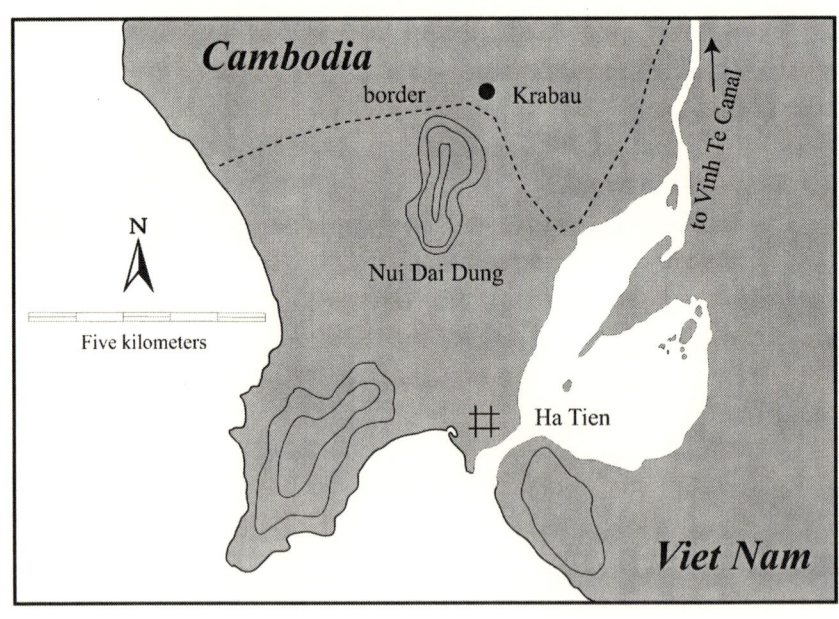

Ha Tien, Krabau hamlet and Cambodian border. Nui Dai Dung mountain dominates the area.

14

Fireworks

The quiet weighed heavy. Frank and Medici didn't talk much. Frank seemed annoyed to be dragged into this Mickey Mouse nonsense. He had left the airborne precisely to avoid this stuff, he reminded Medici.

It grew chilly down at the waterline of the paddy as the sun fell low, then set behind Moon Eye. Curious Vietnamese passersby gathered at the intersection of the dike roads. They puzzled why two Americans had abandoned their perfectly good but filthy Jeep and insisted on lying against the dike slope at the waterline. They discussed the situation in shrill tones among themselves, then laughed lustily. It pissed Medici off. He hoped another near-miss mortar round would send them screaming in terror from the road.

The major's Jeep arrived driven by his Vietnamese interpreter, Nuong. He brought the grenade launcher, 20 fat little bullets for it, and the Ba's inedible fried chicken. When Frank and Medici politely refused the chicken, Nuong sold it to the Vietnamese standing around at the intersection.

Medici observed that none of the Americans accompanied Nuong even though the bombardment had stopped more than an hour ago. Nuong claimed air support was on the way. Great, Medici thought. If Nuong knows, every North Vietnamese within 50 miles of the border knows. Nuong left.

They were nearly asleep in a semi-alert state when an OV-10 tactical fighter roared down Route 8A so close above their heads they could see the flames from its engines' exhaust. It showed no navigation lights, flew along the road a mile into Cambodia, gained altitude, came back out, and circled on station. Medici heard the radio bark. The pilot was talking to the major on another frequency to which he directed Medici. Switching over, he heard the first pilot chatting to the pilot of a second OV-10 Black Pony arriving on station.

"I don't see shit down there. No tracers, no nothin'. How you?"

"Negative here. I see the mountain, though. Nooey Dah Dung, it says." A heavy southern accent.

"Pony Boys, this is Barbados. If you drop a couple of parachute flares, I'll walk you into the target," Medici said.

"Roger, Barbados. Just tell me where."

"The slope of Die Young closest to the smaller mountain south of it. Mortar fire came from a cave there."

"Roger, Barbados. Popping two." Two black canisters fell from the aircraft, trailed small parachutes, then burst into startling white light as the phosphorous ignited. The landscape came to life like the split second of a close lightning bolt, where the image hangs in the mind's eye for hours. The pilot flew over the top of Die Young into Cambodia, then came out in a wide loop.

Medici trained his binoculars on the foot of Die Young. As the flares fell lower, he could see the outline of the mouth of the large cave. He oriented the first pilot who located the cave, lined up, slowed, came in low, fired his five inch Zuni rocket. Medici imagined he could see it flying in the dark, then saw the flash as it hit outside the mouth of the cave. Seconds later the concussion hit him with a rude slap in the face. His ears rang. He hadn't known that a Zuni could boom that loud from three kilometers.

The second Pony followed. In the last light of the flares he dropped his fiver right into the cave. Medici couldn't see the explosion directly. He saw an indirect glow from the cave's mouth that silhouetted flying debris. One piece looked like a stuntman shot from a cannon. A large concussion, then a smaller one followed the flash. The pilot had caused a secondary explosion with the direct hit.

"Oooeee, mama!" the pilot yelled. He flew wagging his wings over Die Young into Cambodia to turn for another pass. As he passed the crest, authoritative red .51-caliber tracers chased him above a spray of puny green AK tracers.

"Fuck this!" the pilot yelled. "You see those tracers!"

NILO HA TIEN

"I'm on 'em, Jack-sone," the first pilot said. He flew across the back side of the mountain at a right angle to the first pilot's course and fired his 2.5 inch rockets at the area from which the tracers had come. The tracers answered back from the ground after he flew by. The fireworks interested Frank so, he crawled up from the paddy to watch. The Ponies made one more pass but could not suppress the machine gun fire coming from the back side of Die Young. They backed off, circled on station, and radioed the big base at Can Tho. Can Tho came up on Medici's frequency and told him they had sent some more aircraft, including "Puff." If he would wait around, he could guide them on target. Medici agreed.

The Ponies circled Die Young from a distance. An occasional red tracer reached out but fell short. They returned bursts of cannon fire to the back side of the mountain when the ground fire got too thick, but always the red .51 tracers came back at them like persistent mosquitoes.

The crowd of Vietnamese at the intersection had grown to nearly 40. Alternately they cheered the Ponies, then the indomitable NVA gunner on the .51. It made Medici nervous.

With his concentration focused on the dark mountain, it took him awhile to realize that it had grown light around them. He turned and saw Frank staring at a burning pile of rice chaff the size of a house that illuminated the junction of the dike slopes. Its light caused the savvy spectators to leave, because they knew they were targets. Medici put a round in the grenade launcher and lay it against his leg aimed toward the blaze, then turned to the mountain.

The parade began. Puff the Dragon, a cargo plane outfitted with God knew how many miniguns, came on scene and hosed the entire target area with a bullet in every square foot. Still the .51 fired back. A-7s appeared with 1,000-pound bombs that they unloaded in and around the caves at Medici's direction, slowing almost to stall speed to deliver their deadly cargo. The 1,000-pounders really hurt Medici's ears. Frank curled up in a fetal position against the dike, bracing himself against each concussion.

Medici found he had numbed himself to them and welcomed the shock and slap. This was living! Between impacts he trimmed the black pigtail on his beret, a first fight ritual. Frank told Medici his grooving on this stuff was nuts.

Some of the bombs overshot and crashed into Cambodia. Medici saw two bombs flash behind Die Young, clearly over the border. He watched a short raging fire of thatch huts after a canister of napalm overshot the slope. "C'est la guerre," he said when Frank worried where it had landed.

A spotter plane arrived around midnight. The spotter told Medici he had done a good job from the ground and that he had been relieved and could return to Phao Dai. The tactical situation in Ha Tien had become first importance in Can Tho and Saigon, he added gleefully, and the command decided to plaster the mountain until opposition was eliminated, probably for the next few days.

A few days! Medici thought. There isn't enough here to shoot at for more than a few hours. The spotter recited woodenly that the security of the Americans on the Ha Tien peninsula had been threatened by NVA gunners in Cambodia for too long, and now something was going to be done about it, by God. Medici and Frank packed up and left.

Medici felt sheepish as he and Frank drove in the dark through Ha Tien, then up Phao Dai. He kept looking over at Frank, but quickly returned his eyes to the road when Frank met his gaze.

"Do you think they're overdoing it, Frank? I mean the response seems disproportionate to the threat."

Frank shook his head but looked straight ahead. "You wanted to stir things up, right? That was the whole purpose of your Navy fire team. Well, NILO, I think you got what you wanted in spades. I think we just provided Saigon and MACV with the pretext they need to roll into Cambodia. Welcome to the newest chapter of the Vietnam War—the Cambodia story," he said bitterly. Medici could feel Frank's cold stare.

Medici felt stupid and sick and drove the rest of the distance in silence.

NILO HA TIEN

Nui Dai Dung under attack. Krabau hamlet lies behind.

Crest of Nui Dai Dung is covered by marble dust
from two weeks of bombing.

15

Cambodia Acts

The bombers kept coming. The day after the incident Medici thought the pilots were simply making sure the caves were emptied and the .51 silenced. But after the fourth day of continuous bombing—BOOM-THUMP-KRRUMP—he knew no threat remained on or around Nooey Die Young. His agents reported that all North Vietnamese and Viet Cong had evacuated the mountain 48 hours after the bombing began.

Yet the bombers never let up. They flew in sorties that arrived every half hour to 45 minutes, dropped their noisy, jarring cargo and returned to Can Tho. The THUD THUD THUDing grew irritating to Medici. He ignored the explosions, but his brain received the low-frequency noises through the ground under his feet and kept him on edge.

Fragile spotter planes patrolled day and night. Army spotters replaced the original Navy spotter. Their small Bird Dog aircraft, olive drab, wing over cabin, would float effortlessly as a dragonfly, investigating the latest bomb's damage and telling the bomber pilot where to put his next load. When they felt frisky, they would shoot a wimpy pair of rockets at an imagined target around Die Young. Medici bristled at the continuous southern drawl on the traffic control circuit, which the major broadcast through a speaker in the team house like a sporting event.

When Medici returned to the border on the fourth day, he was shocked that Die Young had been bomb-sculpted to the point that it didn't resemble the old mountain. Huge pieces of its soft limestone features had been eradicated as if by a sculptor's trowel. Familiar outcroppings were simply gone; depressions were filled in with debris, chalky, bony white. It saddened Medici. Why did these guys from somewhere else in the delta have the right to alter his landscape permanently? He already remembered fondly the old days when the NVA and Americans mostly left each other alone, and at night he watched helplessly as truck convoys laden with Soviet weapons drove down 8A from Sihanoukville.

He drove to the spot where he and Frank had spent the night on the dike slope only four days before. That stretch of road had been hairy, a no-man's-land each time he drove it. Now, to accommodate the tourist traffic that stopped there on the drive to Ha Tien market from Cambodia, a thatched Coca-Cola stand had been set up by an enterprising Vietnamese. A few old ammo crates were spread around, so customers could sit and sip and watch the continuous fireworks on Die Young. The aura of danger was gone, replaced by the banality of carnival commerce.

Medici drove further up 8A to the border. Just before the border, at a thickening of the dike that made a wide shoulder, a Vietnamese Army unit had trucked in three immense 155mm artillery pieces, the biggest Medici had ever seen. They were located so close to the border they could shoot directly into the caves on Die Young and control any movement in the staging area on the back side. Medici drove by them in awe. The barrels were almost as big and high above him as the 6-inch Naval guns he had fired on the cruiser *Tulsa*.

One barrel erupted above him as he drove past. The concussion made his ears ring, which he barely noticed, and physically blew the moving Jeep three feet sideways so its wheels were off the pavement. He pulled to a stop and watched for the round to land on Die Young. A dirty gray puff of smoke erupted at an unremarkable point on the closest slope, not near any cave, yet caused the ARVN gunners to shout and cheer. Big fucking deal, Medici thought. They can hit the side of a mountain at two clicks.

The second gun of the battery fired, showering Medici with smoldering bits of paper wadding from the powder cartridge. He brushed the bits out of his hair. The cordite smell made him queasy. He raised his binoculars to observe the impact on Die Young, but the projectile went wide and exploded in a tree line of splintered palms to the left of the mountain. Medici didn't remember seeing the tree line before. He focused the big binocs, then listlessly dropped them on their neck strap. The splintered tree line was the remnant of Kraubau hamlet in Cambodia, just beyond Die Young. Four days of bombing and artillery had eradicated it. Charred black corner posts of huts were all that remained. The oasis of palm windbreak that had identified the hamlet site had been obliterated.

The ARVN sergeant asked if he wanted to go closer to Die Young with him during a pause in the firing. Medici nodded. The sergeant jumped in the Jeep and directed Medici to a small dike road a few hundred yards across the border that led to the foot of Die Young. They parked, the sergeant loaded his rifle, and they walked toward the cement gray hill. Medici thrilled to be so close.

Huge gray boulders and unexploded 500-pound bombs created a surreal landscape. Medici saw a melon-sized piece of shrapnel with jagged edges that looked like fool's gold crystals. They heard AK rifle fire from the back of Die Young and agreed they should leave. They walked to the Jeep across a stretch of paddy and around a bomb crater filled with milky-gray water from which a human leg in a black cotton trouser protruded. The sergeant hooked it with his rifle and pulled until it came loose. He dragged it out of the water and laid it on the mud where, at his prod, the flesh fell away from the bone and hundreds of maggots wiggled out. "Black pajama, VC, numbah ten!" he said.

They returned to the battery and the sergeant waved goodbye. Medici turned the Jeep toward Phao Dai and didn't flinch when one gun of the battery fired as he passed under the barrel and the crew howled with laughter.

Two days later Medici's agents reported the obvious: Krabau and another Cambodian hamlet further away from Die Young had been "accidentally" destroyed by the incessant American bombing. The villagers who weren't killed fled to surrounding hamlets a safer distance from the mountain. The bombing had sanitized a two-kilometer swath around Die Young of NVA, Cambodians, and Vietnamese.

Another agent reported that village elders from the destroyed and surviving hamlets raged at the North Vietnamese who for years had traveled peacefully along the border corridor in Cambodia. The unarmed Cambodians threw rocks at North Vietnamese units and refused to give or sell them any rice, which they needed to live. The North Vietnamese had started to take rice at gunpoint and leave the villagers handfuls of pretty, worthless Provisional Revolutionary Government money, which would be honored as soon as the war was won.

The villagers blamed the NVA for the destruction and disruption of the hamlets: If the NVA hadn't fired on the Americans across the border, the reprisal air strikes would not have come and the hamlets would not have been destroyed. The decade-long compact—you don't disrupt our lives and we'll allow you peaceful passage through Cambodia—had been violated by the North Vietnamese. Cambodians rioted against North Vietnamese presence in Tuk Meas and Kampong Trach, two large Cambodian border towns.

Saigon found these reports "politically significant." No shit, Sherlock, Medici thought. But he felt troubled because events were out of hand, dehumanized and abstracted into moves in a global chess game in which real people and their towns and ancestral homes didn't matter anymore. A vague sense of guilt for starting it clouded his mind, but his sense of duty suppressed it. "You gotta' do what you gotta' do," he told himself.

Frank Brown had barely spoken to Medici since the night of the mortar incident. Two weeks later, while the bombing continued, Frank brought a report from his agent on the Cambodian cabinet and threw it on Medici's desk.

Medici looked at Frank's tight jaw, then read silently. A mob of Cambodians, some from the border provinces, had rioted, then sacked the Provisional Revolutionary Government (Viet Cong) and North Vietnamese embassies in Phnom Penh, demanding that the NVA quit Cambodia. Speeches demanding NVA departure were made on the floor of the Cambodian National Assembly, and Lon Nol demanded the NVA's complete departure from Cambodia. Since Prince Sihanouk was in France, he couldn't calm the uprising of the usually placid Cambodians.

"Frank, this is great! It looks like the Cambodians are realizing their folly in allowing the NVA to wage war from Cambodia. This couldn't be better news! And Sihanouk's not here to calm troubled waters," Medici said.

"Right, NILO. Couldn't be better," Frank grunted. He turned and walked out of the room.

Medici went to his locker and got his last bottle of Scotch. He went to Frank's room and found him lying on his bunk watching a gecko hunting mosquitoes on the peeling plaster wall.

"Why are you so uptight, Frank?" He pounded the Scotch bottle down on the desk.

Frank turned to him with a how-can-you-be-so-stupid look. "You know what's next, NILO?"

"The Cambodians may try to oust the North Vietnamese from Cambodia. Just what we want.

"Do you think a vote of the Cambodian National Assembly means anything to Hanoi? Who's going to kick the North Vietnamese out if there is such a vote? The Cambodes are outgunned, outmanned, and untrained. They couldn't kick a dog out.

"You think this is Civics 101 and the Assembly's acts are important? Prince Sihanouk runs Cambodia. Who's gonna' take care of him? Do you think the NVA can sit back and give up the Sihanoukville connection? How about the Cambodes? Some of their generals are getting half the communist weaponry that comes in, and they stay filthy rich reselling it."

"So?" Medici said. "I can't see why you're so upset when things are finally going our way...."

Frank was on his feet now. "Because this whole house of cards is going to fall. Hooray for Ha Tien, right? We nudged Cambodia into a crisis that we can exploit. But what about Cambodia? Did anybody ask them?" He looked out his window at the firefly lights of fishing junks putting out of the bay.

"Frank, this is what we're here for. The whole reason Ha Tien exists is as a listening post. Depriving the North Vietnamese of their safe haven and pipeline for weapons into Vietnam is what the game's all about." Medici laughed. "What are you turning into? Some kind of hippie peacenik?"

NILO HA TIEN

Secret-Order-of-the-Cambodian-Border memorial Scotch bottle.

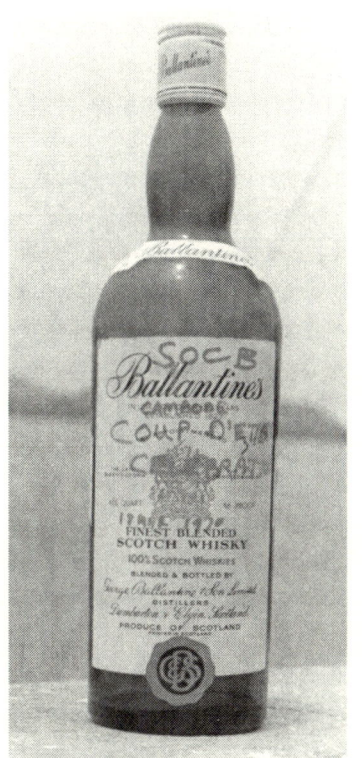

"Fuck you, NILO." Frank glowered at him. "You think this is some fucking game we're playing? Listen to me: Cambodia is in for a world of shit no matter which way it goes. Do you understand, you silly Ivy League asshole?"

Medici stung with the insult. He worried about Frank's attitude. He fought back his anger, calmed himself, then went to the desk and poured out half glasses of Scotch, neat. Frank refused the glass with a wave of his hand, then took it and tossed it down in one gulp.

They said nothing for a long while and just drank. The liquor loosened them up, and they started joking about how fat little "Snookie," Prince Sihanouk, would react to the developments. Probably he'd throw a jazz concert for the North Vietnamese, Russian, and Chinese ambassadors in Paris. They laughed hysterically. Medici took a red magic marker and wrote on the Scotch bottle in a drunken hand "S.O.C.B."

"Wha's tha' mean?" Frank said.

"Secret-Order-of-the-Cambodian-Border," Medici said. They laughed. The major in the next room yelled, "Knock it off, you guys!" They moved to the empty team room and sat at a table to continue drinking.

At 1:30 a.m. they were surprised when the screen door to the team room creaked open and out of the dark slipped Frank's net handler. He never came directly to the hill for fear of being identified by local Viet Cong. He looked pleased but nervous as he nodded politely to Medici, then went with Frank to the radio room in order to speak privately. When they came out, Frank had a wistful expression. He thanked and dismissed his net handler and slid the rice paper toward Medici. It read:

"On March 18, Sirik Matak, President of the National Assembly, and General Lon Nol called a special evening meeting of the Cambodian Cabinet. The recent riots against the North Vietnamese were discussed as well as the trouble at the border caused by the NVA attacks and the American air strike response. The debate concluded that the conduct of the North Vietnamese was no longer peaceful and unobtrusive, and that they should be asked to vacate Cambodia within 48 hours. Lon Nol emphasized the long-standing cultural antipathy between Cambodians and Annamites (ethnic Vietnamese) and concluded that the Vietnamese interference in Cambodian affairs permitted by Prince Sihanouk could no longer be tolerated. A hastily convened Assembly, what could be mustered of it, voted to depose Sihanouk as head of state of Cambodia and to place the royal family under house arrest. General Lon Nol was appointed acting premier until measures could be taken to form a republic and hold new elections.

"Since Sihanouk is in France, it is a propitious time for the Sirik Matak-Lon Nol elements to play their hand. Further reports as the situation develops. End of report."

Medici looked at Frank. They both sobered. "I think this is FLASH priority, don't you?" Medici said. Frank nodded.

Medici got his pad and pen to write a message to Naval headquarters in Saigon and uncapped the red marker. Before he began he picked up the Scotch bottle and added below "S.O.C.B." the inscription "March 18, 1970."

16

Corvette E-311

In April, two weeks after Lon Nol deposed Sihanouk, Medici erroneously reported the arrival of the Cambodian corvette as a "small destroyer." It appeared larger than it was from his vantage point on Phao Dai when it first steamed slowly past the Pirate Islands into Vietnamese waters and stood for two hours a mile from the American Navy LST, then returned to Cambodian waters. Captain Brown of the LST sent a messenger by boat to Phao Dai to ask Medici what he should do if the Cambodian Navy ship came back. Medici said he would guard a certain radio channel day and night, so Captain Brown could contact him in case the Cambodians returned.

The coming of the Cambodians left the captain nervous, since the message traffic had indicated it was uncertain in Washington whether the Lon Nol government was friendly or hostile to the U.S. When the Cambode ship approached his LST off Ha Tien in daylight, the captain put his ship at general quarters to be safe. The klaxon's blare that sent his sailors to battle stations drifted across the placid Gulf and scared the timid Cambodians away without incident. Besides summoning Medici, the captain reported the contact to Saigon and asked for guidance. Staff's brief, helpful response was "MAINTAIN VIGILANCE."

Forty-eight hours later during a muggy Gulf night Medici awakened, startled by the hiss-crack of the radio handset next to his bed. It called plaintively for "Barbados." He answered and the radio operator on the LST put Captain Brown himself on the channel.

"Barbados, they're back. Standing off at 2,000 yards. They continue to flash on their signal light the NATO code letters for 'request you send messenger.' I'd like you out here as soon as possible."

It was four in the morning. The captain agreed to send

a newly repaired river boat to get him. First light was breaking as Medici boarded the PBR. He was aboard the LST in 20 minutes. The Cambodian vessel loomed ominous in the twilight. It excited Medici.

Captain Brown, always gracious, had fresh coffee and eggs ready in the wardroom where he and Medici talked alone.

"Any sign of hostile intent, Captain?"

"None, Tom. Their sailors ambled around the deck with guns unmanned, flashing the code all night long, until we acknowledged a messenger would be sent at first light."

"Any indication that they speak English? I don't speak Khmer, and my Vietnamese is weak."

"Nope. Just the NATO signal. Almost every Navy in the world is privy to those signals now."

"Well… Guess I'll go alone."

"Wait a minute," Brown said. "I'm not going to allow you to be captured and paraded around Phnom Penh like those river boat sailors were last year. I want you to take an armed guard."

"Captain," Medici said sternly, "what you heard was the concocted story, that they were innocent sailors on a routine patrol of the Bassac River when they accidentally drifted into Cambodian waters, were captured by a patrol boat, and marched around Phnom Penh to depict the flagrant violation of Cambodia's neutrality." Medici paused. "The truth is, they were a SEAL team on a covert operation to kill some VC cadre in Cambodia who run guns down the river into Vietnam. Their mission was compromised. The VC knew they were coming and arranged for the Cambodians to catch them. Sihanouk was still boss. The capture made it appear his navy was on the ball, so he agreed to a little parade in Phnom Penh as suggested by the North Vietnamese to embarrass the U.S. The sailors were returned to Saigon a few months after."

Brown shifted his weight in the chair.

Medici said, "The government has changed and these guys are requesting this meeting in formal, proper fashion. I'll wager it's not a setup."

"What'll you bet? A return bus ticket from Phnom Penh?" Brown said.

"If I need the ticket it'll be from Hanoi," Medici laughed.

Cambodian Navy Corvette E-311,
site of U.S. - Cambodian weapons agreement.

"I'll go alone." He stood to leave.

"If I'm not back in four hours, send the PBR back to the corvette with a load of armed deckhands. Have them stand off, look stern, and hail to come alongside. Instruct them that if I don't come out to wave acknowledgment, they should insist on boarding to get me."

"Okay, Tom. Good luck." Brown shook his hand and they walked out onto the main deck to the ladder that led to the boat. Medici saluted and climbed over the side to the PBR.

The Cambodian corvette drifted to 1,000 yards from the LST. From sea level, Medici saw the ship was nowhere near the size of a destroyer. It had a destroyer's profile and proportions, but it was half the size, an old corvette the French Navy had sold to Cambodia years ago.

Medici told the coxswain to approach slowly so as not to suggest hostile intent. They surged directly alongside and the deckhands threw lines to the corvette. It bore the hull number "E-311." Medici noticed the gunmounts were unmanned. The Cambodian deckhands, small, brown, monkeylike seamen in olive fatigues, sat listlessly on deck, eyes glued with curiosity on the American PBR. Medici stood perfectly erect on the PBR with his hands clasped behind him amid the bustle of activity of the deckhands.

The corvette lowered a Jacob's ladder six feet to water level. Medici scurried aboard and looked around the deck. He saw no one with the appearance of authority. Then a watertight door clanked open and a smiling young Cambodian with officer's shoulder boards on his wash-worn uniform came forward, offered his hand to Medici, and then gestured toward the door.

Medici shook the officer's hand and waved off the men in his boat. He stepped through the door, guts growling, wondering how quickly he could draw and fire the .45 in his waistband if he needed to.

The passageway smelled like fish sauce and garlic. Cases of glowing lime-green soda stood stacked in the passageway next to a door. The officer knocked twice then held it open for Medici. They entered a small cabin, shoddily paneled in dark wood with a round teak table at which a chunky Cambodian officer sat. The captain, Medici guessed by his colorful ribbons and ornate shoulder devices.

The captain gestured for Medici to sit across from him. The young officer sat to Medici's right. Medici sat far enough from the table to allow himself the delusion that he had room to draw the pistol if necessary.

Everyone smiled a lot. The captain said something incomprehensible to Medici in Khmer. Medici mimed non-comprehension, raised his hands palms up, and shook his head to convey lack of understanding.

He tried his best butchered Vietnamese: "Do you speak Vietnamese?" They smiled and responded with his "do not understand" gestures. Just as well; he only remembered 20 words.

The captain pointed to a case of the vile lime soda in the corner of the cabin. Medici smiled and nodded acceptance. The younger officer rose and carried three bottles to a small counter behind the captain. He began to open them with a rickety bottle opener when the neck of the first bottle shattered and cut the soft flesh between his thumb and forefinger. "Merde!" the young Cambodian shouted. The captain turned and frowned disapproval.

"Vous parlez bien Français, n'est-ce pas?" *You speak French well, don't you!* Medici exclaimed. He jumped to his feet.

The two Cambodians turned toward him and smiled broadly. "Ah, oui. Nous avons étudiés à l'Académie de la Marine de Brest! Nous avons trouvés une langue commune!" *Ah, yes. We studied at the Naval Academy in Brest. We have found a common language!*

Medici could feel the tension break. Of course, French. For the elites, Cambodia was still a francophon country, and bright Cambodian Naval officers would be sent to the French Naval Academy at Brest. French was their second language. And Medici's.

"We have great difficulties we must share with our American friends. Lon Nol himself has sent me to discuss these matters with your government through you, Lieutenant Medici, is it?" He read the name tag. "A grand Spanish name, n'est-ce pas?"

"Actually Italian. And I'm not sure how great. My grandparents left because they had little going for them in Italy." Both men laughed. "Your name, Captain?"

"Captitaine de Corvette Som Sary. This is my exec, Lieutenant Ang Ly Kim." Medici nodded to both men.

"What are the difficulties with which we can help?" Medici asked in formal French, getting down to business.

Som Sary withdrew a map from a drawer, spread and smoothed it upside down so Medici could see. It was an old, multicolored French map that covered all Cambodia from the Thai to Vietnam borders. Medici knew the area intimately. Something was wrong with the map's proportions, but he couldn't put his finger on it.

"Since the Assembly voted to depose Sihanouk"—this was the first Medici had heard about collective responsibility for Lon Nol's removal of Sihanouk since Frank's agent on the cabinet had reported exactly this, that the Assembly had removed Sihanouk—"the North Vietnamese forces in our country have dropped all pretense of neutrality. They have stolen food from our villages and have perpetrated overt hostilities that have caused your forces to respond with attacks, which have accidentally destroyed some of our border villages and hamlets."

"Like Krabau?"

"Yes, exactly, Lieutenant. But of greater strategic importance to us, the North Vietnamese have moved their forces inland to protect their border sanctuary and to control our roads and ferries. They place their hand on Cambodia's throat and threaten to choke her if we refuse to permit them to continue their activities against Vietnam. Worse yet, in some areas they have already pinned down our battalions, which have few weapons and no ammunition." He pointed to the town of Kep on the map, 20 kilometers north of Ha Tien on the coast.

"Here two marine battalions of the Navy are surrounded by elements of the 101st VC Regiment and 9th NVA Division. They resisted the initial skirmishes, but depleted their ammunition and are armed only with grenades. The NVA have surrounded our marines and cut off resupply. Our battalions are under siege. They cannot fight their way out with only grenades."

They wouldn't be unarmed, Medici thought, if you bastards had kept more of the weapons you stole from the Soviets and Chinese as the price for infiltration through Sihanoukville. He told himself to keep in mind he was a diplomat now.

"How bad off are they? How many days' food do they have?" he asked.

"They are already out of food and living off the land in these hills around Kep. Their commander says they can last no more than a few weeks this way at near-starvation subsistence, but they will have no fighting capability."

"How many men? What is a Cambodian battalion size?" Medici drew out his small pocket notebook with the Vulture Squadron cartoon cover and began to write. He had a headache now. He had not spoken French in five years, and the process of dredging up vocabulary exhausted him.

"Five hundred each in these marine battalions, but we need more than 2,000 rifles and ammo if you can help." Som Sary brought out his own list. "If we can arm soldiers in our Second Military Region here, along the coast, to resist the VC and NVA locally, we can release General Sosthene Fernandes' 8th Mobile Brigade. The brigade has been temporarily assigned to the region, but we must return it to Phnom Penh for the defense of the city, Ponchetong Airport, and the Mekong ferry crossing at Neak Luong. We have reason to believe the NVA will attempt a siege of Phnom Penh soon.

"Lieutenant, on behalf of my government and Lon Nol personally, I request that your government supply us weapons and ammunition to allow our marines to fight their way out against the NVA, and to help us defend our capital. This is what we need." He placed a single sheet of rice paper in front of Medici, a shopping list of weapons written in fine French script. It read:

"Pour Deuxième Région Militaire (6.000 hommes):

.45 pistoles	405
Fusées machines (Thompsons)	1.296
Fusées (M-1, M-2)	3.222
Fusées machines (M-60)	270
Fusées machines (.30 calibre)	72
Mortiers (60mm)	54
Mortiers (81mm)	18
Fusées sans rebondissement (57mm)	27
Fusées grenadiers (M-79)	270

Pour Forces Régionales (2.000 hommes):

.45 pistoles	12
Fusées machines (Thompsons)	315
Fusées (M-1, M-2)	1.659
Fusées Machines (M-60)	14
Fusées grenadiers (M-79)	14

Whew! Medici thought. These guys don't beat around the bush. Washington tells us it's in the throes of debating whose side we will be on since Sihanouk's gone, and they want armed assistance right now. The press will have a heyday if this gets out. Cambodian neutrality, my ass.

"Capitaine," Medici said, "you realize this is a matter of great sensitivity for my government. The request must be transmitted discreetly to avoid embarrassment. But I give you my word as a combatant that I shall do all in my power to help your marines." He paused, smiled and risked, "I think we shall be good allies, n'est-ce pas?"

"D'accord—I think so, Lieutenant. But must you conduct your ship to another location?"

"No. It is not my ship, but Captain Brown's. I live in Ha Tien and will return there."

"So you are a Naval commander there?"

"Not exactly. I'm a … a Naval liaison officer. Saigon will listen to your request. You'll have to believe me on that."

He stood to leave, checking once more the longitude and latitude shown on the French map to locate the beleaguered marine battalions. Hesitating, he fingered the aero photo map in the pocket of his fatigues, thought what the hell, and withdrew it.

"Capitaine, I think these old French maps are inaccurate. See here, yours shows an extra 60 kilometers between Kep and the Chaine d'Éléphante Mountains. It must have been drawn from French visual surveys decades ago. I'll get you some new ones like these. It's hard to accomplish Naval gunfire otherwise." He laughed as the astonished Cambodians compared the maps.

They went on deck and hailed the LST to send a boat.

"Please return in 48 hours. I should have a report back by then," Medici said.

Captain Brown waited in his cabin on the LST and appeared relieved when Medici entered.

"Got any aspirin, Captain? They speak French as a mother tongue. I haven't used it for years. … gives me a hell of a headache." Brown rang for his steward who returned with the aspirin. Medici took four.

"What did they want?" Brown asked.

Medici stared at him with a cold appraising look that said, "What are you, out of your fucking mind? I can't tell you."

"Captain, I need to send a top secret message to Saigon. Can I use the crypto shack?" He rose to leave.

The captain, obviously embarrassed, rose with him. "Of course, Lieutenant. You know where it is…."

"All I can tell you is that their intentions do not appear hostile, but you are responsible for the safety of your own ship. They will probably return in 48 hours. Try not to scare them off. I'll be back then."

Medici sent his message. Brown watched him go over the side to a PBR for the ride back to Ha Tien. Funny bastard, Brown thought, then went to the crypto room and got the communications technician to let him read Medici's top secret message to Saigon about the Cambodian arms request.

17

Shore Bombardment

Saigon did not respond directly to Medici's request on behalf of the Cambodians. N-2, staff intelligence at Naval headquarters, acknowledged receipt of Medici's message with their own TOP SECRET, which told him to report any future "encounters" to N-2, Saigon Command Intelligence, and the CIA Station Chief at the Saigon embassy. The embassy would forward his information to the "highest level."

That eliminated 12 addressees from his standard report list, including his administrative boss, the Walrus. The Walrus will be pissed, he thought. N-2 did not mention the word Cambodian nor did it encourage him to make any further contact. Covering their asses, Medici thought. They won't tell me to contact the Cambodes for fear of violating the neutrality policy, but they're drooling for direct Cambodian intelligence.

Forty-eight hours later, the Cambodes were back in Corvette E-311. Captain Brown hailed them with bonhomie, asked them to stand off, and sent a Seawolf helo to fetch Medici. He flew to the LST, then went over in a flat-bottomed LCP to be greeted warmly by Som Sary.

He didn't know what to tell him. He reported that he had sent the message to Saigon and that it had been acknowledged, but that Saigon refused to give him a direct answer.

Som Sary waved it off. Not to worry, he said. Everything is OK. His answer struck Medici as cavalier in light of the desperate tone of the first discussion of the marine battalion's siege. Something was going on that no one would tell him about, he concluded. The usual intelligence game bullshit. I can't tell Captain Brown; Saigon can't tell me. The "no need to know" conundrum.

"Do you desire to accompany us up the coast for Naval gunfire in support of our marine battalions near Kep? We can go further up to Kampot or even up to our Naval base at Ream if you like."

"Now?" Medici asked.

"Yes."

He swallowed, "Sure. Can I send a flashing light message to the LST to let them know I'm going?"

"But of course, Lieutenant."

Medici raised the LST on the flashing light and sent the following message to Captain Brown:

"Under way to tour Cambodian coast with Captain Som Sary on RCE-311. Return in a few days. Cheers. T.N. Medici."

They got under way with much ceremony and blasting of their steam whistle to impress the American ship. Finally they chugged at four knots back into Cambodian waters toward the Kep peninsula, 20 kilometers north of Ha Tien. With binoculars they could see the outlines of the governor's palace and the stubby treasury building. In three hours they were circling off Kep.

Sary contacted what he said was a Cambodian Naval gunfire spotter on the ancient radio and shouted shrilly at him in Khmer for several minutes. Finally he turned to Medici, smiled, and said, "Now we are ready." He pulled the ancient French map out and started calling coordinates to the spotter, rather than the spotter to him. Curious, Medici thought.

The gunners aimed the three-inch according to Sary's orders and fired a round. Medici saw it hit the hillside 1,000 feet above Kep between the curlicued white spires of two Buddhist stupas.

The spotter screamed angrily over the radio at Sary who shouted angrily back. Must have dropped it close by the spotter rather than the target, Medici thought. He tried hard not to smile. They heard the thump of a second round that landed clear over the hillside. Further argument ensued between the spotter and Sary, to no clear conclusion. Sary fired a third round, spoke with the spotter, turned off the radio with a gesture of exasperation, and fired three two-round salvoes in quick succession. Then he ordered the helmsman to steer northwest toward Kampot and went to his cabin.

Medici, alone in the small compartment that served as chart house and radio room for the ship, could see the backs of the conning officer, Kim, and the helmsman through the narrow door that led to the bridge. He looked around the radio room. Spy time, he thought. Rolled charts stuck out of pigeonholes on the forward bulkhead. The ancient radio gear, bearing the label "RCA Global Communications," covered the portside bulkhead. A mechanical cryptography machine and a pad of foolscap communication paper sat on the desk in front of the bank of radios.

He scanned the pad quickly. It contained the routing and priority indicators used by this Cambodian ship. Medici bent closer and saw the clear inkless imprint of French words on the sheet that had lain under the previous message Som Sary had written, encrypted, and sent to Phnom Penh.

The wheels began to turn in his head and his heart beat faster. He knew Naval Security Group monitored all the Cambodian's encrypted radio transmissions. This imprinted sheet could be filled in with graphite powder, read in clear text, and matched against the Cambodian encrypted message on the security group computers, cracking the code.

Glancing at the bridge, he saw Kim and the helmsman occupied with course settings. He listened carefully for any noise from Sary's cabin. With his heart in his mouth he reached down and began to tear the imprint sheet from the pad a fiber at a time. The task took 15 seconds but seemed like a lifetime. His palms sweated. He kept his gaze on the back of Kim's head as he folded the paper, stood slowly and stuck it down in his skivvies.

The waist band of his fatigues loosened and his .45 slid down his pants leg toward the steel deck. He jammed his knees together, bracing for the noise that would make Kim turn and expose him. His calves pinched the pistol, painfully jamming the hammer into his left leg. He gritted his teeth from the spurring, slid the pistol back up and had secured it in his waistband by the time Sary entered the chart house from his cabin.

"Lieutenant, we must dine well tonight in honor of our countries' friendship. Kim!" He barked Khmer to the X/O. Kim nodded and ordered the helmsman to change course for Kas Kong, a green island visible to port. Medici took a long slow breath as Sary reentered his cabin.

He watched the island draw closer until they were 1,000 yards off the beach and he could see oxen grazing near the water. He walked aft on the main deck to the small stateroom Sary had assigned him and slept as soon as he laid down.

A timid Cambodian seaman gently shook Medici's arm until he came awake. "Le diner," he said, and pantomimed shoveling rice into his mouth from a bowl. Medici nodded and sat up. The seaman left. Medici washed his face, stood out on deck in the gentle sun and looked down the side of the ship. Where the lifeboat bobbed alongside, lurid red-brown stains covered the ship's hull and the boat's deck. The sight made his stomach twitch.

He walked along the deck to Sary's cabin, knocked and entered when Sary answered, "Entrez!" The small table was set for two with white tablecloth, scratched silverware and spiffy white, blue-trimmed china bearing the single anchor crest of the Cambodian Navy. Sary motioned for Medici to sit down and poured him a small glass of dark Cambodian rice wine that he cut with seltzer water from an old-fashioned fizz bottle.

Medici toasted Sary. "À votre santé!" *To your health.* The steward entered, laboring under the weight of a huge platter piled with steaming bloody meat, enough for six men. Medici swallowed hard. He could feel another bout of gastroenteritis coming and didn't need this. 'When in Rome…,' he thought and took a big hunk of the red meat and dropped it on his plate.

"Fresh meat in the Gulf of Thailand!" He mouthed the first bite. It tasted unlike any meat he had eaten before, gamier than venison or elk. "Where did you get it?"

Sary smiled. "Some peasants on the island graciously donated one of their oxen to serve our honored guest. My men butchered it alongside the ship within the last hour. Here, Lieutenant, try some Maggi. It masks the gamey taste of green meat."

Medici blanched. Nausea churned in his stomach. He smiled slowly, painfully, then raised the next forkful in a gesture of pleasure before he ate it. The things he did for Naval Intelligence.

The next day they covered the coast to Kampot, and the day after proceeded to Ream but did not moor at the Cambodian Naval base. Sary received an urgent radio message to return Medici to An Thoi on Phu Quoc Island. They steamed the 42 miles in seven hours and moored off An Thoi. A Swift Boat came alongside for Medici. He saluted Sary and thanked him. Jim Thompson, NILO An Thoi, met him at the dock.

"You're in deep shit, Tom. Saigon went nuts when they heard you got under way with the Cambodes. We still don't know where we stand with the new Lon Nol government. And N-2 doesn't want a NILO to spend time in the Hanoi Hilton, if you dig."

Medici looked surprised. "I had my pistol...."

Jim laughed again. "That doesn't mean shit. They **got you** if they want you out there all by yourself. Come on."

They walked past the end of the Marsden matting **airstrip. A** 40-foot black container box sat on the edge of the matting. **Medici** noticed tiny white stencils that said "U.S. Air Force."

"What's that, Tim? It wasn't here before."

"Sorry, Tom. I'm not supposed to talk to anyone **about it**."

"GODDAMMIT Jim, why can't we talk about this stuff to each other! The fucking VC know exactly what's going on, but we can't say shit to each other."

"Okay, okay, Tom." Jim looked around to be sure no one was within earshot. "It's two thousand M-2 carbines and a bunch of ammunition for the Cambodes. No one's supposed to know we're helping them at this stage, while officially we're supposed to be figuring out what the relationship between our governments is going to be. That's really all I can say now."

Medici fumed. He walked off in a huff. He had arranged the request for the weapons with the Cambodians, and his own people wouldn't tell him that they were to be delivered. Fuck this secrecy shit, he thought, and took a long walk to cool down.

18

Briefing

The field telephone growled while Medici sat in the Phao Dai team room reviewing agent reports. No one else was around, so he answered it. Hayward spoke, his friend and senior advisor to the Vietnamese Navy in Ha Tien.

"Let me talk to NILO," Hayward said.

"Who do you think this is, Ho Chi Minh?" Medici said.

Hayward laughed. "Rainy Day actual and Orange Juice actual are on their way in. They want you to brief them on the Cambodian situation when they go from the hill to the new Vietnamese base. Okay?"

"Hayward, what is this code name bullshit? What's going on?" Medici didn't feel like playing Navy games today.

"Tom. This is serious. Think!"

Medici searched his memory. He knew "Rainy Day" was his boss Admiral Zumwalt's code name, commander of Naval forces in Vietnam. But "Orange Juice" drew a blank.

"Come on, NILO. HICOMM."

Medici dug into his subconscious. It took him back to the staff communications room on *Tulsa* when he stood the token watch required for officers of the deck. The endless banks of communications equipment fascinated him. Once an hour the comm officer let him pick up the red handset labeled "HICOMM" and say clearly and slowly, "Orange Juice, Orange Juice, this is Camelot, Camelot. Radio check, over." After a pause, the scrambler circuit beeped and cracked, and a nasal, electronically reconstituted voice answered slowly, "Camelot, Camelot, this is Orange Juice, Orange Juice. Roger, over." To which Medici responded, "This is Camelot. Roger, out."

The drill ensured viability of the emergency radio circuit

101

between the Seventh Fleet admiral on *Tulsa* and CINCPACFLT. The circuit carried "White Rocket" messages from the White House to all U.S. forces on one subject: nuclear war. The eerie echo of the circuit, the molasses delay in speech, the inhuman voice that resulted from scrambling and unscrambling, both thrilled and scared Medici. Even stranger was that while he spoke on the circuit, he envisioned 200 headsetted Kremlin analysts listening carefully to every word.

"Roger on Orange Juice, Hayward. I'll be ready." He hung up.

The big Sea Stallion helicopter dropped crisply into the circled H. Medici mused about the color, a heathery, violet-gray, different than the olive drab and slate-gray choppers that worked in-country. A shipborne helo, it was clean and waxed and its pilot wore a carrier flight suit and helmet. The crew acted nervous. Door gunners jerkily scanned Phao Dai hill for what? Snipers, ambush teams? Inexperience, Medici thought.

The helo shut down and three men got out. First, a tall, distinguished man with gray hair and bushy eyebrows, unmistakably VADM Zumwalt. Next, a heavyset, balding man a head shorter than Zumwalt. Medici recognized Admiral Hyland who served on *Tulsa* as C/O, then Seventh and Pacific Fleet Commander. A thin, sandy-haired young man limped from the helo. Medici noticed he wore a wash-khaki uniform, lieutenant's tracks and four rows of ribbons. His weary face looked vaguely familiar.

Medici waited until Hayward greeted them, introduced them to the river division commander, then led them to the PBR for the ride to the Vietnamese Navy base. Medici joined them at the boat.

Admiral Zumwalt returned Medici's salute and shook his hand. "You're doing a great job here, Tom, and I think you know it." He smiled. Medici grinned. "I think you know Admiral Hyland...." Medici saluted and shook hands with Hyland. "And an old *Tulsa* shipmate, my flag lieutenant, Mel Walters."

Medici startled. Two years ago he had replaced Walters on *Tulsa* as assistant navigator, the plum job for promising junior officers. Mel still wore a self-effacing boyish smile, but a touch of wistfulness and resignation was apparent. The story on *Tulsa* was that Mel had been transferred to river boats in the Mekong Delta.

Medici had not heard about his promotion to flag lieutenant.

The two chatted before the boat shoved off. The scuttlebutt on *Tulsa* was true. Mel told Medici that he got shot in the butt, literally, which accounted for the limp. After convalescing, he returned to Saigon where Zumwalt chose him as flag lieutenant. He seemed utterly unchanged except for stiffness and a limp in his leg. Deep down, Medici felt like crying for his friend's wounds. He knew he was really lucky to be in one piece, and not to have to patrol the river every day.

The boat pulled away. Its twin GMC diesels growled and blubbered erratically at low RPMs. Medici stood in the stern with Zumwalt, Hyland, and Mel. The boat picked up speed, raised her bow, lowered her stern, and tossed a rooster tail four feet behind the jet drive. Gunners scanned the shore carefully for any sign of ambush.

Medici had the uncomfortable recollection of the lone plane carrying Japan's Admiral Yamamoto during the Second World War. American fighters had shot down and killed Japan's Naval commander as he flew to a remote Japanese base in the Pacific. Medici felt nervous about all this brass as a target in one boat, but the ride wasn't far.

Zumwalt asked the coxswain to slow so the diesels would run quieter. As they moved slowly across Ha Tien Bay, he said, "Tom, I'd like you to sum up for Admiral Hyland the situation in Cambodia as you see it."

Medici swallowed. He had rehearsed a glib, formal narrative, but it seemed inappropriate in this group of friends. He looked ahead to the mangrove wedge beyond the new Navy base, the "V" where Cambodia lay an easy mortar shot away, then he cleared his throat and looked Hyland in the eye.

"The situation is turning to shit, Admiral. Since Sihanouk was dumped and the White House is 'reevaluating' our relations with Cambodia, whatever the hell that means, the NVA have moved steadily to secure and defend storage areas and border crossing corridors into Vietnam.

"Before, they left the Cambodian villagers alone as they passed through on their way to Vietnam. Now they steal the rice, rape the women, kill the meager Cambodian district forces, and shoot at us with impunity from the border. Usually we can't return fire under the Rules of Engagement, except in clear cases like two weeks ago." Medici's throat tightened and he coughed, remembering the mortar incident and its aftermath.

"It's really bad news. Our forces on the border are sitting ducks. We'd better do something to protect our own skins, to say nothing of the wretched, outgunned Cambodians who're getting mauled.

"I know the president's in a tight spot politically because of the neutrality issue, but we really have no choice the way things have come down. We've got to go in soon, at least to clean out the weapons caches before the North Vietnamese move them." Medici stopped. He looked at the three men, realizing with horror he was haranguing Hyland.

Hyland nodded gravely. "I know, son. Your report tracks exactly what we're hearing from Washington. Believe me, we're doing what we can to get off the dime." He stared out over the bay.

Zumwalt stepped aside, motioning Medici to him. "Now that Cambodian intelligence is so important, some of my staff think a senior officer should take over Ha Tien to deal with the Cambodes, because of the political sensitivity." He scanned the riverbank with hawk eyes, then looked at Medici. "I'm not going to do that. You're my man in Cambodia and you're going to stay. Keep up the objective reporting. I'm counting on you." Zumwalt held Medici's shoulder. Mel smiled.

Medici blushed. He said to Mel, "Well, I guess we didn't do badly for two old *Tulsa* sailors."

"You mean three," Hyland said. They all smiled while the coxswain maneuvered alongside the bulkhead at the new base.

VADM Zumwalt and General Abrams at Ha Tien.

19

Kaoh Tunsay

At precisely 9 a.m. the Seawolf helo set down on the pad for 30 seconds while Medici boarded, put his AWOL bag under the seat and plugged in his intercom. The pilot, John Rains, leaped the helo over the berm, reached transition speed, and gained altitude before he spoke.

"Three-zero-zero magnetic okay, NILO?"

"Fine. It's the biggest island off Kep. Head up along the coast until you see a green island about two kilometers wide, due south of Kep. It's called Kaoh Tunsay, Tunsay Island. Sihanouk used it as an R&R spot for diplomats. The province governor, Samuth, invited me. He promised to let me look around. Here's my map. It shows it," Medici said.

"Not necessary, NILO. It's real clear on my aero chart. Where do you want to land? It looks like one big mountain."

Medici paused. "We'll have to eyeball it, John. I've never been there."

"Click-click" on the intercom. Rains signaled acknowledgment.

They flew in silence along the coast for 15 minutes in the cool clean air above the gulf. When they spotted the roofs of the Kep town buildings, then the stolid facade of the tiny treasury, Rains banked left and the island loomed directly in front of them. It reminded Medici of a tiny Tahiti. One prominent peak rose 500 feet from the center of the island. Its green slopes glided to a flat margin of palm and brush that disappeared into the Gulf.

They spiraled to 150 feet above the shore and the door gunners came alert. They were deep in Cambodia now and anything could happen. The helo circled the island and Medici saw a cluster of cottages and a large white stucco building. Stone patio walls and

NILO HA TIEN

trellises dripped with glowing, ultraviolet bougainvillea all around the white building.

"Where am I supposed to land, NILO?" Rains said. The 10-foot-wide strip of beige beach between tree line and water was not wide enough for the rotor disc. They came in lower, and Medici spied a frail dock that stretched 20 feet seaward to fishing weirs.

"Can you hover over that dock?" he asked.

"Sure thing. But I can't land. It looks like it barely carries its own weight."

"Hover as close to it as you can, and I'll drop down from the skid."

"Okay. But no flying Wallenda stuff...."

Click-Click.

Rains corrected expertly for the wind's set and drift. He hovered the Huey at an angle to the dock, keeping his eyes on the tall palms at the edge of the sand. His rotor wash blew water, sand and palm fronds inland. The helicopter hung like a rock eight feet above the dock.

Medici slapped the door gunner's arm and told him to drop the AWOL bag to him after he was down. He thanked Rains with a thumbs-up, took off his flight helmet and left it on the seat. Then he crawled out on the skid and watched the dock swing slowly from side to side below him. When he got the rhythm of the motion, he hung in a chin-up position from the skid and released his grip.

The helo lurched upward when he let go. He fell two feet to the dock and bent his knees to absorb the shock. His left leg broke through a brittle plank to mid-thigh before he caught himself with his hands. He pulled his leg out of the shattered plank, crawled beachward and stood, then gestured for the gunner to toss the AWOL bag. The gunner threw it well and Medici caught the bag like a skilled wide receiver.

He waved the helo off. Rains pulled pitch, backed away from the palm trees over the water, and disappeared around the curve of the island back to Ha Tien.

An eerie quiet enveloped Medici. It dizzied him to think he was alone, deep in Cambodia. No one knew, no one could protect him. He moved to the tree line to get out of the open, knelt behind a coconut palm, withdrew his .45 pistol from the bag, cocked it and held it with both hands in front of him as he moved inland toward the resort.

The trail was easy to follow. Bathers had worn a path from the compound to the dock where Medici landed. There was no sound or sign of human presence as he walked quietly through the cool jungle shade along the clay path.

The trees thinned and he saw the mossy stucco walls of the main building; he crept toward it Injun-style from tree to tree. A part of his mind told him he ought not be so cavalier about traveling alone this far into Cambodia, but his sixth sense told him he was safe.

He came upon the clearing and heard voices. He peeked around a heavy stand of bougainvillea and saw a silver-haired civilian in bush clothes with a group of officers. Two Cambodian boy-soldiers stood a limp and ineffective guard.

Medici dropped the hammer on the pistol, hid it in his waistband, then strode into full view of the men, waving and smiling. He shouted, "Bonjour," to Governor Um Samuth who rose to greet him.

"We heard your helicopter," Samuth said in French, "and wondered where you would land."

"Had to drop in for this visit." Medici responded quickly in French, laughed, and extended his hand. "Gouverneur Samuth? I'm Lieutenant Medici. U.S. Navy."

"Enchanté, Lieutenant. Capitaine Som Sary told me about you when he arranged this meeting. Our new government needs more friends like you."

"My pleasure, Gouverneur." Medici dismissed the subject by turning to the building. "What's this building?"

"It was the administrative facility for the Tunsay resort. The hacienda. The offices were here; meals were prepared and taken by guests at these tables. Sihanouk put in this tower and planned to relay television all the way from Phnom Penh."

Medici looked where Samuth pointed. A triangular steel tower rose 70 feet above the roof of the hacienda. At its peak stood a long aluminum antenna with many narrow cross elements. Coaxial cables ran down the tower from the antenna and through the hacienda roof. Medici noticed the antenna pointed at Ha Tien.

Medici walked inside the hacienda and found the hole where the coaxial cables came through the ceiling behind a sturdy steel rack. The shelves were covered with dust except for clean rectangles outlined in black rubber smudges. A table next to the rack also bore dust prints, but Medici noticed the shapes were pentagrams instead of rectangles.

Medici reached around the rack for the thick black cables. They were marked with orange Cyrillic letters and numerals. With his knife he cut a six-inch section from each cable and slid them into his pocket. He returned to the patio.

"May I see the cottages?" he asked Samuth.

"Of course, Lieutenant. The island is yours."

Medici walked 200 yards further inland to the guest cottages which were sited in a loose semicircle. Each had its own tiny patio screened by low bushes.

He walked into the first cottage. The tile floor kept it cool. He was struck by the complete absence of furniture or fixtures. Divots of plaster had been ripped out of the walls exposing the wooden lath underneath. Medici examined the plaster. Freshly broken, its edges still powdery. A large mapboard had been torn from the wall of the cottage, he guessed, from the roughly rectangular pattern of the missing plaster chunks.

He entered the second cottage. No furniture here either, and fresh scratch marks on the tile and aquamarine door frame. The walls were discolored where large sheets, probably maps, had been taped. Smooth white paper ears remained under tape scraps at the corners. The paint under the map bore the ball pen imprint "117.74 MC," which Medici wrote down in his notepad. Someone boogied quickly from the old resort, he thought.

The third and fourth cottages were also empty and showed signs of hasty departure. Intuitively, Medici returned to the second cottage for a last look and was surprised to see a three-inch triangle of paper on the floor under a dust ball. He picked it up and peeled off the dust. It was a scrap of newsprint, the top center of a page. The printing was Cyrillic but he could clearly make out the masthead:

HL Serra

"PRABDA 5 Mai, 1970" *PRAVDA MAY 5, 1970*
Less than 10 days old.

He carefully placed the newspaper scrap in a small plastic envelope he carried for evidence, pocketed it, and returned to Samuth's group.

Samuth stood as Medici approached. A smile revealed enormous teeth in his oval brown face. He held out two clear plastic bags fogged from the contents. Inside Medici saw daubs of red, green and yellow. Spines poked through the bags.

"Chom-chom!" Medici exclaimed. He caught the first bag Samuth threw and tore it open on the plank table. A shower of spiny, egg-shaped rambutan spilled to the tabletop. Medici took his knife and began husking shells from the fruit. A clean cut exposed grapey flesh around a large pit. He slid it in his mouth and savored its sweet, lightly metallic juice, then concentrated on stripping the husks from the flesh, popping the fruit into his mouth, and flicking the split husks onto the table, like so many small brassieres.

"Lieutenant, you are easily seduced," Samuth laughed. "A few chom-chom and you serve Cambodia."

Medici looked at him, raised an eyebrow and kept eating.

On the table, two plates of red, sweet Cambodian sausage drew a small cloud of flies. Half a dozen cold bottles labeled "Coke" in English and Khmer sweated between the fruit sacks and sausage. They sat.

Medici watched Samuth give instructions to his lieutenants. Medici recalled from Samuth's dossier: a distinguished 50-year-old architect, more comfortable with suits and the boulevards of Paris than bush jackets and the resorts of Tunsay. Som Sary had told Medici he would like Samuth's savoir faire. Sorbonne trained, Samuth had practiced in Paris, then returned to Phnom Penh where, as a remote relative of the royal family, the Norodoms, he made the acquaintance of Lon Nol.

Unable to abide Sihanouk's neglect of the duties of state, Samuth joined the deposers. Lon Nol appointed him governor of the provinces of Kampot, where the North Vietnamese already engaged the Cambodian marines, and Bokkor, high in the Chaine d'Éléphante Mountains, where marauding Khmer Rouge troops were entrenched.

Despite Samuth's dicey assignment, Medici viewed the turf as privileged. Sihanouk had vacation palaces in both provinces.

Samuth smiled placidly. "Capitaine de Corvette Som Sary speaks highly of you, Lieutenant." Medici nodded politely. "He has informed me of your soldierly concern for the plight of our marine battalions." He gestured behind him toward Kep. "Besieged" would be a better word, Medici thought.

"A professional sympathy for combatants in distress," Medici said.

Samuth poured Medici a Coke. He offered to stiffen it with Cambodian rice liquor, but Medici declined and took some sausage. It tasted delicious and sweet, despite the clots of pigskin and hair in each piece.

"I am pleased your country will come to Cambodia's aid, if the rifles for the marines are any indication." Samuth looked directly at Medici. He searched his face for any sign that the U.S. had decided to intervene. Medici didn't move a muscle.

"I wasn't aware that decision had been made, mon Gouverneur."

Samuth smiled. "Let us say we are optimistic. With your help we can defeat the Vietnamese aggressors in a matter of six months, with Cambodian soldiers carrying American weapons. Then peace and tranquility will return to our lovely country." He smiled. The man truly believed what he said, Medici thought.

Samuth's statement had unnerved him. For all his sophistication, Samuth was dangerously naive. Did he really think U.S. intervention against the North Vietnamese in Cambodia would take care of the problem in six months? For an instant, Medici had a vision of what Cambodia would look like in six months. Bomb craters in the paddies, burned-out villages, impassable mined roads, and horrendous casualties among the boy-soldiers now training with broomsticks in Phnom Penh. The disparity of their visions chilled him. What are we getting these people into?

Samuth continued. "You must understand, Lieutenant, our people have met and defeated the Vietnamese aggressor before, and defeated him soundly."

Medici swallowed. He keyed on Samuth's continued use of

"Vietnamese aggressor," not *North* Vietnamese aggressor. If Samuth couldn't make that distinction, could his peasants and troops?

"In fact, the last time we met in combat, we captured their three top generals"—Samuth began to laugh hysterically—"buried them up to their heads, and lighted cooking fires around them so our generals could boil tea water while they decided what to do with the captured troops." Tears rolled from Samuth's eyes. "The Vietnamese generals did not enjoy that party as much as ours did."

Medici's stomach rolled. He was horrified by the barbarism that lay beneath Samuth's civility. He feared this might be a privileged glimpse into the Cambodian cultural personality.

"When did this occur?" Medici asked.

Samuth stopped laughing. "During the great war, of course, about 800 years ago." He wiped tears of laughter from his face.

It's going to be a long war, Medici thought.

The conversation dwindled. The faint pup-pup-pup of an approaching helo reached them. Samuth looked at Medici who sat eating chom-chom.

"Yours, Lieutenant?" he asked.

Medici nodded. They watched Rains' olive drab Seawolf circle the island then stand in a hover 50 feet above the small boat dock at the beach.

Medici wiped his hands and stood. He saluted Samuth, shook his hand and smiled.

"Wait!" Samuth ordered. He withdrew a sleek black 9mm pistol from his holster. Medici tensed. *Oh, shit*, he thought.

Samuth turned the pistol and handed its grip to Medici. Medici's eyes widened as he took it.

"That is from me," Samuth said. "And this is from Lon Nol." He reached into a canvas map case and withdrew a weightless olive Cambodian Naval beret that bore a single brass anchor. He handed it to Medici.

Medici smiled and put it on. It fit perfectly.

"You are a friend of Cambodia," Samuth said.

Medici thought quickly, then reached into his uniform blouse

NILO Ha Tien

and proffered his customized .45 pistol. "The Gouverneur must accept my pistol in return, in keeping with Cambodian custom." A gunner's mate at Ha Tien had told him that, for Cambodians, the exchange of pistols by combatants was like the blood brother ritual of the American Indians.

Samuth beamed. "You know much about Khmer customs, if not our history. Thank you." He took Medici's pistol.

Medici filled his AWOL bag with chom-chom and the pistol, a Belgian Browning. He ran to the beach and waved to Rains as he broke from the tree line onto the sand. He moved along the dock, squinting to keep the sand from his eyes. Incredibly, Rains brought the bird down to hover two feet above the dock. Medici stepped aboard from the skid, waving the bag of succulent fruit triumphantly to Rains and his crew. They grinned as Medici strapped himself in for the ride back to Ha Tien.

In 20 minutes they landed on the LST off Ha Tien. Medici gave half the chom-chom to the air crew and left the other half for the wardroom. He went immediately to the crypto room where the watch officer let him in with a wave. At a desk he wrote a secret message to Saigon:

"P 140615Z May 70
FM: NILO HA TIEN
TO: COMNAVFORV
     USEMB SGN, OSA
     COMUSMACV
BT   S E C R E T
NILO HA TIEN SPOT REPORT 12
BLACKBEARD

1. ON 14 MAY NILO INSERTED ON KAOH TUNSAY ISLAND, CB (VS 2853) FOR PURPOSE OF MEETING GOVERNOR UM SAMUTH OF KAMPOT PROVINCE, CB, WHO THIS WEEK ESTABLISHED FORWARD BASE OF SECOND MILITARY REGION COMMAND STAFF ON TUNSAY.

2. ISLAND WAS RESORT FOR VISITING FOREIGN DIGNITARIES SENT FOR RELAXATION BY PRINCE SIHANOUK. IN NILO HA TIEN SPOT REPORT 8, COLLECTION TEAM FIVE AGENT REPORTED SMALL GROUP OF EASTERN EUROPEANS PERMANENTLY OCCUPYING RESORT FACILITIES FOR LAST 18 MOS, AND SUSPENSION OF NORMAL TRAFFIC OF DIPLOMATIC GUESTS.

3. NILO VISUALLY INSPECTED MAIN BUILDING. BUILDING TOPPED WITH SEVENTY FOOT RADIO TOWER HOLDING FOREIGN MADE YAGI ANTENNA FOR UHF AND VHF FREQUENCIES, AIMED AT HA TIEN AREA 6 MILES TO SOUTHEAST. COAX CABLES BEARING CYRILLIC LETTERS RAN INTO OFFICE OF MAIN BUILDING WHERE EVIDENCE WAS FOUND OF RECENTLY REMOVED BANKS OF RADIO EQUIPMENT. FOOTPRINTS OF ONE PIECE OF REMOVED RADIO EQUIPMENT MATCHES EXACTLY IRREGULAR PENTAGONAL FOOTPRINTS OF U.S. NAVY RIVER BOAT TACTICAL VOICE CIRCUIT SCRAMBLER. SECTIONS OF COAX CABLES WITH CYRILLIC MARKINGS FORWARDED BY POUCH TO EVALUATION CENTER SAIGON FOR ANALYSIS.

4. NILO INSPECTED INDIVIDUAL COTTAGES OF RESORT. EVIDENCE FOUND OF HASTY REMOVAL OF FURNITURE AND WALL MAPS. WALL UNDER MAP BORE BALLPEN IMPRINT '117.74 MC,' U.S. NAVY SECURE VOICE TACTICAL FREQUENCY. ALSO FOUND SCRAP OF NEWSPAPER IN ONE COTTAGE, FROM MAY 5, 1970 EDITION OF SOVIET NEWSPAPER "PRAVDA." SCRAP FORWARDED BY POUCH TO EVALUATION CENTER SAIGON FOR ANALYSIS AND VERIFICATION.

5. NILO COMMENT: NILO SURMISES THAT TUNSAY ISLAND WAS SITE OF SOVIET RADIO INTERCEPT STATION REPORTED FREQUENTLY BY COLLECTION TEAM FIVE DURING LAST TWELVE MONTHS. INTERCEPT STATION

NILO Ha Tien

REPORTEDLY MONITORED RIVER BOAT, AIRCRAFT AND ARMY SECURE TACTICAL FREQUENCIES. IT PROVIDED REAL TIME UNIT LOCATION INFORMATION TO NORTH VIETNAMESE ADVISOR WHO WAS IN RADIO CONTACT WITH NORTH VIETNAMESE AND VIET CONG UNITS ALONG CB BORDER. IT IS LIKELY THAT ALL SECURE TACTICAL COMMUNICATIONS AMONG RIVER CRAFT HAVE BEEN MONITORED AND COMPROMISED IN PAST. EQUIPMENT LIKELY REMOVED SOMETIME IN THE LAST SEVEN DAYS ON ADVANCE KNOWLEDGE THAT SECOND MILITARY REGION COMMAND STAFF OF NEW LON NOL GOVERNMENT WOULD OCCUPY ISLAND. NILO WILL TASK COLLECTION TEAM FIVE TO LOCATE NEW SITE OF SOVIET RADIO INTERCEPT STATION.

GP-4
BT"

Medici thought of the river minesweeper whose positions for sweeping operations were broadcast over the scrambled circuit at the time of the bloody ambush at The Bend in which one sailor was killed and five were wounded. Now it was no mystery. *Detente*, my ass, he thought.

20

Shooting Coconuts at Kep

Medici marveled at the ocher French colonial mansion framed by tall coconut palms. There on the flatlands of the Kep Peninsula, surrounded by the Gulf of Thailand, the governor's residence appeared as stately as Versailles, though closer inspection revealed that it was constructed of colonial stucco and pocked by NVA bullets. Um Samuth, governor of Kampot and Bokor Provinces of Cambodia, stood quietly next to Medici and Non Kim, his regional military commander. All three absorbed the beauty of the peaceful Asian day, the aquamarine of the gulf, and the Chaine d'Éléphante Mountains rising lazily from the horizon behind the palace.

"Je ne sais pourquoi," *I don't know why,* said General Kim. "We now have official channels in Phnom Penh to deal with your government. Why should we deal with you directly?"

"Mon Général, 85 percent of North Vietnamese supplies destined for the delta are introduced by sea between here and Sihanoukville, and then transported across the border. Already those weapons are not merely shipped through Cambodia but have been turned on your soldiers and civilians."

Kim blinked and stared. Emboldened by the impact of his remark on the Cambodian, Medici continued. "Now that Sihanoukville is closed to Communist weapons shipments, this infiltration is specifically the business of Naval Intelligence. I respectfully request your direct cooperation in collection activities. I don't think we are in a position yet to officially provide weaponry to make up for the shortfall until matters are arranged between our governments, but I have friends who can and have provided you guns on an emergency basis."

Kim shifted his weight from one foot to the other and slid

his M-16 from his shoulder to the ground and leaned on it as if it were a walking stick. His troops were woefully outgunned by the NVA in Cambodia. He had not looked Medici straight in the eye since the subject of the infiltration had come up.

Um Samuth sensed the tension and Kim's awkwardness when Medici confronted him bluntly. Cambodians seldom dealt bluntly and directly with important or sensitive issues. Samuth wished Medici would use some tact at this critical time. He sought to break the tension.

"Lieutenant, do you like my mansion?" Samuth asked, beaming. "It is better sited than Sihanouk's summer palace in Kep, *n'est-ce pas?*"

"*Oui, mon Gouverneur, sans doute,*" Medici said, smiling appreciatively. "I am only sorry that the security situation prevents you from occupying it."

"Ah, but that is temporary. Soon there will be great changes in our relations, and the Cambodian people with American help will expunge the Vietnamese bandits from our land. I told you six months—no longer," Samuth said, earnest as a child.

Medici shuddered at the governor's fatuous and naive remark. It irritated him every time he said it. In his mind's eye, the only future he could see included huge B-52 bomb craters all over the grounds and the mansion reduced to a pile of rubble.

"Do you see the double set of French doors on the right corner of the third floor? That will be your suite, Lieutenant Medici!"

"You are extremely gracious, mon Gouverneur," Medici said gratefully. If only Kim could be won over, he thought. Samuth was on his side, despite Medici's bluntness. Kim was a harder nut to crack. St. Cyr trained, he had worked his way up through the Khmer forces to become commander of the Cambodian Second Military Region, covering the Cambodian coast. In military matters he had the last say, even though Samuth was civilian commander as governor of the same area.

"And such coconuts," Samuth laughed and gestured expansively with his left arm. "Nowhere in Kep are there such large and flavorful milk coconuts as right here in front of the mansion." He pointed to the tall, slender fruit-laden palms 70 meters away. "We must have some green coconut milk with luncheon. Have you tasted it, Lieutenant?"

Medici nodded. In the distance he heard the dhuh-dhuh-dhuh of AK-47 fire answered by the brrrritt of an M-16.

"General Kim will send a man up to collect some," Samuth said, placing his hand on Kim's shoulder in an attempted gesture of bonhomie.

Kim looked impassively at the governor, then broke into a smile and said, "I shall do better, mon Gouverneur—we shall have them immediately!"

Kim raised and shouldered his M-16 in the direction of one of the palm tops, clicking the safety to semi-auto. He drew a bead on a large coconut and slowly squeezed the trigger. The rifle cracked once and expelled its hot brass shell casing into Medici's cheek, leaving a small welt. He did not flinch. The large green coconut husk fell 50 feet to the ground, spilling shards of husk and part of its milk as it tumbled. Kim's finesse with the weapon was not lost on Medici. For an American general to have maintained such proficiency with a rifle was unlikely.

Samuth looked admiringly at Kim, then turned to Medici. "My general is, how do you say *en anglais*—a crack shot? Do you care to try, Lieutenant?" At Samuth's gesture Kim offered the rifle to Medici. Shit, he thought, an embarrassment is just what I need right now. Kim read his thoughts.

Medici smiled openly at Samuth and Kim, "*D'accord mes amis*. But it is necessary to lose less milk, *n'est-ce pas?*" and they laughed. He accepted the M-16 from Kim and shouldered it. He took a deep breath, held it, and squeezed off one round in the direction of the same cluster of coconuts, no particular target in mind. A frond rustled and one perfect green husk, clean and smooth, dropped motionless to the lawn below with a thud. Kim's driver ran to pick it up, brought it back to the three men and handed it admiringly to Medici. The wiry stem that connected it to the tree had been cleanly severed; the husk was undamaged.

Medici laughed a coarse belly laugh at his clear dumb luck, and the Cambodians joined in the mirth.

NILO HA TIEN

On their way to the Jeep with the prize luncheon coconut, Kim, looking out over the gulf, casually said in a low voice, "Lieutenant, I believe we shall cooperate on the infiltration information you seek. The details we shall discuss at luncheon." Medici kept walking straight ahead and let out a long quiet breath.

21

Incursion

"Hey, NILO. Look at this!" Frank Brown yelled. He stood at the end of the hall and looked through the open door toward Ha Tien village.

Medici flip-flopped down the hall, rubbing sleep from his eyes. "Wha'?" he said.

"I guess after six weeks of indecision we've decided to invade Cambodia," Frank said. He looked at the blister lens over the date on his watch. "April 30, 1970. A day that will live in infamy," he said in a deep radio voice, then laughed. "Let's drive down and watch."

Medici grunted acknowledgment. He stared at the sinuous pontoon bridge that had grown across the river during the night and connected the road from the south to 8A, the direct highway into Cambodia. The tenuous floats swayed under the weight of endless AMTRACS that ground slowly across, spewing a fog of blue diesel smoke over the river.

They drove to the village and parked Medici's Jeep off the side of the dirt road that ran along the Ha Tien quay. Both ends of the bridge were clogged with traffic. Personnel carriers, half-tracks, and big diesel trucks jostled and locked with each other, despite the staccato curses of Vietnamese sergeants. Medici saw few Americans. Here and there an advisor shouted through cupped hands into his Vietnamese counterpart's ear. And somehow the mess oozed slowly north to the border.

"All Vietnamese Army, Frank. Says 'Ninth Division' on most of the rolling stock," Medici shouted. The din, dust, and diesel smoke overwhelmed them.

Frank nodded. "My exec in Can Tho called to tell me American divisions are invading Cambodia at the Parrot's Beak and the Fishhook. Only Vietnamese Army invading down here in the asshole of nowhere. He took pains to tell me to call it an incursion,

NILO HA TIEN

not an invasion. Orders from Saigon command. It's supposed to suggest a violation of the border limited in time and space. As if the effect of 100,000 GIs in the Cambodian villages will be less harmful if we call it an incursion." Frank sneered. "Sorta' like it isn't really rape if you call it a temporary penetration."

Medici shook his head. He felt offended by this massive violation of Cambodia, his private preserve, by a wehrmacht of American and Vietnamese grunts, and helpless to prevent the defiling of the Magic Kingdom. And he felt obsolete, now that anyone could walk in. "How far are they going?"

"Thirty kilometers. Thirty days. No more. Those orders came straight from the White House. Slam, bam, thank you, ma'am."

Medici spread his map on the steering wheel. "That's far enough to reach the weapons storage areas, if the North Vietnamese haven't already moved the stuff farther in." They both laughed.

"Last week I briefed an Army Intelligence advisor from the delta command on the location of Secret Zone III. Now I see why he was so interested," Medici said. "Jesus, Frank. Look at those armored cars go."

A full column of armored cars cleared the bridge and shifted into high gear on Route 8A's smooth macadam. Oval blue puffs of smoke hung where they shifted gears. The big knobby tires whined above the diesels' throaty growl. The lead vehicles accelerated to 50 miles per hour.

"Christ, they'll be in Angkor Wat for dinner at that speed," Medici shouted. He started the Jeep and drove back to Phao Dai.

The Walrus had left a message for Medici while he and Frank watched the Ninth ARVN Division. It said:

"Helo arriving your location 1600 hours 1 May '70 to transport NILO HA TIEN to field HQ, 9th ARVN DIV across the line vicinity TUK MEAS, CB. Cooperate and effect maximum liaison with COL. LE COMPTE, MACV Senior Advisor to 9th ARVN DIV.

PLOVER, LCDR"

The helo arrived early, the Red Baron at the stick.

"Now we can go anywhere we want in Cambodia, right, NILO?" he said on the intercom. His cheerful tone suggested that he had forgiven Medici for the hot flights around Nooey Die Young.

"Up to 30 kilometers. But that doesn't mean they won't shoot at us. We don't control Cambodia," Medici said.

"Roger that. I'm forewarned this time." The Red Baron laughed.

"Follow the highway to Tuk Meas," Medici said. "The division will race along it to make speed. The swath of the road will be secure and lead us to them."

Click-Click from the Baron.

They flew above Route 8A across the border then turned north and followed Cambodian Routes 17, 36, and 16 to Tuk Meas. There they found the headquarters tents of the 9th ARVN Division inside a wide circle of armored personnel carriers. The sight of the circle of APCs with manned turret guns looked to Medici like a wagon train preparing for attack against Indians in an old Western movie.

They circled three times to make sure the area was secure before they landed. The Red Baron said he'd wait for Medici, who noticed him warming to the idea of goofing around legitimately in Cambodia after the dicey illegal entries.

A harsh-faced Vietnamese officer with close-cropped hair strode smartly to the helo, identified himself as Major Hung, and asked Medici's business. Medici bristled at the officer. He hated tight-ass, spit-and-polish types, regardless whose Army they were in. He introduced himself, then curtly asked to see Colonel Le Compte.

Hung led him between enlisted men's cooking fires to a cluster of safari khaki tents, not Army olive drab. A real Tim Tyler outfit, Medici thought. The clearing, debrushed and swept smooth, formed a tiny parade ground. They approached the largest tent. The canvas fly swept open with a pop and an orderly stepped out to attention.

A smooth-shaven American officer in spit-shined cavalry boots strode from the tent at a martial pace. Medici gaped. The officer's hair was slicked back, European-style, and he wore taupe twill riding trousers tucked smartly into his boots. A stream of smoke trailed from the bowl of his briar pipe. The man marched in measured steps till his face was within a foot of Medici's, then stopped with a click of heels, standing ramrod straight. Up close, Medici noticed he looked much older. A missed daub of shaving cream stuck to his right earlobe.

"Colonel Le Compte, I presume?" Medici said. He tried not to sound like a facetious Mungo Park.

"Leftenant Medici? So good of you to come. Your reputation precedes you. That's why I asked for you to report here. This is rather your neck of the woods, isn't it?" the colonel said. He drew hard on his pipe between sentences. He looked to Medici like a house afire.

"You could say that. I had the fortune to be here before Cambodia became so popular."

"Jolly good! But that's exactly why we have intelligence specialists, isn't it? To lay the groundwork for when it's needed by operational forces?"

Medici blinked. The truth was he had never really thought of his NILO post that way. So involved in Cambodia-watching, he'd forgotten the reason for his post until now when the colonel stated it. He had not done much groundwork lately, since getting caught up in the whirl of Cambodian political events. The colonel seemed sensible, if eccentric.

"Come with me, Leftenant. I've something to show you."

Le Compte led Medici to a neat set of white tarpaulins and white canvas ground cloths. An American journalist was photographing an impressive array of spanking new Communist weapons laid in neat rows on the tarps. Medici estimated one large truckload of weapons and ammunition laid spread before him: 108mm Czech mortars and recoilless rifles, 82mm and 61mm Chinese mortars, Chinese B-40 rocket propelled grenade launchers, big Soviet 122mm rockets, Czech and Chinese AK-47 assault rifles. Medici had not seen so much enemy hardware in one place. Nor guns so clean and new that he could smell the cosmoline. But all of it amounted to only one truckload. The colonel beamed.

"Colonel, this is very impressive, but I hope you got more

than this," Medici said. He spoke in a quiet voice so the journalist could not hear.

The colonel took his pipe from his mouth. "Of course, Leftenant. This is only a representative sample. The division has already trucked much of the ammunition and equipment back across the border." He put the pipe back in his mouth.

And probably already resold it to the Viet Cong, Medici thought. "Colonel, where did the division get this stuff?"

"Why, from your notorious Secret Zone III. I sent a reinforced battalion to scour the Zone today on our way to Tuk Meas."

Medici took out his map. "Colonel, your guys move over the ground faster than Air-Cav units do." He performed some mental calculations. The headquarters company and the AMTRACs had traveled 70 kilometers from Ha Tien since yesterday morning. The reinforced battalion covered another 30 kilometers to Secret Zone III and back, plus the time to find, capture, and load the weapons onto the trucks. "That's alot of quick hauling," Medici said.

The orderly appeared with a silver tray of anchovy canapés and two glasses of sherry. Medici couldn't believe it. Le Compte smiled.

"The whole purpose of modern cavalry, light mechanized assault, is speed. We fly past enemy lines and position, strike like lightning where we choose, then get on to further objectives. The enemy cannot respond quickly enough to set up against us."

And the poor grunts are left to plod after you to mop up and get their asses kicked while you drink sherry and eat anchovies, Medici thought.

He sipped from his glass. They toasted the division's formidable two days of progress and chatted purposelessly for a few minutes. Then he asked, "How many tons of weapons and ammunition did your division find?"

The colonel cleared his throat. "Well...truckloads."

"But any idea of tonnage?" Medici persisted.

"I shall ask Major Hung. He led the battalion into the Zone." The orderly fetched Hung. They squawked pidgin English and Vietnamese, then gesticulated. All they got from Hung was "many tons." Hung left.

NILO HA TIEN

"Colonel," Medici said, "the best agent reports I've read over the last six months indicate entire *shiploads* of weapons from Sihanoukville were stored at Secret Zone III. Thousands of tons. At best, Hung described five or six truckloads, 80 to 100 tons at most. As a matter of logistics, you know your battalion didn't capture much tonnage today."

The colonel lowered his head to his chest and revealed several chins of smooth skin. He sucked on his pipe. "Are you saying my Vietnamese officers are lying, Lieutenant?" he asked.

"Maybe a little," Medici said, "but that's not the point. I'm really suggesting they should have found staggering amounts of stuff. Even if the agent reports exaggerated quantities, there were so many of them from different sources that the Zone had to contain vast amounts of weapons and ammunition. The issue is the magnitude of the discovery." He looked around the camp and the formidable ring of AMTRACs, then looked directly at the colonel.

"The North Vietnamese moved most of the stuff out before you got there. They left a creditable amount to make it look like you caught 'em with their pants down. We've been had. During the six weeks' delay before we crossed into Cambodia, they could have moved the Queen Mary north past the 30-kilometer limit." Medici tossed the rest of his sherry on the ground.

Le Compte stood straight and stared off at his AMTRACs.

"That was my suspicion, and why I summoned you here. The amount of captured weapons is disappointing for all the heat we're taking back in the States for entering Cambodia."

"Have him take a lot of pictures from different angles, Colonel." Medici gestured at the journalist with his thumb. "Maybe it will look like more." He saluted and returned to the helo.

Captured NVA weapons near Tuk Meas, Cambodia.

22

Public Relations

The camouflage paint on the 10th Swift Boat felt nearly dry. Medici climbed a ladder to make sure the white, five-pointed American star atop the pilot house wasn't visible through the fresh paint. Near the waterline, several daubs of American haze gray showed through the olive drab. Close enough for government work, he concluded.

Medici looked at his watch—0830. Behind him a chopper warmed up on the An Thoi pad to take him back to Ha Tien. He had a noon rendezvous with two reporters whom he had been ordered by Saigon to take on a guided tour of Cambodian coastal waters "to demonstrate the existence of Extended Market Time patrols by solely indigenous Vietnamese personnel, sealing off Cambodian waters from Communist waterborne weapons infiltration." In plain English, they wanted him to convince these reporters that the Vietnamese Navy had blockaded the Cambodian coast against Communist weapons smuggling, which was not yet true.

The boats were officially turned over at 4 a.m. before repainting. The Vietnamese boat captains and crews received a crash course in Swift Boat operation from the displaced American crews. The boat captains and engineers gestured and yelped shrill Vietnamese and pidgin to explain Onan generators and sideband radios. The Vietnamese understood diesels and guns, nothing else. Medici personally removed the secure radios from the boats. Since his mission to Tunsay, the Navy assumed compromise if their Vietnamese allies got American crypto gear. Medici ordered the sailors to respray the old hull numbers so they were invisible at close range, a necessary part of the gambit.

As a final act Medici rebriefed the Vietnamese. They grunted understanding of the mission as Medici explained it a fifth time. He could do no more. They were on their own. He saluted them and boarded the chopper for Ha Tien.

At noon a new UH1-Lima helicopter with powerful whining engines fell to a hover 50 feet above the Ha Tien pad. The door gunners searched the hill with jerky movements of their heads. The helo sat quickly on the pad and two civilians jumped out and ran at a crouch up the path to the hill, while the helo leapt and retreated over the water. Medici met them halfway.

"Hi. Tom Medici, liaison officer. I'll be your guide to Cambodia today," he said with a radio voice. He hated the role.

The dark-haired one said, "Jim Strong, New York Times," and shook Medici's hand.

"Bob Kempf, Washington Post," the other said. His lips were tight.

Great, Medici thought. These guys are here to ream us. He reminded himself to choose his words carefully.

He took them to his Jeep without giving them a chance to speak with any of the American locals, and drove them to the new Navy base where a Vietnamese Navy Swift Boat waited alongside the floats. They got under way in 40 seconds, pursuant to Medici's previous orders, and skimmed across the bay at top speed. The crews of two fishing sampans gave them the finger when they were nearly swamped in the boat's large wake. Medici didn't attempt to speak over the diesels' roar until they were well offshore and moving north along the Cambodian coast.

"Either of you gents speak Vietnamese?" he asked.

They both shook their heads no. Whew, Medici thought, they can't chat with the Vietnamese crew to ask what's going on. Unless they're lying.

He gestured to the boat captain to slow down so they could talk over the engine noise.

"We should see the first Vietnamese extended Market Time patrol shortly. She's stationed in the Zone centered at Kep, just up the coast a bit." He looked at his watch, hoping the repainted boats had left in enough time to beat them to stations over the horizon.

NILO HA TIEN

"They've got one every 5,000 yards up the coast to Sihanoukville," Medici said. "Since Lon Nol closed the port to Communist weapons, seaborne trawlers have been the only alternative. The Vietnamese Navy seems to have taken care of that loophole nicely," he said. He scanned the sector in front of them with the boat's binoculars.

"There she is!" he yelled. He ran to the pilothouse and pointed for the helmsman. "Not too close," he whispered and winked to the helmsman, who spoke perfect English. The helmsman barely dipped his chin.

The Swift passed 500 yards from the first picket. The Vietnamese sailors aboard it looked to be on serious patrol duty in flak jackets and helmets. They waved unenthusiastically at the reporters. The reporters peered at the chart, looked for landmarks on the shore, conferred and jotted in their small notebooks.

The wind picked up as they went north. Strong borrowed the binoculars and scanned north for the next picket. The combination of monsoon swell and wind chop made the Swift buck and weave from crest to trough. The waves made it impossible to see farther than 250 yards from the boat, except on the higher seventh wave crest. Thank God, Medici thought. The boats will have time to reach station without the reporters watching them come from behind.

They passed beyond the next picket before they saw it off their port quarter. As they circled, Medici could hear the rough, irregular idle of hot diesels throttled down from prolonged full power. He saw billows of heat rise from hot diesel stacks. But the crew performed flawlessly. They looked bored from having patrolled so long.

"Any chance we can stop and talk to them?" Kempf asked.

Medici appeared to gauge the depth of the swell and wind speed, then shook his head. "No, sir, I'm sorry. Considering all the ordnance they have on board and the thin aluminum hull, I don't think we should try." A rogue wave top slopped over the windward side and doused them, as if to confirm Medici's decision. The reporters forgot their pique at the decision as they absorbed themselves in drying off.

They cruised north one more picket, but the Swift pounded now and they made headway with great discomfort. The reporters, who had been playing "Do You Know" with Medici about Princeton classmates, grew silent. Medici noticed the Vietnamese coxswain steer a course that was out of phase from how he should be running the waves. Medici thought he saw an incipient smile on the coxswain's face. He knew exactly what he was doing. He wanted the reporters to miss none of the fun.

Finally Kempf looked at Strong, commented how green he looked and wondered if they had seen enough. Strong agreed and they asked Medici if they could go back. Medici looked at his watch, then the sun, then the Cambodian shore.

"We could probably pick up two more pickets and still get back to Ha Tien only two hours after dark," he said.

The reporters waved off the suggestion. The boat turned around and they rolled back toward Ha Tien in an awful beam sea. Medici offered the reporters C-rations, which they declined. He opened a C-rat case and discovered the Vietnamese crew had carefully removed the can of fruit cocktail from each carton. With ceremony, he devoured a scrambled eggs with ham. Kempf looked green.

By the time they got to the flat water at the Ha Tien channel mouth, both Kempf and Strong looked better. As the Swift tied up at the base, Strong asked formally, "Well, Lieutenant, in your estimation, how do we stand on stopping coastal infiltration?"

Medici scowled and pulled on his chin. He looked at the reporters with a straight face and said, "Gentlemen, I believe for the first time we're able to see light at the end of the tunnel." He held his expression for 10 seconds while the reporters looked at him and each other in disbelief. Then Medici belly laughed until tears came to his eyes, the reporters caught on and the three joked all the way to the team house.

Three weeks later Medici saw a *TIME* magazine. Its international section showed a half-page map of Indochina with small black silhouettes of Swift Boats all around Vietnam and along the Cambodian coast to Sihanoukville under the caption "The Noose Tightens." The article touted the Vietnamese Navy's blockade of communist weapons into Cambodia since intervention. Good news for the folks back home. Medici figured it was worth a day's trip in a rolling Swift.

23

Let's Do Takeo

In the morning Medici had a throbbing hangover from carousing with the river rats and junk sailors the night before. He couldn't eat breakfast, so he sat unshaven and shirtless in fatigue cutoffs, drinking soda. He slumped in a wood crate chair, flip-flops propped on the patio wall, gazing at the Gulf of Thailand. He felt like a sleazy lizard, poisons oozing from his pores while the sun slowly raised his body temperature. His eyes squinted behind dark aviator sunglasses that seemed entirely inadequate this rotten morning.

Something appeared in the line of sight between his sweating legs. At first he thought it was the cobra, but then a human head appeared and bobbed higher with each step. It belonged to a tall, blond, meticulously uniformed American Army colonel followed by his puffing aide-de-camp.

The colonel reached a point on the path where he could see over the wall into the patio. He sized up its height then vaulted the wall on one hand, landing lightly on the concrete. The pudgy aide clattered over the wall and rolled onto the patio, breathless.

"Morning, soldier," the colonel said. "Know where I can find NILO Ha Tien?—Navy Lieutenant Medici."

Medici blinked at the colonel, turned his head left then right to survey the patio, and returned to the colonel.

"You talkin' to me, grunt?"

The colonel's nostrils twitched. "Is this Advisory Team 5, Ha Tien?"

"Yup."

"I would like to speak to your commanding officer."

"Sure. He's Vice Admiral Zumwalt at Naval headquarters in Saigon. I can get him on the radio in about 15 minutes if you really need to talk to him."

"Are *you* Lieutenant Medici?"

"Yup. Thomas N., 728471, United States Naval Reserve. Who the hell are you?" Medici read the name Carruthers on the colonel's uniform patch.

"I'm Colonel Carruthers, C/O of the 525 Military Intelligence Group for the delta." He extended his hand to Medici who sat up and shook it. "My aide, Captain Torgeson."

Medici waved at the captain who returned the gesture. "Sit down, Colonel, it's too hot to stand."

The colonel pulled up an ammo crate chair. He put his feet up on the wall and surveyed the Gulf from the river mouth, north past the Pirate Islands to the profile of the Elephant Mountains. He took it all in slowly and gave Medici the feeling he was intuiting what Ha Tien was about.

Quick study, Medici thought. I'll do business with this guy.

"This beats the shit out of Can Tho," Carruthers said. "Frank Brown told me about you. I thought I'd come up to see what this wildman NILO Ha Tien could show me about Cambodia." He laughed.

Medici grinned. "I'm feeling less than wild this morning." He rubbed his temples slowly in an attempt to snap out of the hangover. "How did you get here anyway? I didn't hear a chopper."

"Came in at the Navy base in town late last night. LT. Hayward told me I could find you up here. I thought we could do a little intel."

Medici sat up, removed his sunglasses, and looked at Carruthers. "What do you want, Colonel?"

"Let's do Take-ee-yo," the colonel said.

Oh shit, Medici thought. Here we go again. He sensed a hollow in the pit of his stomach. "Colonel, it's pronounced Tah-KAIYO, not TAKE-ee-yo. Why there? It's been pretty quiet since the 9th Vietnamese Division swept through two months ago."

"No real operational significance. Just—well, curiosity."

Right. Curiosity. Medici replaced his sunglasses and gazed seaward. "Sorry, Colonel. I don't do things for mere curiosity anymore. I'm gettin' short. Sort of. Four months left."

"Commander Holland thought you'd be willing to help a friend of his," Carruthers said. He stared off at the islands.

Medici swallowed. Carruthers had him. He'd played the one card Medici would respond to, his loyalty to Holland.

"You talked to Holland?"

"Yes. For two days."

Medici drew his lips against his teeth and nodded his head rhythmically.

"You got a chopper?"

"All mine. Down at the Navy base. When can you be ready?"

"Ten minutes."

Medici directed the helo pilot along the coast to Kep where they found Governor Um Samuth in a headquarters tent on the lycée soccer field. Security had degenerated. The town and the governor's mansion were unsecure, dangerous even in daylight. Bands of Viet Cong and Khmer Rouge roamed the area but left Samuth and his men alone on the soccer field, in the funny avoidance strategy of the guerilla.

Samuth was gracious, but Medici noticed he became edgy when Carruthers mentioned Takeo. He actively discouraged Medici and Carruthers from going, giving as a reason danger from North Vietnamese troops. It did not make sense. Medici's agents had not reported any North Vietnamese activity around Takeo.

He assured Samuth they would not risk a visit, but instead would travel to the refugee collection point on the Kampot coast where ethnic Vietnamese of Cambodia sought repatriation to Vietnam. Samuth agreed that was a better idea.

On the way to the helicopter, they saw one of Samuth's new Land Rovers parked in the shade of an enormous banyan tree. The paint looked unmarred from the rear, but as they passed the front, they saw the windshield had been blown out and the boxy left front fender twisted from an explosion. Medici examined the fender and saw a small entry hole and spattered bronze metal welded to the inside frame. The tire was flat, the rim bent, the seat covered with glass shards.

Medici said to Samuth, "Ambuscat B-Quarante?" *B-40*

ambush? The governor nodded.

Carruthers said in French, "I didn't know a B-40 would do so little damage to a Land Rover." Medici noted with surprise that Carruthers could speak the language. Samuth told them that Viet Cong ambush teams were raiding Cambodian convoys on all the major highways in an effort to disrupt supply.

As they watched, Cambodian soldiers, working like a pit crew, unbolted the twisted fender box, changed the flat tire, removed the shards of windshield from the seat, then drove the Land Rover away. The astonished Americans applauded with admiration for the shade tree mechanics. Carruthers said what they had seen would make a great ad for Land Rover back in the States.

Medici directed the helo northwest to Kampot. When they were over Kampot, Medici told the pilot to head northeast along Highway 3 to Takeo.

"You told Samuth we weren't going there." Carruthers smiled.

"So I did. But now *I'm* curious. Samuth was lying."

Fifteen minutes later they were over Phnum Puos Pong, a small hamlet located where Dambang Mountain's escarpments came within meters of the road. Medici figured the French engineers who built Route 3 veered it to the east at the hamlet to miss the small mountain range of which Dambang was the tip. The mountains were a welcome change of scenery. The trip so far had been flat delta mud and paddies, as far as the eye could see.

They flew high enough to avoid rockets and gunfire. The pilot followed the strip of road as if it were a freeway. He edged to the right as they approached Dambang's cliffs to stay away from updrafts. Then they saw a small convoy of Cambodian trucks and Land Rovers heading south, bearing the emblem of Forces de l'Armée Nationale Khmer, the FANK—Lon Nol's Army.

They watched the nine vehicles move like elephants along the base of the mountain. Medici noticed automatically the bottleneck created by the mountain on one side and the foliage of the hamlet on the other. The lead vehicle slowed to avoid children and pigs at the constriction.

A white tendril of smoke wove from the foot of Dambang Mountain to the first Land Rover. A second tendril found the middle truck, and a third met the last truck of the convoy. The action unfolded slowly as viewed from the air, like a water ballet. The first Land Rover became enveloped in thick black smoke, drove off the road and overturned. Great red tracers flew from the hamlet to the trucks. Pigs and children fell.

Medici said, "Hey, look at that," without concern. The colonel was already on the intercom telling the pilot to descend and have his door gunners help.

"NEGATIVE!" Medici shouted.

The colonel gaped at him.

"What d'ya mean! They're getting ambushed!"

"Too risky with all that firepower. They have .51 calibres. The door gunners can't help unless we get close. Otherwise we may hit Cambodes. And you have an SCI clearance. You shouldn't be here anyway." Medici told the pilot to maintain altitude and circle.

A big .51 calibre machine gun continued to fire at the convoy. All the vehicles were stopped now, hemmed in by small arms fire heavy with green AK-47 tracers. One truck burst into a giant fireball after a black clad guerrilla ran to it and threw a satchel charge inside. The greasy smoke rose toward the helo. The pilot circled wide to stay out of it.

Two men in civilian clothes ran from the last truck at the explosion. They staggered down the bank from the road and ran toward the scraggly cover of the tram when a crossfire of automatic weapons cut them down, then pounded and rolled their bodies after they fell.

Carruthers looked at Medici who closed his eyes and shook his head. Green AK tracers flew by the helo and fell back to earth. The colonel ordered the pilot up and away toward Takeo.

Medici pulled out his pocket notebook with the Vulture Squadron sticker and flipped to the page on which he had listed the Cambodian tactical frequencies. He had the pilot dial in Takeo's emergency frequency and then called, "Tiger, Tiger," for five minutes in French, then English without response. The Cambodians were not monitoring. He quit, sat silent, and looked straight ahead.

The helo arrived over Takeo, then spiraled down. The town site, at the intersection of Route 25 and old French Route 2, consisted of three major buildings: a saffron-colored province headquarters with a turquoise iron gate; the provincial governor's mansion; and a small hospital. Two hundred yards to the west they saw a schoolyard rimmed by a square of bunkhouse-like classroom buildings.

Medici told Carruthers he had visited Takeo before with Samuth to discuss defense of the town with the Province Governor. The governor had not seemed as bright as Samuth but was apparently dedicated and loyal. Medici discovered the governor had taught 9th grade religion before the lycée closed. He had served them a peanut curry with rice wine and coconut milk while artillery crumped in the distance.

With panache the pilot put the helo down in the small schoolyard, amidst a cloud of buzzing flies that the rotor wash dashed against the buildings.

The place didn't smell too good, Medici noticed as he stepped onto the earthen schoolyard. Away from the kerosene odor of the turbine, he noticed the smell got worse, especially around large brown blots that stained the yellow dirt. Medici started to feel sick when he realized how much of the yard was covered with stains. He knew where he'd encountered the smell before. On the ambushed minesweeper. He grabbed the colonel's arm and led him away from his aide.

"Do you know what the smell and spots are from?"

"I think so. You tell me."

"Recent massive bloodstains." Medici walked into an open classroom; dried blood smeared the walls. Bullet holes confirmed his guess.

"My guess is one hell of alot of killing has gone on here in the last few days," he said, slowly surveying the yard and extent of the stains. A burning nausea formed in the back of his throat. He was surprised he could no longer control it as he had months ago.

"Let's see if we can find your friend, the province chief," Carruthers said.

They left the pilot and gunners with the helo and walked to the province headquarters and up a flight of steps.

"It's too quiet," Medici said. He had the sense of awe commonly experienced at hallowed places where many had died, like Donner Pass, or the Princeton battlefield, or the *USS Arizona* memorial at Pearl Harbor. One hell of alot of killing, he repeated to himself.

They yelled "Alloooh" twice before anyone stirred within the offices. Finally a 15-year-old Cambodian soldier came out. He dragged an AK-47 by the muzzle, its butt scratching and thunking on the tile floor. Medici asked in French where the governor was. The boy's face remained blank. He tried Vietnamese and the boy scowled and brought the AK to his hip. Medici finally mimed a formal salute to an invisible, much taller man, and the boy caught on. He withdrew to the rear of the building and returned minutes later leading the governor by the arm.

The governor was stoned out of his mind. He did not recognize Medici until Medici repeated, "Samuth, Samuth." Then he smiled wanly and said, "Yah, yah." Medici asked him directly how all the killing had occurred at the schoolyard, and the governor responded in rehearsed English, "Crossfire, crossfire," jabbing his forefingers across each other to make Xs. He pretended not to understand any more of Medici's or the colonel's questions, but kept asking if they wanted "coca" to drink.

"I don't think he's going to tell us anything more," the colonel said. Medici agreed. They saluted, shook hands, smiled politely at the governor and walked back down the stairs and toward the school.

Medici said, "This way," and turned the colonel toward the hospital. They were met at the door by a short Cambodian orderly in a white, bloodstained hospital coat. The orderly understood some French and assured Medici that there were no patients in the 20 beds.

The hospital had large open windows. Medici saw neat, white-framed hospital beds made up, empty. His head began to buzz. When he stuck his head inside the building, the buzzing got louder. He charged past the orderly and ran between the rows of beds with the colonel close behind. The orderly protested, "Ce n'est pas possible d'entrer!" *It is not possible to enter!*

They reached the back door of the hospital, and the buzz exploded to a din. Medici saw a black swarm of flies 50 yards behind the building. Then a powerful, sweet stench engulfed them. They covered their noses and mouths and ran toward the flies. At the edge of the cloud, they saw a tiny yellow Komatsu bulldozer that had excavated, then backfilled an area 10 meters square. Between the tread tracks, swollen arms, hands and feet protruded, some already black with decay, all covered with flies. The drone of the flies seemed to surge like two aircraft engines out of sync— Rhuh-Rhuh-Rhuh. It mesmerized them.

Medici looked at the colonel, then at the trembling orderly. "Qui sont les morts?" *Who are the dead?* he yelled over the din. He grabbed the orderly by the whites and shook him.

"Vietnamiens. Vietnamiens ethniques de Takeo," *Ethnic Vietnamese of Takeo,* he said. He looked at the ground.

"Combien de personnes sont tués?" *How many were killed?* Medici lifted the small brown man off the ground.

"Deux ou trois douzaine," *Two or three dozen.* The orderly gasped as the white collar pressed his windpipe.

Medici set the orderly down when the governor's boy-soldier ran out of the hospital's back door and chambered a round in his AK. Medici stood his ground, shielded with indignation, and afraid any fast move would cause the boy to fire.

"Le Gouverneur demand que vous departez maintenant. Allez-vous en!" *The Governor orders you to leave now. Get going!* the boy-soldier said in perfect French.

Medici nodded to the colonel and they left the hospital with the boy-soldier behind them, AK aimed at their backs. As they walked straight to the helo they saw the governor at the top of his stairs watching them without expression. Medici figured they weren't going to be shot. In that case, the governor would have stayed out of sight to avoid being a witness to any more killing.

When the helo was airborne, the colonel told him that

journalists had reported executions of ethnic Vietnamese in all the Cambodian border towns. The Cambodian command sought political loyalty through ethnic purification by eliminating the Vietnamese in Cambodia. Yesterday he had seen hundreds of floating bodies of ethnic Vietnamese rafted against a floodgate of the Mekong at Tan Chau where they had washed downstream from Cambodia. Today, MACV sent him to verify the rumor of slaughter in Takeo.

"Thanks," Medici said on the intercom. "It's been one hell of a nice day." On the flight back to Ha Tien, Medici wondered if the massacres meant further ethnic paroxysms by the Cambodians. Cambodia had been in the war only a month.

The colonel left Medici at the foot of Phao Dai at the old Navy helo pad.

"Thanks, Lieutenant. I'm off to Can Tho to report the Takeo slayings."

"Technically all we saw were portions of a few dead bodies, unidentifiably Vietnamese. We shouldn't jump to conclusions without eyewitness verification," Medici said in defense of his Cambodians, but his heart told him otherwise.

He plodded back up the dusty brown path to the top of the hill. The sun was setting and a pleasant chill from the Gulf of Thailand settled over him. He strolled up to the team house in the light of dusk, for some reason not caring or worrying about anything. It had been a frightful day, but he was home, alive, and desensitized again.

His boots thumped on brick steps. He entered through the screen door and saw Frank and the major whispering intently in the major's small office. They both glanced up and seemed relieved to see him.

"NILO, you're back. You won't believe what's happened!" Frank said. A cigarette jittered in his hand. Medici walked into the major's office.

"NILO, my net just reported that A-34, my agent on the Cambodian Cabinet, was killed on his way to the border today. I can't believe it."

Medici felt a chill. A-34 was the main source of their good

information from Cambodia. After months of courting, Frank had recruited the recording secretary of the Cambodian Cabinet as an agent. Within twelve hours of a Cabinet meeting, they received an imprint carbon of his minutes.

Medici took the rice paper sheet from the major's sweaty hand. It read:

"... While riding in a FANK convoy on Route 3 this afternoon, A-34, a highly positioned member of the Lon Nol government, was killed when the convoy suffered an ambush near Dambang Mountain. Villagers at the hamlet reported two civilians tried to flee the convoy during the firefight, but were shot by heavy automatic weapons fire. It is not known at this time if the ambush was a pretext for A-34's termination. He was reported merely to have been hitching a convenient ride instead of taking the slow province bus."

For the third time that day, Medici felt the nausea grow as realization overtook him. He stared blankly at the wall, then at Frank, then the major.

"I saw him get it. I watched our best agent shot to death from the helo and did nothing to save him. Shit, I didn't even know it was him—wouldn't have recognized him anyway."

The major laughed, "Jesus, I guess this ruins your reputation as tour guide in Cambodia...," until Medici's glare stopped him midsentence.

Medici breathed deeply four times then spoke rapidly for 20 minutes about what else he had seen in Takeo.

24

The Invasion of Kep

Both crash-room beds at An Thoi on Phu Quoc Island had stiff new sea bags on them. One said "Florio, LCDR, N-3, CTF 115," the other "Flaherty, Commodore, CTF 115." Medici hissed as he threw Flaherty's sea bag next to Florio's on the other bed and lay down.

Fucking Commodore, pretentious motherfucker, Medici fumed. There hadn't been a commodore in the Navy since World War II when the rank, the Navy's equivalent of Army brigadier general —a one-star flag officer—was abolished. Technically the appellation was available for the functional job of task force commander, such as the officer in charge of a destroyer squadron, like the term "captain" was used for the commanding officer of any ship regardless of his rank. But for the commander in charge of the Swift Boats on Market Time patrol in Vietnam's coastal waters, the term Commodore was ridiculous and inappropriate. He fumed for a while then dozed off.

"ATTENTION ON DECK!" someone shouted.

Medici thought he was dreaming about *Tulsa* with the Seventh Fleet Admiral coming aboard. He blinked his eyes, rolled over on his elbow and saw four knees in crisply starched new fatigues in the small space between the two beds. He followed them up to two faces, one a heavyset Italian-American with a "Florio" name patch, the other a tall, thin man with shiny bald head and rosy cheeks. Both smelled of Old Spice cologne in the air-conditioned room.

"Hi," Medici said, rubbing his eyes.

"Is that all you can say, sailor!" the fat one bellowed. "This is Commodore Flaherty, commander TASK FORCE 115. Hit the deck!"

Medici focused coldly on the fat man's eyes but didn't budge off his elbow. The commodore stood at attention, a bemused expression on his face from watching the exchange. Medici rolled off the bed, put his feet on the floor and stood. He ignored the fat one and extended his hand to the commodore. "Lieutenant Thomas Medici, NILO Ha Tien."

The man shook Medici's hand. There was a thin enigmatic smile on his face. "Good to meet you, son. You've got a lot of guts from what I hear," he said quietly.

Medici didn't know what to say. He couldn't tell whether Flaherty meant he was a wiseass or courageous, or both.

Flaherty continued, "That's why they assigned you to me as my N-2 for Task Force 115.3. You are now my staff intelligence officer for the invasion of Kep, Cambodia."

Medici was flabbergasted. "I just got back from Kep. I'm NILO at Ha Tien. I can't be your staff intelligence officer...."

Flaherty withdrew a sheet of communications paper from his pocket and handed it to Medici. It was a request from Flaherty to Medici's administrative boss, the Walrus, to assign Medici temporary additional duty as staff intelligence officer for newly formed TF 115.3 for the duration of "secret ops in Cambodian waters." The request was unctuously approved by the Walrus and rubber-stamped by Saigon with the proviso that Medici not be kept away long from his duties reporting on Cambodian intelligence.

"Why are you invading Kep?" Medici asked, a look of disbelief on his face.

"I'm not sure I am yet," Flaherty smiled. "I've requested permission for an amphibious landing of a U.S. Marine battalion to rescue the Cambodian battalions you described in your first message after meeting with the Cambodian officers. Saigon's reviewing it now for approval. We're going to start the planning right now if you're awake enough."

"Kep's too shallow water. You can't get an LST closer than 4,000 yards from the beach or a landing craft ashore. The VC have dug spider holes all along the beach. They're dug in the hillside above Kep within easy mortar range of anyone coming ashore in landing craft. Kep's not the place for an amphibious landing,

Commander" Medici said matter-of-factly.

Flaherty was undaunted. "We'll figure out how to do it somehow, Lieutenant. By the way, my staff calls me 'Commodore.'" On the way out of the room he said, "That's LCDR Florio, my staff OPS officer. You'll work closely with him. See you in TAC PLOT in 10 minutes."

Medici turned to Florio. The man glared at him for having been ignored. Medici could never understand why he had such a difficult time with other Italian-Americans. He never got along with them. "I just told him an amphibious landing at Kep is foolish and impossible. I've just been there and seen the beach and coastal waters. And he intends to try it anyway?"

"The Commodore's a tough sailor. He'll find a way if there is one," Florio said fatuously. "He volunteered his services in Cambodia as soon as he got wind of your contact with the Cambodians," Florio said proudly, a far-off stare focused on glory.

Oh, shit, Medici thought. These guys are up here to jerk off and get some medals while Cambodia is still a novelty. There would be no military logic to the operation. Just enough to get them in somewhere so they could write each other up for medal awards. Trouble.

Flaherty was already studying the big wall maps of the Cambodian coast when Medici and Florio entered TAC PLOT. There was virtually no detail of underwater contours along the coast of Kep.

"How do you know an LST can't beach here?" he said to Medici without taking his eyes from the map.

"See that jetty that sticks out into the bay about 100 yards? At low tide it and the bay bottom are high and dry 100 yards seaward. They bring in Chicomm trawlers to offload weapons. Agents report a trawler beached short of the jetty at high tide and had to kedge itself off at the next high water. I had Som Sary sound with a line when we went in for gunfire support. No more than four feet 2,000 yards off the beach at high tide. Forget it, Commodore." Medici crossed his arms Injun-style.

143

"What's the bottom like? Gravel or mud?" Flaherty said without taking his eyes from the map.

"Mud, or more properly muck. I'm afraid even LCUs would get sucked into the stuff and be sitting ducks for the hill gunners. I'd call an LSD in and helo drop the marines with three or four choppers at a time. It looks peaceful and there are lots of school fields and mansion grounds on which to land if the VC zero in on any one site with mortars," Medici said earnestly.

Flaherty turned toward him with one raised eyebrow and tight-lipped mouth. "You're as tough minded as they say. 'Got your shit together' is the expression." He looked back toward the map. "My flagship will be here at 2300 hours tonight, a turbine fast gunboat, the *Antelope*. We will depart as soon as she gets here to recon the coast ourselves. I want you both ready to leave by 2200."

"I'm ready now," Medici said.

"I'm sure you are, Lieutenant. That was for LCDR Florio's benefit," Flaherty said waspishly. Florio blushed and looked at an irrelevant part of the map.

Flaherty turned his attention to the Rach Giang Thanh River just north of Ha Tien village. NILO Jim had drawn in a large red cross-hatched area labeled "Tra Bang Storage Zone" in Cambodia based on Medici's report from his debriefing of an NVA transportation battalion soldier.

"I have temporary operational control of River Division 55 at Ha Tien. It appears from the map there is a small tributary of the Rach Giang Thanh that runs through the Tra Bang Storage Zone. That's a weapons storage and transshipment area for the NVA, correct, Lieutenant?"

It was obvious Flaherty had read and remembered Medici's reports on the area. "Yes, sir," he said tentatively, guessing what was coming next.

"Good. I'd like to send an exploratory flotilla of river boats up that tributary to see if they can capture any weapons or make any contact..."

"COMMODORE! That 'tributary' is a streambed barely wide enough for a PBR to get through during wet season. There's no room for them to turn around if they get in a firefight—and they will up there! I've flown the area scores of times and even walked it a click upstream. The NVA use needle-thin sampans to float a case of ammo at a time down to the canal for night crossing. We'll get creamed up there..."

"Listen up, Lieutenant! You're like all the rest of these pussies. Can't do this, can't do that. Always afraid of making a little contact with the enemy. Well, by God, Lieutenant, I'm here to tell you making contact with the enemy is what this Navy is all about in Vietnam. And I'll send them up there at gunpoint if that's what it takes!" Flaherty was livid. Veins bulged in his forehead. "Damn field guys," he muttered and strode out of TAC PLOT.

Medici couldn't believe it. This guy was going to get involved in some boondoggle Cambodian operation at all costs, even river sailors' lives. He bet Red O'Brien would tell Flaherty to go to hell and be relieved of his river division command before undertaking such a foolish operation as one up the tributary.

This was dangerous stuff. This guy had to be watched carefully. He'd sacrifice anything to get himself a good medal for his brave efforts in sending others into Cambodia. This was his one chance during his Vietnam tour to get off the floating city, a personnel barracks ship on which his staff was based in Cam Ranh Bay, and make a name for himself. Very dangerous man, Medici thought.

"Lieutenant. I'll remind you not to raise your voice to the Commodore. He's your immediate superior for this op and we will definitely file a special concurrent fitness report on you at its completion. If you get my message," Florio huffed.

Medici glared at the presumptuous butt-sucker. "Fuck off, Commander," he said and left TAC PLOT.

At 2230 they were on the small pier at An Thoi waiting for the *Antelope*. Huge purple-black puffs of rainsquall cruised over An Thoi as another monsoon storm blew through. Out of one squall the *Antelope* steamed without lights. Shortly they could hear the high tinny whine of her turbines, an aircraft noise, not a ship noise, Medici thought. *Antelope* backed down dead in the water 500 yards off the pier. The coxswain cranked over the diesels of the PBR and Medici, Flaherty, and Florio made the short trip to the *Antelope*. She was a sleek-lined gunboat, about 80 feet in length, with a single three-inch gun mount topped with a radome located forward of the bridge. There were no stacks like a real ship, just turbine vents aft. Medici could smell the kerosene fumes from the jet engines before they were aboard. It reminded him of an airport's smell, or Yankee Station when the carriers were engaged in flight ops.

The entire crew was unbelievably young, even the senior enlisted man, a chief, who greeted them and took them to the small wardroom. In it sat a tall, muscular man, extraordinarily good looking, in a white skivvy shirt. He stood. "Hello, Commodore," he said.

"Good evening, Captain. This is my new N-2 for this op, Lieutenant Medici. Lieutenant, this is LCDR Mazzini, commanding officer of *Antelope*." Medici smiled and shook hands with Mazzini.

"Call me Joe," Mazzini said.

"I'm Tom," said Medici.

"Captain, are you ready to get under way? I want to be at Kep by first light. I've got an LSD steaming to rendezvous with us by tomorrow afternoon if we need to insert Marines. They'll use four of the big Sea Stallion choppers to land," Flaherty said. Medici stifled a smile.

"Yes, sir, Commodore. I've already plotted the course. We'll arrive at 0500, in time to watch first light on the beach. Chief Allard will show you and LCDR Florio to my cabin. I'll double up with my X/O." He turned and looked at Medici. "I didn't know LT. Medici was coming. I'll arrange a bunk aft for him...."

"That's okay, Captain. I'll just crash on the wardroom floor, if you don't mind," Medici said. It was icy cold and dry in the wardroom. The carpet was spongier than Medici's bed in Ha Tien. "I'd like to go over navigation with you first."

Mazzini took Medici to the small, well-laid-out chart house behind the bridge. Flaherty joined them. There was not enough room for Florio, who stood outside in the passageway. Medici briefed Mazzini on the coastal depths, how far in the Cambodian corvette had stood for gunfire, and where the NVA gun positions were. He showed him the grid coordinates where the Cambodian Marine battalions were under siege—no, in hiding actually. Flaherty gave a little speech about hostile forces and the possibility of the ship being fired upon. Mazzini said they had .50 calibre machine guns and the three-inch to protect them. They went to the bridge.

The squalls started in earnest. The lights of the Naval compound at An Thoi blacked out completely in each rain burst the ship passed through.

The bridge was like nothing Medici had ever seen. It was more of a cockpit than ship's bridge. It swept around a spaceship-like red leather chair in which the chief strapped himself like a helo pilot. Before him sloped a complicated instrument panel glowing red, orange and green around a go-cart-size steering wheel. The steering column slid back and locked into position in the chief's lap, so his elbows could rest on the contoured armrests. Two thrust controls like on a jetliner were within easy reach of the chief's right hand, two thrust reverse controls on the left. The exotic instrument panel sloped upward to meet a wraparound windscreen that angled rakishly back above them and gave the *Antelope* her sleek racy look from the outside.

"What's the seatbelt for, chief, high-speed turns?" Medici joked.

"That's exactly what it's for, Lieutenant. Everyone on the bridge please hold on to a grab rail," he said. "Prepare to turn," the chief said after flicking on the ship's intercom with a switch in the armrest, then, "Turning." He slowly rotated the small wheel 45 degrees to the right. The ship heeled immediately to port as its bow sliced to starboard. They felt the turning surge and held on. The chief came to course and eased the wheel back to amidships, leveling the gunboat.

A heavy squall drummed on the pilothouse. The chief reached for the panel and flicked on a bank of high-speed windshield wipers that kept the wraparound windows clear. The portion of the windshield directly in front of him held a clear rotating disc that spun rapidly, threw off the rain, and left a clear porthole into the night.

When they cleared the anchorage at An Thoi the chief advanced the two thrust levers. The ship's turbines whined higher in pitch and soon *Antelope* lurched forward like an accelerating ski boat. The surge exhilarated Medici.

The burst of speed didn't last long. As soon as they were clear of Phu Quoc Island, the chief reduced speed to six knots in order to cover the 55 kilometers to Kep in steady, slow steaming and to arrive precisely at dawn. Captain Mazzini explained he didn't want to arrive early, steam around in circles, and give NVA gunners time to set up on them before first light. Medici agreed. They discussed their angle of approach to the coast, then Medici went down to the chilly wardroom, used a cushion from the small easy chair as a pillow, laid on the plush carpet, and slept for the few hours until dawn.

MWAAHM, MWAAHM, MWAAHM. "General quarters, now general quarters! All hands man your battle stations. This is not a drill. This is not a drill!"

Medici bolted upright, disoriented. He was in an unfamiliar compartment on *Tulsa* and had to think of the path to his battle station, Director One, where he fired the big six-inch Naval guns on which the ship depended in counter battery. He did not recognize the room. He did not know why he was sleeping on the carpet. He was chilled to the bone. The metal band of his watch slid down several inches on his cold, dehydrated wrist. Then he heard turbine whine, and from that bit of information his brain reconstructed the events of the night before. He was on *Antelope*, steaming for Kep at first light.

He looked at his watch: 0430. The captain was taking no chances. From the high-speed whine of the turbines and the ship's surge, he guessed they had lain over the horizon from Kep and were sprinting in at general quarters to hit rendezvous precisely at dawn to maximize surprise.

He walked from the wardroom to the ladder for the bridge. He smelled coffee and detoured to the galley where a Filipino steward gave him a full steaming mug, smooth warm white porcelain with green stripes around the top. He balanced it and lithely inched up the ladder to the spaceship bridge.

Full house. Flaherty and Florio were there, crouched low on

the land side, peering toward the dark beach through glass fogged by air conditioning.

"Why don't you go out on deck?" Medici asked, then realized from their expressions that they were afraid. They would have no steel around them for protection. He laughed.

"Where's the Captain?" he asked Chief Allard in the pilot seat.

"Above us on the open bridge," Allard replied.

Medici went aft to the door that opened onto the main deck and the ladder to the open bridge. He purposely walked past the bridge window behind which Flaherty and Florio cowered, waving at them with a goofy smile as he headed up to join the captain.

Mazzini was carefully scanning the dim gray beach with big 7 x 50 bridge binoculars.

"Good morning, Captain," Medici said with a smile.

Mazzini lowered the binoculars and smiled back. "Hi, Tom. Situation too tense down on the enclosed bridge?" he said, and both of them broke into laughs.

"I don't believe those guys," Medici said. "They're scared shit that we'll take some fire from the beach, so they hide down there!"

"Lot of good it'll do 'em. We took a recoilless round through that metal bulkhead down at Seafloat. That's how I lost my last X/O. But we won't tell them that!" They both laughed again.

"I don't expect much in the way of fire," Medici said. "Close to the beach we may get some small arms, but my guess is they'll hightail it for the hills as soon as they see us."

"Flaherty wants us to put over boats so we can recon the shore. What do you think?"

"Why not? Have you got some M-16s and grenade launchers?" Medici said, more curious to go ashore than ensure the safety of the landing party.

"Sure. I thought we'd wait until it was light for half an hour so any bad guys along the beach can split...."

"Good idea," Medici interjected, then sipped some more coffee.

"But watch this first. A little surprise for those at the windows." He spoke quietly into a handset and the 3-inch gun mount turned slowly toward the beach. Mazzini told the gunner to drop one round in the grassy area close to the beach where they would land the boat. He gave them range, had it verified on fire control radar, and ordered the gunner to prepare to fire. Medici hung over the open bridge rail far enough to see the heads of Flaherty and Florio through the window.

The sharp report of the 3-inch had a much higher pitch than the six-inch guns on *Tulsa*. Medici was glad the captain gestured to put his fingers in his ears. The bridge windows rattled and Medici saw Flaherty and Florio literally fall over each other at the noise. No one had warned them in advance. Mazzini and Medici had a good belly laugh, then watched to see the round's impact. Right on the money, and no one fled the area.

"No one there," Medici said.

Antelope put two large Boston Whalers over the side to transport the landing party to the beach at Kep. The tide was low and they proceeded at cruising speed until they could see the bottom. Then they idled at troll speed until they had to pull the outboards up, get out and drag the flat-bottom boats further along the putrid mud. They sunk to their boot tops, the mud sucking at each step, then sloshed and squished for 100 yards until they hit the sand beach. Two men from each boat stood perimeter guard with M-16s at full automatic as the group moved across the mud flats and up the beach to a wide grassy area. Two sailors stayed to guard the boats while the group walked with their rifles aimed ahead, slung from their shoulders John Wayne-style, nervously fingering triggers and handgrips.

The coxswain walked point with Medici 10 feet behind him. The rest of the group, including Flaherty and Florio, who each wore French wraparound bubble sunglasses, held back 50 yards in case of mines.

"Lieutenant! A foxhole," the coxswain yelled, then leaned over the edge on his rifle.

"STOP!" Medici yelled. Everyone froze.

"I was just going to see how deep it is," the coxswain said apologetically.

"It's a spider hole, a foxhole for one man. The VC booby-trap them with grenades if they leave hastily." Medici crawled up to the edge of the hole. It was 20 inches wide and three feet deep. He looked carefully around its perimeter, then down the earthen walls. About eight inches from the bottom was a crisscross of black monofilament thread. Medici pulled out a pen-sized flashlight. He shielded his eyes and traced the thread to the places it entered the dirt wall. At one point he saw the tip of a crudely made cotter pin. He stood up.

"You play baseball?"

"Yeah, why?" the coxswain said.

Medici pulled a concussion grenade from his pocket and handed it to the coxswain.

"Toss this in the hole from about 20 yards, then hit the deck," he said.

"Okay," the coxswain said. They backed up 20 yards.

Medici yelled, "Fire in the hole." The group lay flat on the ground.

Without pulling the pin, the coxswain took aim and lofted the grenade underhand at the hole. The grenade bounced four feet from the hole, and rolled until the spoon caught a clod and stopped a foot shy of the spider hole.

"My turn," Medici said. He retrieved the grenade, walked out five yards and cavalierly tossed it back over his left shoulder in a high arc. He took another slow step then leaped into a run and dove for the coxswain's safe ground. As he slid to a halt the spider hole went "PHUMMPT-PHUNT" and spewed a cone of dirt and black smoke. Medici got up, brushed the dirt off, and avoided rubbing the spot on his groin where his pistol had poked him during the dive.

The group walked slowly on the pebbled road along the quay wall that led to the few town buildings. They approached the treasury building, a two-story, white stucco wedding-cake structure with awning-covered balconies on each floor. The windows were shuttered and they couldn't see inside. The white stucco fascia on the second floor was blemished with a two-foot-wide powder burn and a small hole where someone had shot a 40mm grenade at it.

The building stood silent behind an aquamarine-painted iron gate, closed but unlocked. They squeaked it open and walked up the path to the front steps. They had to walk around a small pergola with stupa-like spires, the roof shadowing an alabaster bust of King Norodom of Cambodia, Prince Sihanouk's father. Two sailors edged their way up the steps and kicked in the door. No sound. They rushed in with 16s on auto, quickly searched the room, found no one. They spread out in the building. One yelled for Medici. He ran in and found the sailor peering into the ground level vault, the doors of which had been blown off by explosives. Medici withdrew his flashlight and eased down into the cool, clammy cavern. Empty wooden cashier drawers lined the room. Medici spied a scrap of torn bill pinched in the joint of one drawer. When he slid it back and forth it came out, the corner of a Cambodian 1,000 riel note. Medici pocketed it and went outside. Flaherty and the group were loosening up, now that they knew there was no threat.

"The VC cleaned out the treasury, then closed up the building nice and neat," Medici said. "Blew the vault doors off the hinges. Must have gotten a pretty piece of Sihanouk's vacation money."

The party continued down the street. They came to a vacant restaurant with enclosed patios that became open air when the doors were swung out. Two cases of empty Coke bottles with English and Khmer characters stood outside the door as if waiting for a deliveryman to pick them up. There were no buildings beyond the restaurant. They hadn't seen a human yet.

They retraced their path on the street to 500 yards beyond the place they landed. They came to the governor's mansion, a three-story, ochre colonial mansion framed by tall coconut palms. As they got closer they could see the stucco was peppered by bullet holes around the entrance. They did not go in.

A kilometer further up the road they came upon a hard-packed earthen quay with oblique stone and mortar sides. The quay jutted into the Gulf of Thailand 100 meters. This was the jetty mentioned in Medici's agent reports, and which the NVA used to unload trawlers of guns and ammunition since Sihanoukville had been closed to them. Medici paced it off, making careful notes of its size and the water depth alongside to report to Saigon.

They walked another two kilometers toward the hilly point that formed the northern jaw of Kep Bay. They came to a large, white, two-story stucco building that bore the escutcheon of the

Norodoms, Prince Sihanouk's royal family. Medici smiled. This was it: Sihanouk's uncle's summer palace at Kep that Som Sary had described to him.

The grounds contained statuary and stately palms spread over a cleared acre. The statues were huge, imprecise plaster replicas of Rodin's works. They looked ridiculous, like caricatures really, and made Medici laugh aloud. He had one of the coxswains take a picture of him sitting in front of a version of Rodin's *The Thinker*, Medici assuming the same pose, chin on fist, elbow on knee.

They entered the building as before, two sailors ahead of Medici. The first floor was empty. The two headed upstairs quickly to examine the second floor while Flaherty, Florio, and the group ambled through the front entrance. The anteroom held a teakwood desk with a small writing blotter. A tall credenza and bookcase combination stood against the wall behind it, 1955 Danish modern. Medici posed again sitting with his feet crossed on the teakwood desk, gesturing expansively around the room. He saw two small oil paintings, one a Klee, in keeping with the Norodoms' taste for modern art. He noticed Florio staring at the Klee. It made him nervous. One of the sailors hailed him from the upstairs landing.

"Lieutenant, you gotta' see this." He pointed into a room.

Medici bounded up the stairs, through a sitting room, then a large bedroom with an enormous double king-size bed, and into a glittering bathroom 20-feet square. It was a wonderland. The floor, ceiling and walls shimmered with thickly glazed, emerald green Italian tile. The fixtures and towel racks were gold plated, the 10-foot tub, bidet and commode were a sparkling, glossy white porcelain. A truly regal room. Medici laughed and posed for a picture lounging in the enormous tub, a bit of hokey history, he said, then photographed both the coxswains in the tub and frolicking in obscene poses on the bidet. They said the pictures made the whole invasion worth it.

They returned to the ground floor. The remainder of the party gathered at the door to leave. Medici glanced at the spot where the Klee had hung. It was gone.

"Wait a minute! Where's the painting that was on that wall?" he pointed. The group was silent. "That's a Klee, and it's property of the Cambodian government. Who's got it?"

153

NILO takes over Prince Sihanouk's desk at his summer palace.

Silence. He looked around at the eight men from his vantage point halfway up the staircase. He noticed that the enlisted men's glances aimed toward Florio. Florio shifted his stance and Medici saw the frame of the Klee under his arm.

"Mr. Florio, put it back, please. It's property of Cambodia."

"MISTER Medici, I'll give the orders around here," Flaherty said. "Besides, if it's that valuable we can't leave it around here for the NVA to steal." He jerked his head toward the door and walked out, the group shuffled after him.

Stunned, Medici walked slowly down the stairs. Florio no longer hid the painting from the others. He grinned wickedly at Medici as they passed and said, "Spoils of war, Lieutenant."

Medici was speechless.

They walked to the wooded promontory on which sat Sihanouk's guesthouse for foreign dignitaries. He and the coxswains searched it and found nothing. They were transfixed by the view north over the Gulf of Thailand to the silhouette of the Chaine d'Éléphante Mountains. Through the thick green plate glass windows of the guest house the mountains appeared as their name, a recumbent Indian elephant's head resting on the shore and rising up to the bulk of its body which lay inland, the highest part of the cordillera.

The sleek modern guest house enchanted Medici. The view, the tranquility, and the languor of the Gulf made him think he would like to conceive a child in this place. The thought unsettled him.

When they returned aboard *Antelope*, Florio informed him that Commodore Flaherty had ordered Medici to make a census of all the Cambodians on Koh Kong Island off the Cambodian coast. Medici would be dropped there tonight and picked up sometime tomorrow. And no, there would be no security detail.

"The Commodore said NILO Ha Tien is tough enough to handle this one alone." Florio laughed.

Waterfront, Kep, Cambodia.

Vietnamese and Cambodian sailors celebrate the invasion of Kep.

Details of entrance to Royal Cambodian Palace at Kep.

NILO HA TIEN

The Thinkers contemplate the invasion of Kep.

The entire Kep invasion force.

25

North Vietnamese Embassy, Manila

"5-5-4 Vito Cruz," Kenck told the driver of the blue Renault. A sign on the taxi door said air conditioned, but like everything else in the Philippines, it was a fraud.

"Makati?" the driver asked in Tagalog. Kenck nodded.

The cab bumped down broken streets. Kenck opened the back window to get a breath of humid, stifling air. After a few blocks he remembered to ask the price.

"Eighty pesos," the driver said, narrowing his eyes and glancing at Kenck in the rearview mirror.

The ride should cost no more than 30 pesos, Kenck calculated. "No, 20 pesos." He watched the driver's face in the mirror. The driver scowled and said, "No, no, no! Eighty pesos!"

Kenck scowled back. "No, thief! Let me out!" He opened the door of the moving cab. The driver braked and Kenck started out the door, until the driver said, "Okay, okay, 30 pesos."

"Okay," Kenck said. His lips curled into a smile.

He resumed his view of the sidewalks. The street scene reminded him that Manila was just another dirtbag Asian city. As bad as Saigon, except the locals wore flip-flops instead of jungle boots, and short white tees instead of camies over their brown bellies. These men bore the languid expressions of the unemployed killing time in the tropics instead of the mirrored-sunglass sneer of Saigon cowboys. Under a palm umbrella along the street he saw a toothless Filipino selling bright-colored sugar drinks to dirty youths with vacuous faces.

The cab rounded a corner and he glimpsed a battered sign saying only "itu Cruz," and Kenck knew they had arrived. "Harrison Plaza Shopping Center," a sign read, and he laughed when he saw three crooked storefronts. Fifty yards further the cab came to a bumpy halt in a cloud of dust.

NILO HA TIEN

The driver pointed to the faded green wall on the right, grunted and held out his hand. Kenck paid him and drew himself from the tiny cab. A blast of sunlight blinded him and he shaded his eyes with his hand. The grimy wall seemed to have no opening. As his eyes adjusted to the light, he noticed a dingy sign high on the wall where vandals could not reach it. Faded red rows of Vietnamese and English proclaimed "Embassy of Democratic Republic of Vietnam." His gaze traveled above the sign. Through the grillwork he saw a wood trellis laced with concertina wire above a four-poster rifle platform commonplace in Saigon, but Manila wasn't at war.

He walked up and down the block, decided on one of the two flat steel gates set in the wall, banged on the gate and yelled twice. No one came. Searching the wall, he found a paint-encrusted bell button and pushed it hard. He thought he heard a bell's muffled ring deep inside the compound. Then came the sound of shuffling, and someone slowly worked the deadbolt of the steel door. It opened and he faced a short Vietnamese with sharp facial features and the harsh expression of the north.

"Uhhh?" said the caretaker.

"I need visa," Kenck said.

"Oh, visa." The caretaker pointed the stub of a finger inside the compound.

Kenck went through the gate and the Vietnamese closed it with a clank. The caretaker's bare feet and toes were gnarled and twisted in their thongs from hard years of carrying heavy loads without proper shoes, probably down the Ho Chi Minh Trail, Kenck thought. He grinned when he remembered he had studied such feet with detachment, usually on the corpses of NVA soldiers. Following the caretaker into a spacious screened porch, he stared through the transparent blue blades of a Sanyo fan. Two tall mahogany doors faced a pair of frail wooden chairs. The caretaker gestured for him to sit and lifted an intercom handset from the wall. He buzzed twice. "Visa," he said, then hung up and left.

Kenck studied the stately doors, an anomaly in the shabby residence. The morning's heat seeped into the porch. He walked to the fan and pushed its buttons without result. The doors opened and a reedy Vietnamese entered the porch. He wore unironed black cotton pants and a plain white synthetic shirt outside his trousers. His face was drawn and shaped by lines of discipline characteristic of northerners. His brush-cut hair was neatly trimmed with close military sidewalls. His only jewelry a thin gold wedding band.

"*Chao ong,*" *Good day, sir,* Kenck said, extending his hand.

"*Chao ong.*" Vo smiled to hide his shock, but Kenck knew he was startled. "Yes, it is already hot." He deftly started the fan with a flick of two fingers. "Perhaps we go inside where it is cooler, and we cannot be seen through the windows."

Kenck followed Vo through the mahogany doors into the musty parlor. That smell again, as if a fruit rat had died somewhere inside a stucco wall and for months oozed the odor of rot while wet tropic heat and microbes slowly did their work. He had been in the room only once before when he began this enterprise after that bastard Medici went to Ha Tien. The rat smell of the inner sanctum flooded him with waves of excitement and guilt. He felt a little dizzy.

"Your visit surprises me. You did not follow normal procedures," Vo said calmly. Kenck watched him rotate the wedding band with quick movements of his thumb. Kenck guessed he was calculating whether the embassy was under observation by the CIA.

"I know," said Kenck. "I used some of my in-country leave to come to the Philippines for a four-day R&R. I must report at Subic tonight. It was necessary to see you." He paused, then cleared his throat. "How would it affect the diplomatic situation if the Americans destroyed the piers and warehouses at Sihanoukville?" God, it's hot in here, he thought. He watched Vo's eyes for a sign.

Vo watched Kenck perspire and said nothing. He maintained a taciturn expression in order not to betray the furious whirring of his mind. He was not much older than Kenck, but knew he carried greater responsibility than the confused American. In his mind he fought not to make the invidious comparison. Bonding and control had to be maintained with turncoat agents. His thoughts of moral superiority made him nervous. But then Kenck had not taken a first at Moscow's University of International Studies, the KGB's college for spies, as Vo had. Nor had Kenck been posted to Vancouver to study the expatriate antiwar Americans in preparation for the most important job in the Intelligence Directorate, handling deep-penetration American agents in Vietnam. Heady responsibility, Vo thought. A gecko climbed diagonally across the wall above Kenck's head. Vo tracked it with his peripheral vision while he thought.

This degenerate American Naval officer was his prize. For the price of Sai Thom's carnal delights, Vo had gained U.S. Cambodian intelligence. Sometimes he roared with laughter at how far wrong American intelligence was, but recent Naval Intelligence reports accurately portrayed NVA activities in Cambodia. Kenck had proven particularly helpful since the overthrow of Sihanouk and the accession to power of the double-dealing whore Lon Nol, who allowed the Americans to buy his loyalty and close Vo's Sihanoukville weapons pipeline. Since the weapons had stopped moving through the port, Vo's agents had to beach trawlers on the Cambodian coast to unload munitions for infiltration into the delta. It was much slower and inefficient, but patience, deep-abiding Vietnamese patience, would overcome this setback.

The truth was, the port served no further purpose for Vo and Hanoi. Vo remembered his irritation when agents reported that the warehouses remained stuffed with *his* Soviet and Chinese weapons, while Lon Nol waited for the right opportunity to spirit them away and resell them to Cuba or Libya without irritating the CIA into cutting off his money. The gecko paused, turned its head at a right angle to its course. A languid water bug waved its antennae a foot away. Vo's eyes widened. The lizard was *stalking* the bug.

Kenck shifted in his chair.

With the piers and warehouses at Sihanoukville destroyed, the NVA siege on Phnom Penh would be tightened, for Sihanoukville was Cambodia's only seaport. Without it, now that NVA gunners had cut the Mekong as a supply route, the capital could not receive foreign supplies. Most deliciously, if blame were clearly pinned on the Americans, even Lon Nol would not trust them.

In the long run, the port would be valuable to Hanoi once it took Cambodia, but that was at least five years away, in 1975 according to the Politburo's plan. Anyway, when the time came, the stupid Russians would rebuild it for nothing to woo Hanoi and press a thorn in Peking's side.

"The port's destruction would be a fortuitous development," Vo whispered. He smiled as the gecko darted and crushed the water bug in its jaws.

Kenck relaxed, glad Vo was pleased and had smiled at him.

26

Come to Saigon

From where he sat, slouched, the red-leaded team room door framed the glistening greens of Cambodia beyond the border. As he watched, a pool of sunlight grew then shriveled around the drenched palms and banyans of Prek Chal hamlet. The colors unfolded from dark Hunan jade to Key lime. Medici remembered greens of such wondrous hues on elaborate Chinese cloisonné.

For an instant, the contrast of green against red of the jamb caused the colors to flash with alternating intensity in his mind, as they did on glossy red and green Christmas cards. He forced his gaze back to the *café au lait* in front of him to break the hypnotic cycle. He mused that the coffee's color was the same as the muddy Giang Thanh River that flowed by the foot of the hill and stained the green waters of the Gulf of Thailand seaward for miles.

Outside, beyond a neat row of carefully parked Jeeps, he noticed the first skirmishes of an approaching monsoon squall. The sky darkened. The waves of rain hissed. When the squall reached the parking area in front of the door, the raindrops appeared to bounce, leaving tiny dust clouds and craters in their trail. Soon the rain pelted the galvanized iron roof with the slow regularity of Russian AK rifle fire: Dhuh-Dhuh, Dhuh-Dhuh, Dhuh-Dhuh-Dhuh. The sound of the squall rose to a deafening metallic trill, subsided for a moment, then quit without warning.

PHLAAMM! The big four-inch mortar fired 20 yards from where he sat. The pressure wave, amplified in the wet air, smacked his face, traveled up his nostrils and ears, and caused the coffee on the table to rise in a tiny geyser.

He noted dispassionately that he no longer flinched. An improvement since his first week in the team house. Then, believing they were under attack when the mortar fired, he bolted out of bed and gashed his head on the bunk above. From force of habit he narrowed his focus to the slice of Cambodia visible through the team house door, hoping to see the impact of the big 4.2-inch round. Again, no luck.

"Oh. NILO. I didn't know you were here," said Yeager, the team radiotelephone operator. Medici awakened from the rain-induced trance. "Commander Plover called to tell you to take the first available air hike to province. *Very* important."

Medici rose, noticing Yeager's ringworm had reached clinical paradigm. He could actually distinguish the little red corkscrew shapes on Yaeger's cheeks, oddly similar to a Calder lithograph he had once seen at the Guggenheim.

"Thanks, Yeager," Medici said. Yeager returned to the radio room.

Medici's gut tightened in anticipation of the new mission. The romance is gone, he thought. I'm getting tired of being summoned here or there like a call girl turning tricks. Show up here. Go there. Take this guy into Cambodia. Ask the Cambodians this. Bring them that. Brief this incompetent on the Cambodian situation so he can pretend he understands it. He heard commotion in the radio room.

Before conscious recognition, he felt through his feet thudding WHUP WHUP WHUPS of a chopper circling in the rain searching for the pad.

"NILO, the swing's here a day early and headed down to Rach Gia. I told them you needed a ride," said Yeager, poking his head into the room.

"See if you can keep them on the ground for a minute, or ask them up for a soda. I've got to pack and talk to Frank before I can leave."

"Roger, NILO," and he was gone.

Medici rummaged through the armoire to see if he could put together a complete uniform of jungle fatigues. Rach Gia was getting to be a chicken-shit town with under-utilized Army officers driving around looking for uniform violations. On his last trip, a colonel, the Province Senior Advisor, had screeched to a halt in his Jeep, backed up and chewed Medici out for wearing the jaunty Cambodian naval beret Lon Nol had sent him through Samuth. Medici told the colonel to fuck off and kept walking. That evening at the safe house the Walrus had lectured him severely about inter-service protocol, how the Walrus had to deal with the colonel daily for intelligence matters, and so on. Medici never said a word, just grinned.

After much digging, he found enough parts for one complete uniform, although the blouse was new and a much darker color than the faded pants. He stuffed the AWOL bag with skivvies, socks, the Browning, 9mm ammo, a bottle of Scotch, and his shaving kit. Now he was ready for anything.

He found Frank in his room.

"What's up, Frank?"

"One of my people in Can Tho says some strange stuff is going on. Rumors that someone's going to destroy the Sihanoukville port facility. Maybe the North Vietnamese. Maybe the Russians...." He looked directly at Medici. "Maybe the Americans."

"WHAT! That's crazy. Why would we do that now? Lon Nol closed the port to Communist gunrunning," Medici said.

"Calm down, Tom. I didn't say it was going to happen. It's just that there is an awful lot of rumor pointing that way. There's usually something to it.

"It would be insane for us to do it," Medici said, deep in thought. "On one hand, I can see that in the near term it would guarantee Sihanoukville could not be used for weapons infiltration if the new Cambodian government changed its mind and made a deal with the North Vietnamese. On the other hand, the loss of the port could drive Cambodia back into a neutral or pro-North Vietnamese position, since they'll starve without the port while the Mekong's closed." He looked at Frank. "No, it's too stupid. I just don't believe it."

"Tom, something's afoot, but no one's saying much. Just be careful," Frank said.

Medici smiled. "Don't worry. I'll reason with them and talk them out of it if that's what the fuckers have in mind."

"Just watch your ass, Tom," Frank said.

Yeager poked his head in. "NILO, the Red Baron wants to leave so's he can get back to Can Tho before dark. You ready?"

"Okay, Yeager. Tell him I'll be right out." He turned to Frank. "See ya, pal."

"NILO, LET'S ROLL!" boomed the Red Baron from the team room. Medici grabbed his bag and left.

A Navy Jeep sat on the flooded dirt strip at Rach Gia, its canvas top and side curtains buttoned against the driving rain. An Air America Pilatus Porter aircraft sat 50 feet away with its prop turning, the pilot peering through the windshield at the rain clouds.

The driver's curtain peeled back and a hulk lumbered from the Jeep. Medici started toward him. The Walrus. Great.

The Walrus took a few steps around the Jeep with his head tucked into his shoulders, then looked up at the downpour. He beckoned Medici over and slid back in the driver's side. Medici opened the passenger curtain and sloshed in, drenched.

"How y'all doin', Tom?" the Walrus said with faux joviality.

Uh-oh, it's got to be really bad.

"Hi, Commander, long time no see. Think we can go over to the Embassy House tonight to watch a movie with Sherm and the other CIA guys?" His voice held a hopeful note.

"'Fraid not, Tom. You're not staying here tonight." He pointed to the Porter. "Sherm arranged for Air America to get you to Saigon tonight. You'll have to change planes at Long Xuyen. They said you won't be on the ground long there. Got your Browning?" Medici nodded. "They want you in Saigon AAY ESS AAY PEE. You'll be briefed at noon tomorrow by Captain Ross. They won't even tell me why. Which is nothing new." He snorted.

"You have no idea what's up?" Medici looked him straight in the eye.

"Honest, Tom, I don't."

Medici looked at the Porter and nodded. "Well, adios, Commander." He grabbed his AWOL bag, slid out of the Jeep and splashed through puddles to the Porter. He was airborne in less than a minute.

27

Next Mission

Medici walked up three flights of spiral stairs with the familiar uneasiness in the pit of his stomach. The inescapable smell of wine mold sickened him. No matter how they scrubbed and painted, the place smelled like a musty old winery.

His time on the staff before Ha Tien made it no easier to come back. He ached with exhaustion from seven hours' travel to Saigon last night after receiving the summons for his next mission. Air America had missed its connection. Three hours' layover in Long Xuyen, where Vietnamese urchins kicked empty aluminum beer cans around the tile floor, didn't help his nerves any.

"What the fuck do they want now?" he said in a bare whisper. Kampot, Kep, Tuk Meas, Kompong Trach and Takeo ran through his mind in a blur. Enough's enough, he thought.

Second floor. He passed the operations office and wondered why they got a new double door and intelligence hadn't. The operations chief must be the new admiral's fair-haired boy. Intel is out, Ops is in. Who cares? I'm glad I'm off this chicken-shit staff with its petty politics, no matter what's in store for me.

Third floor. N-2. Spook city. Now if I can just slide down to the captain's office at the far end of the corridor without running into any of my old staff buddies, I'll be all right.

Not that he didn't want to talk and catch up, but he had come to fear those moments when they feigned ignorance of his next mission and its danger. "You are in deep shit and I have a nice safe staff job. Don't you wish you'd stayed?" their eyes would say but their lips couldn't. They didn't have the heart to play that bitchy game with a field agent who might not return.

End of the hall. Made it. He stood between the sinister steel door of the "back room" and the intelligence chief's office, trying to gain composure. The door to the back room swung open with a nerve-shattering clank, and Dave, a survival school buddy, exited. Shit, Medici thought. But Dave held a candy-striped Sensitive Compartmentalized Intelligence folder and nodded to him without speaking, in accordance with SCI rules. Medici calmed himself, opened the wooden slat door and walked into the chief's office.

Worth, the pompous fat yeoman, sat at reception. At least he didn't have to deal with Brooms, the regular yeoman, a three dollar bill.

"Is the captain in?"

"Yes, Lieutenant Medici, he is."

"He's expecting me."

"Just a minute, I'll check," Worth said. He waddled to the partition that obscured the Chief of Staff for Intelligence from Medici's view.

"Captain, NILO Ha Tien, Lieutenant Medici to see you." A pause, then Worth motioned Medici in as he backed out. Five steps to bad news. Grace under pressure, right? You begged for the post, Medici told himself. He swallowed hard, rounded the partition and cool, hang loose "NILO Cambodia" strode into the man's office.

"Afternoon, Cap'n. What've we got?"

Ross took the meerschaum pipe out of his mouth and stood, smiling, while smoke leaked from his mouth. Medici realized he was a really huge man as he proffered a hand the size of a baseball glove across his desk for a handshake.

"Tom, m'boy. How are ya'? Keeping out of trouble?" Ross seemed unduly jovial.

"Trying to, Captain. Everything looks the same here."

"The staff's always like that: the more things change, the more they stay the same." Ross sat down and beckoned Medici to a chair. "Seriously, Tommy, any big problems up there? I mean from the standpoint of your personal security and comfort?"

Medici fumed: No one called him "Tommy." And when Ross led off with creature comfort stuff, it usually meant a shit-bad mission.

"Oh, the usual rats, snipers, sappers, and lousy food, Captain. Nothing out of the ordinary."

Ross bellowed an inappropriately loud laugh at the quip.

Must be a real bad detail, Medici thought.

"You know, Tom, you've got quite a 'can-do' reputation here on the staff. Just before Admiral Zumwalt went back to Washington to become Chief of Naval Operations, he personally told me how pleased he was with your 'outstanding and professional job,' those were his words, in conducting the original negotiations with the Cambodian government. And in French!

"You should know that there was quite a little tussle on the staff after you made the first secret contacts. Several of the other Chiefs of Staff wanted to send a more senior officer to conduct the negotiations, a captain or commander. Admiral Zumwalt listened to the debate for several minutes, then said, 'I've heard enough. I want to leave LT. Medici out there. He knows the turf and he's already effected liaison we never expected. He stays.' Those were his exact words, Tom. There was even a message to that effect from him to you. Did you receive it?"

"I think so," Medici said. Unconsciously he tapped the pocket in which he kept a copy. Too much, he thought. Where the fuck are they sending me? Hanoi?

"There is one thing that concerns us, Tom. You seem to be taking extraordinary risks in some of your forays into Cambodia. That time you disappeared for a few days on one of their ships was a bit cheeky."

Cheeky? Did he actually use the word cheeky? Jesus!

"Nonetheless we are at the same time grateful here in N-2 that you're willing to do what's necessary to get the bacon, if you know what I mean. I have to admit our fortunes on the staff have improved considerably since you've generated original Cambodian intelligence product."

Medici needed to piss. He couldn't listen to any more of this guy's horse shit.

"But in fairness I must warn you, Lieutenant, that if you're caught up there, where no Americans are supposed to be, well, we'll treat you like the colored relative who shows up at the wedding and deny your existence."

"Captain, I'm aware of what I do at my own risk. The thing I really like about the Navy and this job is that you let me make my own decisions on those matters." He paused. "Could we get on with the next mission? I'd really like to know where I'm going."

"Certainly, Tom." Ross looked embarrassed. "I apologize for pussyfooting around." He opened an SCI file. "Have you been to Sihanoukville yet?"

"Sihanoukville! No. That's where all the weapons infiltration went on. Soviet and Chicomm ships unloaded weapons and ammunition for shipment across Cambodia into Vietnam. That's a long way up there, Captain." Medici couldn't hide his excitement. He remembered, then dismissed Frank Brown's warning.

"It is. We're sending you up on an American LST. Its ostensible mission is to ferry a shortwave transmitter for Lon Nol to use as a second Radio Phnom Penh. The North Vietnamese have silenced the real station outside the capital, so the alternate transmitter will broadcast from Sihanoukville, which is more secure right now. The delivery gives you an excuse to do port photography, locate channel buoys, piers and warehouses for our charts. And most important, to snoop around and determine how to take out the entire port, should we need to."

"Take it out?" Medici was flabbergasted. So Frank's rumors were right on the money. He swallowed, then said, "I thought we were friendly with Lon Nol's people."

"Now, yes. But the scene can change quickly there. We want a contingency plan to take out the port permanently to prevent a recurrence of the 'Sihanoukville Connection,' as you've aptly named it in your reports. Something a little more elegant than B-52 bombers. That's your mission."

Medici blew out a slow breath and stared at Ross's desk. He flashed on a vision of himself alone aboard a Cambodian ship, when word comes that the U.S. and Cambodia are now enemies, and that Sihanoukville had been destroyed. Medici becomes their prisoner instead of their guest. Or worse: Som Sary, the C/O, walks into Medici's cabin on the corvette with a cocked pistol and a black expression on his face and shoots him.

"Tom?" Captain Ross said quietly.

Medici snapped out of the reverie. He looked at Ross.

"I was saying you should go to see Commander Holland so

he can brief you on mission details. You'll have to leave quickly because you rendezvous with the LST 0300 Sunday morning. Any questions?"

"Not that I can think of now, Captain. Good to see you." Medici stood and shook Ross's hand. He turned smartly and walked out.

28

Mission Orders

"Check in with the Cambodian Shop before you leave tonight, Tom," Commander Holland said. "LTjg Kenck will give you the one-inch-to-fifty-foot-scale charts of the Sihanoukville pier and quay basin facilities. You'll want to take bearings and verify the accuracy of the pier and warehouse locations and photograph them when you're there. The stuff we have is at least seven years old. We need to update the port information just in case this Lon Nol doesn't remain favorable to us or gets dumped. If the weapons infiltration is restarted by the Chinese or the Sovietskis, we'll simply take out the port this time." His jaw tightened. "The White House has decided not to tolerate that shit anymore, détente or not."

Medici sat looking at Holland with a placid expression. Holland was the one person on staff with whom he could be completely candid. Medici didn't have to adopt the NILO persona with Holland. Holland was a mustang. He came up the hard way from the enlisted ranks. But he had the gentlest personality on the N-2 staff, and Medici had warmed to it from the time Holland got him the Cambodian border post. Medici often suspected the staff left the explanation of dirty details of each new mission to Holland precisely because he told it like a gentle bedtime story:

"…Then, Tom, you may have to get out on your own. It's a long way overland to the border, so you might think about commandeering a fishing junk to take you to Thailand or Singapore…." Or "…The only way you can reach the island without a boat is to be dropped from a helicopter. There's no beach wide enough for the rotor disc…." The man's gentle tone had a soporific effect on Medici. Even though his mind registered danger in each briefing, the pit of his stomach radiated no alarm when Holland spoke.

Medici thought the contrast odd. He always felt ill at ease and nervous when his mission briefings started with the Chief of Staff for Intelligence. He guessed for that reason he adopted the NILO bravado. In those pep talks he seldom paid attention, merely tried to maintain exterior emotional control, to make sure his knees weren't knocking. The chief never said anything of significance, only drivel about the fine job Medici was doing, how pleased the intelligence staff and the admiral were with his operations. If he were to be captured in Cambodia, the Navy would, of course, strenuously deny its affiliation and any prior knowledge of his whereabouts, da-dah, da-dah, like that.

Medici wondered why the chief even spoke to him. He suspected so that he could tell the admiral, generals and other buddies at lunch that "my Cambodian agent was in today and he said...." Basically cocktail gossip.

But, damn it, he couldn't blame Holland. Several things were unspoken but perfectly understood between them: This was a serious job, Medici had volunteered for it, Holland had gone out of his way to get it for him. Holland's expectation was that Medici would perform in impeccable fashion and set a standard that would reflect the wisdom of sending a staff man to the border.

When Holland briefed him, Medici remained calm and unafraid because personal fear had absolutely no place in their professional relationship, and both knew it. Each created a comfort zone for the other. Holland had complete confidence in Medici's ability to do the job and, incidentally, to protect his own neck. He knew that Medici would never compromise a mission either by being too cautious or foolhardy about his own safety. Their mutual confidence was Dumbo's magic feather: Medici didn't worry about his personal safety because his mentor, Holland, had complete faith in his judgment.

Holland finished speaking. Medici wondered how long he had been lost in this reverie. He guessed it wasn't too long because Holland smiled and said, "It beats staff duty, anyway!"

Medici laughed. "Want anything from Sihanoukville, Commander? Like a pink cup-and-saucer set engraved with 'Souvenir of Sihanoukville, Cambodia.'"

"Just photos and a plan to take out the port if we have to." Holland laughed and stood. "It's quarter of six. I told Kenck to stand by with the charts for you. I'll call and tell him you're on your way over. It's Friday night in Saigon and the staff pukes deserve their night out, too."

"I'm on my way, Commander. Just need to stop at the Annapolis to pick up a poncho liner, then I'll see Kenck. I intend to tip a few tonight myself. I've got a reservation on the Jolly Green Giant back to the border tomorrow."

Holland reached over the desk and shook his hand. "Stay out of trouble, Tom."

Medici smiled and left. Now, *this* was his Navy.

29

Payroll

Medici took a pedicab to the Annapolis, the Navy's transient hotel and supply center. He wandered between disoriented newcomers to the supply desk where he had been issued his fatigues and M-16 on the way to Ha Tien. At the time there were no poncho liners—camouflage, feather-light synthetic blankets—for issue because the office-bound staffers in Saigon had drawn them for souvenirs. Medici accepted this as a fact of life then. Now he was going to get one.

A chubby yeoman third class sat behind the counter reading a *Harvard Alumni Magazine*. He wore tailored fatigues, starched and shiny, and gold wire-rim glasses. Medici stood quietly, waiting for him to look up. He waited 90 seconds.

"Huh. What d'you want?" The yeoman glanced at Medici's rumpled fatigues, then returned to his magazine.

"I'm NILO Ha Tien and I want to pick up a poncho liner. You were out of stock when I went into the field."

"You'll have to show me your service record," the yeoman said from behind the magazine. "Too many guys are taking them for souvenirs. I have to make sure you weren't issued one already."

"I told you, you were out of them when I went out to the field. Look in your own records. I need the poncho liner to sleep under. That's what they're for," Medici said

"I suppose I could check in our records in the back, but it'll take me 45 minutes and I'll need to know the exact date and time we issued your equipment...."

Medici slammed the butt of the Browning on the counter and the yeoman jumped off the stool. "Get me a fucking poncho liner right now or you won't live to see your fifth reunion!" Medici shouted. He felt the blood surge into his face.

The yeoman paled. He knocked over the stool on his way

into the back of the warehouse, whining, "Okay, okay!" He came out in less than a minute with a bright new poncho liner and tossed it from a distance to Medici.

"Where do I sign?" Medici said quietly.

"Don't worry about it. Just go. Please."

Medici nodded thanks with a thin smile and walked to the door. He heard the yeoman say timidly, "You know you're fucking nuts, don't you? Fucked up field guys." On the street, Medici laughed himself to tears.

Medici saw charts laid out on the big rosewood table when the black steel door groaned open. He entered and Kenck slammed the door.

"It's about time, Lieutenant. I broke a dinner engagement to wait for you," Kenck said.

Medici didn't look at him, but walked to the table. "If you prefer, Lieutenant jay gee Kenck, we can reschedule this for four o'clock tomorrow morning before I take the helo back to the border." Kenck didn't answer.

Medici looked around the shop. The walls were completely covered with full-color aerial photo maps of Cambodia in four big northwest to southeast slices. The first slice covered the entire Cambodian coast from the Thailand to the Vietnam border. Thin lines of red tape showed coastal infiltration routes reported by Medici's agents. He felt satisfied that the long looping lines were his intelligence product and tracked the lines on his map in Ha Tien. Overlaying the map were clear acrylic sheets showing enemy unit information on one layer, Communist bloc ship names, ports and destinations on another, and range arcs of American bombers in Thailand on a third. Medici walked to the wall map and gauged the distance from Sihanoukville to An Thoi where he would board the LST. Shit, he thought, I'll be way up there this time. He walked back to the table where Kenck was peeling back charts.

Medici stopped short. His eyes widened. "I didn't know we had maps this detailed," he said.

"Neat, huh? If you look closely you'll see they're hand drawn.

Did you ever hear of the Navy rating Cartographer? Well, we've got two on the staff. They do special assignments and hand draw these from photos and the detail from word-of-mouth reports. Pretty good, eh?"

"Are these the one-inch-to-fifty-footers Holland mentioned?"

"They sure are."

"How the hell can they be that detailed in large scale and be inaccurate?" Medici asked.

"They start with pantograph expansions from the old aerial maps. They're modified from observer reports. Some dock worker paces off the length of a new warehouse and eventually we get some version of his guesstimate. The aerial photos used to help, but we haven't been flying low-altitude missions because of Cambodia's neutrality. The satellite pictures don't tell us where the entries and doors to the go-downs are, or where the channel is in relation to the end of the seawall. Strong currents cause shoaling around there. That's why I wanted you to go and photograph everything yourself."

"How about giving me a photocopy of the pier and warehouse area on this one? And the largest scale chart you have of the channel and quay basin. I can get the LST's navigation guys to shoot bearings on everything as we proceed slowly into the channel. We'll get a good fix on the channel buoys, the corners of the warehouses, and the opening in the quay wall. That should tie all this together. I'll take pictures of everything."

"You've got 'em, Lieutenant," Kenck said. Medici thought he heard sarcasm on the word lieutenant.

He looked at Kenck. The young man had not weathered staff duty well. His complexion was pasty and he had remarkable acne for a 26-year-old. He was pudgy all over, and his pectorals appeared breast-like under his wash-khaki shirt.

Medici looked over to the alcove in which Kenck's desk stood. Yes, they were still there: Danish porno magazines with photos of women in various postures of autoeroticism. On top of the armoire and jammed against the ceiling was a blow-up "love companion" Kenck must have purchased from a classified ad in the back of a porn magazine. It was the kind with a pouch between the legs to receive "all of your gifts of love to her," according to the ad Medici had glimpsed.

"You still fucking that Popeye punching bag, Kenck?" Medici asked. "Why don't you get a decent whore, clean her up, and get her to service only you?"

"Very funny, Medici. Why don't you worry about your problems? Like the price on your head. I hear it's $10,000US now—that's why you got mortared," Kenck yelped. "You know, you're damn lucky to be going to Sihanoukville. I don't think there's been an American there in seven years. I've been reading everything I could lay my hands on about the city for the last eight months. It's really an exotic place. It even has a casino.

"They really should have sent me on this mission, since I'm so familiar with the port from my study. But you know Kease. If it's a collection mission he wants a NILO to do it. He says you guys are more attuned to personal security and the details of collection. I just wish they'd let me do this one...." Kenck drifted off in a Walter Mitty fantasy of heroic exploits in Cambodia, Medici guessed from the glazed eyes and crooked smile.

He grinned. The staffers were the same this way. They fantasized they could do missions better than field guys, especially when they knew there was no chance of their being sent into the field to prove it. It was easy to sit in an air-conditioned office in Saigon and bad mouth the NILOs. It was a staff sport with no consequence for the players.

Kease was right. The NILOs became canny about personal safety and ways and means to accomplish collection missions. To be honest, Medici knew he had become more effective once he got the romance out of his system and looked at the job in cold, calculating terms. Otherwise he'd be making mistakes that could cost his life. He'd learned something today.

Kenck photocopied the portion of the charts Medici wanted. Medici folded them into his thin vinyl briefcase, then zipped it and put it under his arm. He turned toward the door.

"Wait. Payroll," Kenck said. He walked to the big wall safe at the end of the room, dialed the combination, opened the safe and withdrew a bound block of Cambodian riels the size of two six packs of beer. He crossed the room and heaved the wad at Medici who caught it like a football.

"What the hell is this?"

"Payroll for your agents, famous Collection Team 5." Kenck laughed. "Take it with you and get it to the Walrus. His net handler pays all the CT-5 spies, or didn't you know that? Did you think they got a monthly green check from the U.S. government?" Kenck laughed, enjoying Medici's confusion.

"But wha—what am I supposed to do with it? I'm not leaving until 6 a.m. tomorrow."

"Sign this." Kenck proffered a form and government ballpoint pen. Medici dropped the raft of currency on the table and signed. "You're supposed to protect it with your life and your fancy 9mm pistol. You've assumed responsibility for $10,000 worth of Cambodian currency, worth three times that much in Vietnamese piastres on the black market. Have a nice Friday evening in Saigon," Kenck grinned.

"What if it's stolen?"

"Then it comes out of your pay. You're penny accountable."

Medici drew a slow breath. Instead of arguing with Kenck he looked around the room for something to carry the bills in. Kenck offered him an attaché case and Medici asked him if he was crazy, and maybe would he like to stencil "$10,000 CASH INSIDE" and really cook Medici's goose. He reminded Kenck of the accuracy of CDR Kease's assessment of the operational shortcomings of staff pukes trying to perform field missions.

Medici surveyed the room. He saw a scruffy shopping bag which contained Twinkie wrappers and wadded Kleenex. The bag looked like it had been washed several times, and used to degrease French fries, judging from the spots on it. Medici dumped the Kleenex and wrappers out on the floor.

"Kenck, you been jerking off in this or what?" he said. Kenck didn't answer. Guess he was, Medici thought. He stuffed the currency into the bag, wadded it under his arm and opened the door.

"See you in a few weeks, Kenckie. Don't get her pregnant." Medici winked, raised his head toward the blow-up doll, and was out the door before Kenck could say anything.

30

Crash Pad

Medici walked back through the park to the NILO crash pad at the Meyercord Hotel. He passed the Cercle Sportif tennis club where he had been invited for membership—three months after he went to remote Ha Tien. The wock of the tennis balls seemed surreal after discussing the destruction of Sihanoukville port. He walked past the Cercle Equestrienne where French-educated Vietnamese Brahmins sent their daughters to learn to ride as the rich did the world over.

When he reached the intersection at the other side of the park, his eyes started to burn before he heard the screams of the students. National Police in a cloud of MACE clubbed student demonstrators who massed in the intersection. Medici, in uniform, passed undisturbed along the edge of the melee—and tucked the brown bag a little tighter under his arm.

A block further on he stood before the Meyercord. The Army had taken it over to billet officers and civilians attached to commands in Saigon, such as the surfeit of colonels (one was assigned as toothpaste officer at the Cholon PX) who had to be berthed in a manner suitable to their rank. While on staff Medici had lived in the Le Qui Don, a nice quiet hotel in the tree-lined embassy section of Saigon. But the NILOs came to Saigon infrequently for special mission assignments, so they had a crash pad, a Spartan white room with six steel bunks and a bathroom, on the sixth floor of the Meyercord.

There were no elevators. An elegant, wide staircase spiraled from floor to floor around a broad atrium. The ground floor housed a small cafeteria with a short-order cook who prepared nothing edible except ham and cheese omelets made from nitrated Danish ham, synthetic cheese, and Army instant powdered eggs. Any other dish meant heavy enteritis. A small PX which episodically sold wine, brandy or *Playboy* magazines stood next to the cafeteria. Medici stopped to buy wash-and-wear shirts and trousers. He would travel to Sihanoukville as a U.S. AID engineer, and the innocuous garments provided perfect cover costume.

A real vacation resort, Medici thought as he rounded the staircase to the second landing. He plodded up the stairs, his jungle boots kahwunking on the tile steps. He passed a Vietnamese whore whose arms encircled a paunchy American colonel. She smelled so yeasty with semen that Medici winced.

On the third floor railing a parrot sat silhouetted against the dull green glow cast by the atrium's skylight. The parrot blinked at Medici, crooked its head to one side and quietly said, "Aaawwk."

On the fourth floor a Vietnamese laundress delivered piles of freshly starched jungle fatigues. Each bundle was carefully tied with a thin vine rather than string. Medici said, "*Chao, Ba*," and she nodded and answered, "*Chao, Dai-Uy.*"

He reached the sixth floor and kicked open the door to the crash pad. He saw his open AWOL bag spilling dirty olive socks and underwear on the bed. Two small bags and a large sea bag sat on other beds. The name "LT (jg) Henderson, 727113, RivRon 5" was stenciled on the sea bag. He had to be a boat driver from Seafloat, the insane floating Naval base on the river that wound through Nam Can, the southern tip of Vietnam.

Medici closed the door. He put the brown bag of cash on his bed and checked the bathroom. The room was empty. He looked carefully into his AWOL bag for any booby trap wires across the opening. There were none he could see. He gently lifted the AWOL bag to see if it was heavier from the addition of a grenade or slice of plastique. It felt as light as he had left it. He held his breath and opened the bag. No click, snap or flash. He was okay.

He withdrew the dirty socks and underwear, and stuffed the underwear down into the brown paper bag to cover the Cambodian riels. Then he slid the bag halfway under the metal bed frame. No coverlet or sheet hung down to obscure vision under the bed. He took the smelly socks and draped them half in and half out of the paper bag so they would be in plain view of all who came into the room.

Walking back to the door, he surveyed his work. It satisfied him. He opened the door and left it ajar, so any passerby on the landing could see in, then walked down the stairs into the Saigon twilight.

31

Huge

Medici had arranged to meet Huge, a staff friend, for dinner at L'Amiral restaurant for the best French food in Saigon. He whet his appetite during the walk to Thuy Do Street, lined with Saigon's best restaurants and the Reuters office.

As he walked, thoughts drifted through his mind. How absolutely beautiful Saigon must have been before the war, how nice it was in certain places still. The Sihanoukville mission excited him, but not too much yet. He enjoyed the buoyancy he always felt after they briefed him, the relief from fear of the unknown. He smiled at the prospect of the evening of reveling that lay ahead.

The idea that Kenck had planned the mission bothered him. How many other missions had he suggested to the intelligence chief? Kenck's part in them gnawed at Medici. It made him apprehensive about the real risks of Sihanoukville. CDR Holland had explained that as far as they could tell Sihanoukville was as safe as Phnom Penh, possibly safer because the NVA hadn't surrounded it or shelled it. Medici remembered that his agents had reported elements of the 9th NVA Division in the area, but no one besides Medici believed the reports.

He couldn't help dwelling on Kenck. He never realized how jealous Kenck was because Medici got the Ha Tien NILO post. His subconscious kept scanning his history with Kenck, all he knew about him, trying to see if there was something he had missed in sizing him up. He remembered Frank's warning about the rumored destruction of the port.

He abruptly caught the movement of a rifle in his peripheral vision. Crouching, he withdrew the Browning from his waistband, then leapt sideways two steps behind a banyan tree that poked through the sidewalk. An Asian soldier in chrome helmet spun his rifle and brought it smartly to a halt in front of him with a cry. Medici stood, put the pistol back in his waistband. The soldier completed the manual at arms and returned the rifle to rest position. The butt cracked sharply on the cement.

Medici blushed with embarrassment and returned the salute. In front of the Korean embassy, a sharp-eyed guard at attention in the twilight spotted his black collar devices and initiated the manual-at-arms salute. The Korean guards were so enthusiastic that in daylight they could spot and salute an officer a half block away. During his month on the staff, their elaborate salute had so annoyed him that he would walk on the far side of the street to avoid the formality.

He couldn't believe he had reacted instinctively as if it were an attack. You really can't put a field man in the city, he thought.

He rounded the corner and found himself on Thuy Do Street. The European architecture reminded him of Paris. The second stucco building modestly displayed a small brass sign, "L'Amiral." A plaintive Vietnamese ballad came from a restaurant further down the street.

He opened the small wrought iron gate and stopped to read the menu posted in a glass shadowbox. He smiled. It would be a good eat. He slipped through the door into a chilled anteroom with a small tapestry on the wall. A faint smell of decay mingled with the smell of garlic and butter.

A Vietnamese waiter in high-cut vest and plastered hair came to greet him.

"Bon soir, Capitaine. Y aura-t-il des autres en votre partie?" *Good evening, Lieutenant. Are there others in your party?*

"Seulement un autre. Un sous lieutenant de la marine, de très haute taille, avec les cheveux rouges," Medici answered. *Only one other. A very tall lieutenant jaygee with red hair.*

"Bien entendu! Il est déjà au table! Monsieur Reffe, n'est-ce pas?" *Of course! He's already at your table. Mr. Reffe, right?*

"Ah, oui! C'est lui!" *Yes. That's him!*

The waiter led him around a wall to a room with two tables. Rick "Huge" Reffe sat, towering in his wash khakis, red hair like a beacon. His massive freckled forearms rested on the table, an empty bottle of beaujolais in front of him.

"Huge! Am I late?" Medici asked. They shook hands and sat down.

"No. I had a particularly shitty day and came over early to get out of the back room. All hell's breaking loose since the shift in emphasis to Cambodia. The stupid middle-level officers just don't know anything about what's going on and they flap around at the slightest crisis." He drank some wine and motioned to the waiter for another bottle. "Of course the upshot is, they give the junior officers scores of emergency projects that take time and keep us frazzled. You're one lucky dude, Tom. I'd give my left nut to go out to the field now, just to get away from this staff bullshit!"

"I guess your SCI clearance from the embassy job in Manila doomed you." Medici laughed. "And you were the one guy in language school who really wanted to be a NILO, got orders, and then was pulled back to the staff. I thought I'd be happy with safe staff duty, and I end up out in Cambodia. How d'ya figure it? Fate?"

"Fuck fate," Reffe snorted.

Medici guessed the irony wasn't so funny to Huge, so he dropped the subject. He poured himself a glass of wine. It was good but had vinegared slightly. Wines shipped to Saigon inevitably soured from exposure to the brutal heat.

The waiter came and they ordered. Medici began his dinner with French onion soup au gratin. Then escargots, a scallop salad, rack of lamb, and glazed carrots. Huge had veal in wine sauce. His eyes widened as Medici, on whom he had a foot in height and 100 pounds, out-ate him three to one. For dessert, Medici ordered a Baked Alaska for two for himself, while Huge had only espresso. After he finished the Baked Alaska, Medici picked a softball-sized mango from the fruit display across the room.

"Where the hell do you put it, Tom! Do you have a hollow leg or what?"

Medici laughed. "I don't know. I've never eaten like this before. The food's shitty in Ha Tien except on Sundays when the Ba is off and we go to the round restaurant and eat shrimp. Maybe it's Last Supper syndrome. Figure I better eat decently while I can." He slid a thick slice of ripe orange mango into his mouth.

They ordered cognac and sat silently awhile. Medici really missed spending time with Huge. They had met in the crash Vietnamese language school at Coronado and had finished at the top of their class.

Huge graduated from Dartmouth and Medici from Princeton the same year, 1967. The Ivy League camaraderie had offered them some insulation from the relentless leveling effect of the service.

Huge's dream was to finish his hitch and start a private book publishing press somewhere in New Hampshire. Medici didn't understand Huge's apparent lack of larger ambition. He was a Phi Beta Kappa, no great feat at Dartmouth, Medici kidded, but seemed uninterested in material things.

"What about the trip home in the Land Rover? Have you looked into that?" Medici asked. The Martell calmed him.

"I did. I think the best plan is to buy it in Bangkok, not Saigon. There's no way we can drive through Cambodia now, even if we bring our own weapons. Even with NILO Ha Tien aboard," Huge laughed.

"Roger that. Do you need a deposit or anything?" Medici said.

"No. Not yet. I've explored the routing. From Bangkok, we can drive northwest to Rangoon, then on up the caravan route to East Pakistan, India, West Pakistan, Iran and through Turkey to Istanbul. From there we just follow the path of the Orient Express back to Paris. Should take four to six months, assuming we get cooperation at the borders. I'm working on getting us both red diplomatic passports."

"Will Naval staff separate us from service out here?"

"Yup. I've already taken care of that with the administrative officer. It cost me several dinners and some Scotch, but he'll do it."

"Great!" said Medici. He and Huge had planned this trip home before they got to Saigon. Part fantasy anyway, their plans suffered a setback when Medici transferred to the border. On trips to Saigon, he made a point of discussing details with his friend, in the hope that they would attempt the trip.

For Huge, THE TRIP represented the derring-do that had been denied him when the staff cancelled his NILO orders because of his special intelligence background. Medici sensed the blow Huge felt and was determined to keep their dream alive.

Medici lived out adventure fantasies regularly in Cambodia. THE TRIP would be fine, but he didn't need contrived adventures anymore. Medici had seen Huge become demoralized from the pressure of staff work and the boredom of Saigon. Unless he could keep his sights on THE TRIP, the year might be unendurable for him. He wondered whether Huge understood this. Then he thought maybe Huge believed Medici's sanity depended on THE TRIP in the same way. He knew neither of them could discuss the issue directly. The dream must be kept alive for sanity's sake. Whosoever's. That was their compact.

The bill came and Medici paid. Over 20,000 piasters with tip, almost $100. Huge tried to contribute, but Medici said, "I ate most. Anyway, I can't spend this stuff out at the border if I try."

Huge, really drunk, made a mock salute and said, "Okay, NILO Ha Tien. Now it's my treat: Monique's!"

"What's that?"

"You bumpkin from the border! The most famous massage parlor in all of Indochina. Monique is half French and half Vietnamese. She's run the parlor since 1954. It's a high-class joint."

"A whorehouse, right? I'm not interested."

"Not a whorehouse. Well, they give hand jobs under the right circumstances. But the girls are really talented masseuses. If we leave now we can be there in 10 minutes."

32

Monique's

Medici saw no sign to distinguish Monique's from the other residences on the neat street of European houses. Huge paid the fare and led Medici to a solid plank door. He knocked. Behind the door an old Vietnamese man sat listlessly on a wooden chair and smoked. An M-16 leaned in the corner next to him. He smiled at the sight of Huge, a regular, Medici gathered. Wooden benches lined the anteroom but no patrons waited. Monique glided gracefully toward them. She was an aging yet stunning Eurasian, the essence of elegance. Every word and gesture was graceful and pleasing to Medici's eye.

They bantered briefly in French. Huge asked if Mimi, his favorite, was available, and Monique led him to a small door in the wall of a larger room beyond.

"Et vous, Capitaine?" she asked Medici pleasantly.

"Just a massage, Monique. SEULEMENT un massage." *ONLY a massage.*

She smiled and nodded, then gestured for Medici to follow her. She moved fluidly down the hall to a dressing area with benches and stall shower, told him to undress and shower, then to encircle himself with a large, terrycloth towel. He complied. A petite Vietnamese girl in an elegant silk dressing gown came out of a room to greet him.

Medici was nervous. On the border he had simply decided not to deal with the sexual issue. Concentrating on his job, he found fear could be directed to suppress rather than excite his libido. He knew Frank Brown went to town to be serviced every 10 days or so. Carlos merely masturbated regularly. They never discussed the subject of how each coped, forbidden under the cryptic but strict code of etiquette of the hill.

The temptation did not upset Medici but, rather, the fact that circumstances might serve to smash the fragile shell of abstinence he had constructed around him as part of his Ha Tien mystique. If the shell broke, there was no telling what arrangements he might make in Ha Tien for his own pleasure.

He remembered the young Navy lieutenant from Annapolis whose father was an admiral. He had survived well as the C/O of the junk force advisors in Ha Tien until he became enchanted by a Vietnamese widow with two children. He moved in with her in a small rented house in Ha Tien village, said he loved her and would divorce his American wife to marry her. He went to hell in a hand basket. The lieutenant's friend, his second in command, assumed the responsibilities of the junk group when a full third of the lieutenant's tour remained. The lieutenant so wore himself out from the stress of trying to maintain a domestic life while knowing he had a family back home and Naval duties, that he contracted hepatitis and was flown back to the States. No one knew what became of his Vietnamese paramour and her children.

Medici didn't trust himself to open the door to that kind of fall. Too many people relied on him and the job he did, not to mention his wife to whom he intended to be faithful. They had never discussed fidelity before his departure, but he decided he would be faithful. It also fit his Ha Tien scheme.

The girl said her name was Lotus; Medici said his name was Tom. She directed him to a padded table covered with fresh white linen. He climbed up, careful to keep his towel in place. Lotus turned him face down, loosened the towel, sprinkled talc on his back and shoulders and started a soothing gentle massage.

Medici relaxed, but tensed and rose quickly up on one arm as the door quietly opened. He realized the Browning was in the pocket of his fatigue blouse in the hall.

Monique entered dressed in a silk robe. She smiled so benignly, Medici felt immediately at ease. Lotus giggled. "You are safe here, Capitaine," Monique said in flawless English. He lay down again and relaxed.

Monique expertly kneaded his leg from foot to thigh. She moved to the other foot and up the leg. Tension drained from him. Lotus worked his back and arms. They gently rolled him over and continued. He didn't open his eyes. Monique worked with talc up his thighs while Lotus worked down to his mid section, kneading gently but persistently. The crescendo effect was incredibly sensual. Medici felt himself arousing inexorably. He experienced a stupor of pleasure. He sensed himself growing hard against the scratchy towel, and Lotus redoubled her efforts around his groin, never touching his genitals.

Completely, uncontrollably erect, he felt the thin shell of abstinence cracking. Lotus rotated his pubis in wide circles, bearing down more with each orbit. Medici could take no more. Tomorrow his Sihanoukville mission began. He sat up, furious.

"I said massage only! Stop now!" he shouted in a frenzy of sexual desire and anger. He jumped off the table, holding the towel in front of him and barged past Monique, her mouth agape.

"Cher monsieur..." she started, but Medici charged out of the room, scowling, his libido completely supplanted by rage.

He tore his uniform from the hanger and dressed in seconds, pulled on his jungle boots and laced them, leaving the wide stovepipe trousers unbloused, dropping baggily to his boots. He tucked the Browning in his waistband and went to the door of Huge's room, banged on it twice, heard a commotion inside, then shouted, "Huge, I'm gone. See you when I'm back from mission," then headed for the door. As an afterthought, he threw 5,000 piastres on the wooden table next to the puzzled guard, who saluted limply. Medici threw open the door and entered the Saigon night.

33

Curfew

Medici closed his eyes until his night vision returned. The street was black and silent. He calmed himself, got his bearings and headed down the street in the general direction of the park and the Meyercord. Before he reached the intersection, an Army Jeep with peep-slot headlights like oriental eyes turned the corner and stopped next to him. The large white letters "MP" covered the door. An enormous black man, six-foot-seven, at least 250, wearing a chrome helmet and cinched with a broad white cartridge belt, jumped out of the front seat. Medici thought he felt through his feet the concussion of the man's landing. Three smaller men followed, two of them Vietnamese. They formed a circle around Medici.

"You know wha' tahm it is, soldja?" The black man spoke from the dark.

"I give up," Medici said. "What time is it?"

"Ah thank we got us a wise guy heah, Lieutenant Waylon. Should we bring him in?"

"What the hell's the problem?" Medici said. "I'm walking back to my hotel."

"Not after curfew you're not," said Waylon. He shined a flashlight in Medici's eyes. He dropped the beam to his collar devices. "Ah, I mean, did you realize it's past curfew, Captain?"

"I didn't know there was a curfew, Lieutenant. I come from Ha Tien out on the Cambodian border. I was just at Monique's...."

"A secon' vylayshun," said the black MP. He relished the admission that further incriminated Medici. "Ah think we should take him to detention, Lieutenant."

Medici's anger had not subsided. Now it surged back. "Care to know what I was doing in Monique's, Lieutenant?" Medici drew his NILO card from his pocket and handed it to the lieutenant who shined his flashlight on it. Next to Medici's photograph, in which he looked 16 and angelic, it said:

"NAVAL INTELLIGENCE FIELD
ORGANIZATION VIETNAM IDENTIFICATION
CARD

This is to certify that Thomas N. Medici whose photograph and signature appear hereon is assigned to the U.S. Naval Intelligence Field Organization Vietnam, Commander U.S. Naval Forces Vietnam, and is authorized to travel after curfew on official business, enter Vietnamese military and civilian facilities on official business, transport indigenous personnel and such other persons as directed. Wearing of civilian attire is authorized as directed. The nature of his duties is such as to preclude explanations to unauthorized persons.

/s/CDR Paul H. Kease
Chief Collection Branch
Card Number: 00100
Expiration Date: 31 December 1970"

Waylon faced Medici after he read it. He looked irritated but concerned. "So you're a spook, Captain. Double-Oh One Double-Oh. A real James Bond," he said. He thought a moment. "This still doesn't explain why you were in Monique's."

"Nor do I have to, as stated on the card," Medici said. Then he lowered his voice. "Will you step over here, Lieutenant?" He moved a few steps away from the group. The Vietnamese MPs were reading the back of the NILO card which recited the same information in Vietnamese.

Medici spoke in a whisper when they stopped out of earshot of the others. "Do you know what a 'dead drop' is, Lieutenant?"

"I'm not sure. Does it have something to do with messages?"

"Sort of. It's a means of transmitting agent reports from spies to their net handlers without drawing attention to the connection. We use Monique's as one of our drops for the really sensitive agents we have within the Saigon government. I shouldn't be telling you this at all, but I felt you were entitled to some explanation. You must not say anything to your squad, especially the Vietnamese. Heads could roll instantly. You know, summary executions at the National Police Headquarters before dawn."

Waylon whistled a breath. "I don't know, Captain. I'm under strict orders to bring curfew violators in. They're cracking down in Saigon."

Medici looked at him levelly. "Lieutenant, I'm armed and on official Naval Intelligence business. If you have any thoughts about taking me in, I insist you call my admiral, Commander Naval Forces Vietnam, to inform him. This is a mission personally initiated by him. His number at the compound is 2-7389. That phone is right next to his bed. Only four people know this number."

Waylon looked back at the Vietnamese, shifted his weight, then fidgeted. "Okay, Captain. I'll let you go this time, but this is your one bite of the apple. You fuckin' spooks cause more trouble around here...."

"How about a ride to the Meyercord? Then you won't get in trouble if someone else finds me walking." Waylon nodded reluctantly. They got in the Jeep. No one spoke during the five-minute trip. Medici was amazed at the eerie quiet of the noisy city after curfew. At the Meyercord he got out, saluted them smartly, then gave them the arm and laughed as they disappeared into the night.

34

Henderson

A light was on in the NILO crash pad. Two NILOs Medici did not know (he could tell they were NILOs from the berets next to their beds) lay sleeping face to the wall at one side of the room. LTjg Henderson from RivRon Five at Seafloat lay in his skivvies in the bunk next to Medici's reading a *Playboy*.

Medici eyed the brown bag containing the Cambodian currency. It hadn't moved. Socks spilled from it. He carelessly kicked it to insure the cash's heft was still there. It was. He sat down on his bed and unlaced his boots.

Henderson glanced up. He looked exhausted, but something Medici couldn't identify gave him an air of alert sobriety.

"Hi. I'm Tom Medici," he said. He pulled off his boots and socks.

"Jim Henderson," the jaygee said. He returned his red-rimmed eyes to the magazine.

"Can't sleep?" Medici asked.

"Nope. Not for three weeks, on and off," Henderson said. He didn't look up.

"You're from the RivRon down at Seafloat," Medici said.

Henderson looked up.

"I saw it on your sea bag. Did you know Joel Feiner? He was the NILO there."

Henderson let the magazine fall on the bed. He stared at Medici. "Yeah. Did you know him?"

"Yup. But not well. I met him at a coastal zone NILO meeting. He was a Yalie and I'm from Princeton. We broke each other's chops about that. We were all shocked when he was killed."

The mask of Henderson's face tightened. "I was with him when it happened. He was my best friend at Seafloat." He paused.

Medici sensed the wave of emotion flooding through him. The guy really hurt.

"That sea bag is mine, but it's full of Joel's personal effects. I came up to send them home to his wife and folks, and to accept the Distinguished Service Medal they awarded him. Posthumously." Tears filled his eyes. He sobbed. "A fucking DSM and a Purple Heart. That's all they'll have to show for his life. Fuck this goddam war."

Medici didn't know what to say. The news Joel had been killed had really troubled him. NILOs were not supposed to get killed. They weren't paid to get killed. They were supposed to live by their wits, and attend to their personal security. It burst the bubble of Medici's notion of personal immortality. Joel had been at Seafloat about five months and loved his work. How anyone could be enthusiastic about Seafloat escaped Medici, but Joel's enthusiasm was welcome.

Medici thought a moment. He knew he must ask Henderson how it had happened. The morbid details were important. He superstitiously felt that if he avoided duplicating the details that led to a combat death, he would escape that bad luck. A foolish notion, but one of the rationalizations Medici used in order to cope.

"How did it happen?" He examined Henderson's face to see if the question would freak him out.

Henderson looked at him for a long time, trying to size him up and judge whether he was worthy of the details, Medici guessed. Then his pained expression eased and he spoke quietly.

"Joel couldn't get enough of the boats. He rode everything and anything that floated. At first I thought he was familiarizing himself with the tactical capabilities of each craft, but then I realized he just loved the wild and woolly stuff. He'd much rather get shot at than do intelligence work.

"He was in a couple of close scrapes on the river but kept riding. Usually with me. He was really loyal that way. I told him he didn't have to ride so much, that his was a different mission...that we had only one NILO, and that lots of boat drivers would be in deep shit if we lost him, especially after he learned all about our area of operations.

"Joel told me he could only learn stuff by being out on the river. What the hell could he do at Seafloat anyway? He could take an occasional VR ride with the Seawolves. Otherwise he'd be left sitting around on the ammi barges out in the middle of the river waiting to get rocketed, if he didn't ride the boats. What can you say to that logic?"

Medici nodded. He had never thought through how the NILO job would be different down there in Indian country, living on a floating target.

"We were out on ambush before Joel was shot. It was quiet, not much contact anywhere in the area, which is unusual. We broke ambush at dawn. We were on our way back to the ammis, within sight of them, skylarking around. We heard the heavy thud of a .51-caliber machine gun—that gets your attention anytime—and the crew scrambled to their weapons positions. We took a hosing with fire from three directions.

"Joel ran toward the stern of our boat to get his M-16. As he ran, he was hit with a .51-caliber slug high on his left shoulder. It tore his shoulder and arm off and smashed him against the gunwale. The bullet sliced the aorta. Blood shot from him like a high-pressure hose." Henderson sat up, tense as a rail.

"There was nowhere to put a goddam tourniquet on him or to find a pressure point to stop the bleeding. We tried to run back to the ammis, but the fire was intense. We had to make three high-speed passes, then the Seawolves came and suppressed the fire. We ran back to the ammis but it was too late. He died in my arms...."

Henderson broke into great heaving sobs. He covered his eyes but tears streamed through his hands and mucous dripped from his nose. His sobbing woke the two NILOs, but Medici motioned them to go back to sleep.

Noting a bottle of cognac on the window sill, he opened it and told Henderson to take a good shot. He took one himself. They said nothing for a long time while Henderson's sobbing slowed. He fell exhausted on his pillow, closed his eyes and slept.

"Joel was a good dude," Medici said to himself. He turned off the light and quietly fell asleep with tears in his eyes.

35

Airport

Medici's internal alarm clock went off. His eyes opened wide, his pulse quickened. He sat bolt upright and took four deep breaths, then looked at his watch. 5 a.m. Holland had arranged for a Navy driver to pick him up in front of the Meyercord at 0515.

The others slept. Henderson looked placid and slept soundly. Medici remembered his emotional come-apart of the last evening. But he was in his NILO mode now, all mission, no emotion. He dressed quickly and quietly. No time to shave and shower. He could do that on An Thoi Island. He tucked the Browning in his waistband. It felt cold and unfriendly after a night on the tile floor. The bag of riels was intact. He stuffed underwear, pants, shirts and money into his AWOL bag and walked silently downstairs.

Not a soul stirred in the hotel. He could have heard a pin drop in the stairwell. Even the parrot slept with his head tucked down into his neck.

The driver waited outside in a black Chevrolet with small covered flag posts attached to each headlight. The Chevy looked like an embassy limo. Medici tapped on the window and the driver sat up straight and unlocked the doors. Medici got into the front seat and threw his bag in the back.

"Are you Captain Medici, sir?" the driver said with surprise.

"Yup. Who else would be out here at 0500, sailor?" Medici laughed.

The driver started down the street. After a block he said, "But you're so young."

"It's the job. Fountain of youth. The longer I'm out there, the younger I get." He suddenly understood the sailor's confusion. "Look, I'm not a Navy captain, I'm a lieutenant. The marine at staff who called in the car reservation always calls me captain, like they do in the Corps. Is that why they sent this fancy limo from the motor pool? I usually get a Jeep."

"Well, yeah. These are normally reserved for big-shot senior officers," said the sailor. He seemed relieved.

"Good. Is there a bar or TV set in this thing?"

"No, sir. But there's a place we can stop where I can get you a beer if you want. We got time. It won't take us 45 minutes to get to Thanh Son Nhut airport this early."

"Good idea. Let's go."

They detoured slightly, got two warm Ba Muoi Ba beers from a sleepy-eyed Eurasian girl in an eight-foot tin hovel and continued to the airport.

At Thanh Son Nhut the Vietnamese guards were stoned. The smell of marijuana filled the car when the driver opened the window to show his curfew pass. Medici became irate at their inattention and self-indulgence while on duty, then swigged his beer and laughed at himself for his equal sin.

The driver dropped him at a small building at the west side of the airport. A sign showed a sailor's hat with the inscription "WHITE HAT AIRLINES." Medici thanked the driver, took his bag and went inside. One small light bulb lit a wooden table in the empty room. A clock on the wall showed 0545. Medici sat down on a folding chair and waited.

After 20 minutes an aircrew chief in a green flight suit ambled in and pulled a clipboard from a nail on the table leg. He yawned, scratched his ample belly and said, "You Medikee?"

"MEDichee," he answered.

"Looks like you're our only passenger today. All our other passengers cancelled. Strange."

"Strange, my ass. You've lost 11 of those old jolly green Sikorskys to mechanical failure in two weeks. You surprised people cancelled?"

The chief looked annoyed. "We won't be flying the jolly green today. They sent us a new CH-47. We're taking you straight to An Thoi, not the usual milk run around the delta. You an important guy or something?"

Medici shook his head. Things were looking up. He followed

the chief out the door across the tarmac to the powerful new helicopter.

CH-47 helo to Phu Quoc Island during monsoon squalls.

36

An Thoi

The monsoon seascape dwarfed the helo. Thick dollops of pearly cloud on slanted pillars of rain blocked their course like huge Ionic columns. The pilot dodged them with a slant to the left, then to the right, and made long slow tacks to Phu Quoc Island like a racing yawl.

The floor cargo hatch was missing. As the pilot edged by the squalls, the craft fell until it escaped the down draft of each rain pillar. Each fall caused a strange effect: in defiance of gravity, rain and chilled air blew *up* into the cargo bay.

Medici watched with fascination as it rained up into his face during the first falls. Then he unbuckled his harness and crept forward to a dry seat against the cockpit bulkhead. The crew chief poked his head into the cargo bay to shout, "Is everything all right, Lieutenant?" His grin told Medici he was not displeased about Medici's discomfort. Medici shivered but forced a smile and gave the chief a thumbs-up—while considering to raise another finger.

They flew direct. With one stop for fuel, they made An Thoi in less than two and a half hours, the fastest Medici had done it. The pilot set the helicopter at the end of the desolate steel matting. The blades drove sheets of spray outward until he eased the collective. The rotor wound to a stop while a squall inundated them.

No one came to meet them. They could see the mess hall and trailers the men lived in, and lights were on in the Quonset hut officer's club. Finally the pilot came into the cargo bay and said, "Fuck this, Lieutenant. If they won't come out to refuel us because it's raining, I'll get fucking JP-4 over at To Chau. I don't have an umbrella to offer you...."

"I get the message. Thanks for the ride," Medici said. He put the AWOL bag over his head, leaped from the stern ramp, and dashed 200 yards in the downpour to the O club. His uniform was soaked before he got halfway. By the time he reached the door, rivulets ran down his back. The helo's whine was drowned by Johnny Cash singing "Folsom Prison" at full volume.

Medici looked around the white empty room. Not empty. Jim Thompson, NILO An Thoi, sat in starched fatigues and read *The Atlantic Monthly.*

"You lazy fuck. Can't you get off your ass to meet helos anymore?" Medici boomed as he shook water off himself like a dog.

Jim didn't answer. He got up, pointed to his ear and shook his head. He walked over to the big Japanese hi-fi set and turned Johnny down.

"Tom! I wasn't expecting you so early. How'd you get here? It looks like you walked across the gulf!" He laughed at Medici's drenched uniform. "Come on over to my hooch. I'll loan you some clothes until the Ba can dry yours. We've got an electric dryer now."

Whoopy-fuckin'-doo, Medici thought. He unzipped the AWOL bag and withdrew the soggy raft of riels. He threw it like a medicine ball at Jim. It knocked him back a step as he caught it in the bread basket.

"Payroll for the network. Get it to the Walrus somehow. Okay?" Jim held the dripping wad at arm's length.

They trotted across wet sand to Jim's hooch, a small trailer supported by cement blocks at each corner, with a huge air conditioner extending through the wall. The thermometer inside read 58 degrees.

"You could catch pneumonia in here," Medici said.

"Not when you sleep with an electric blanket." Jim smiled and Medici fumed. They didn't have it this good in Saigon. Jim put a tape on a deck the size of a TV: Country Joe and the Fish blasted the "Vietnam Rag" out of five-foot speakers. Medici accepted the beer Jim took from a tiny refrigerator.

"War is hell," Medici said. He stripped off his wet clothes and put on the shorts and tee shirt Jim gave him. He chilled in the cold. "Let's get out of here. Is it too late for breakfast? I'm starved."

"I'll have them open the mess for you. But check this out

first." Jim pulled a leather bag from under his bunk, opened it and withdrew a sinister and complicated burnished metal camera. It looked very German.

"What's that?" Medici said.

"It's for you, especially for the Sihanoukville mission. A Leica, with all the Zeiss lenses you could need. It uses 35mm film and can get higher resolution than any other camera its size. I'll show you how to work it later. You've got 25 rolls of high-res Pan X to shoot."

"How'd you know I'm going to Sihanoukville?"

"Got a SECRET from the Cambodian Shop to me and the *Garrison County*, the LST you'll ride. We're to rendezvous with her at 3 a.m. about 10 miles west of here. That way she won't have to make An Thoi at night and Russian trawlers won't see an unusual course change. We'll ride a PBR to meet her."

Medici wondered how many others Kenck had told of the mission: The more traffic on the radio circuits, the greater the chance they would know he was coming. He felt his stomach knot up.

Medici ate a late breakfast and spent the day lolling in the O club and Jim's hooch, fidgeting with the Leica to keep himself occupied. The rain continued intermittently until dusk when it became a long, slow deluge. They ate dinner in the mess hall, and Medici noticed clear acrylic pepper mills along with the usual condiments.

"Phu Quoc white pepper," Jim told him. "A small war was once fought over the rights to harvest and export it to France. We figured we should have the spices of Asia on our table."

When dark fell they returned to the O club. Medici grew nervous with the rendezvous only hours away. He returned to Jim's hooch several times to make sure he had packed the camera gear, his civvies, the Browning and ammo in his AWOL bag.

He knew he was wired when he returned to the O club around 11 and observed intense color and detail of the room that he had not noticed before. His adrenalin flowed now, slowing real time down and causing objects to appear lucid in three-dimensional relief. He stood in the doorway, transfixed, and stared halfway up the curve of the Quonset roof. Along the arc of the roof, like a panel in the Sistine

Chapel, hung a photograph poster of Neil Armstrong descending the last step of Eagle's ladder, about to place the first foot on the moon. Wow. Then he noticed the spiral dog turd below Armstrong's foot.

Medici poured a double brandy which he nursed to calm his nerves. Jim sucked down beers one after the other and was joined by Chief Hanson who had been assigned to take Medici out to meet the *Garrison County* in the PBR. Hanson had been drinking all evening and didn't stop while they continued their waiting.

"How long you figure it'll take us to get 10 miles offshore in this rain, Chief?" Medici interrupted Hanson in the middle of another war story.

"Hell, Lieutenant, those babies can clip along at 30 knots."

"Not in the southwest monsoon. You got 8- to 12-foot swells with short chop out there tonight. No way we're gonna' do 30 knots. My guess is we're lucky to do 10 over the ground. And the swell means we'll actually travel 12 miles over a course of 10 even if we maintain a straight course, which we won't. I'd like to leave an hour and a half before rendezvous time, just to be safe."

The chief looked bleary-eyed at Medici. His soused brain tried to track Medici's calculations but gave up. "Okay, Ell Tee. Any way you want," said Hanson.

"Good. I'll get my bag. We should leave the dock in 15 minutes." Medici got up and walked out. The chief and Jim stared at each other and their watches.

"Arrogant little wop, ain't he?" Hanson asked. "Did he really calculate all that shit?"

"My guess is he did," Jim said. "He used to be navigator and small boat officer on a cruiser. He's ridden the PBRs and Swifts lots of times over at Ha Tien. He just doesn't want to miss that rendezvous. We better get going."

They chugged the rest of their beers and walked to their hooches for rain gear.

37

Rendezvous

Medici peered into the PBR cockpit. The engineman performed final tuning on one of the diesels that pumped water to the jet drive.

"She ready to go, snipe?" Medici asked.

"To hell and back," answered the engineman without turning. He didn't care if there was an admiral on the pier, Medici thought. He had done his job well and was confident.

Medici jumped into the cockpit and the pool of light thrown by the snipe's lantern. "Where can I put this so it stays dry?" he asked. "It's got camera gear and stuff in it."

"You must be the NILO we're takin' out tonight. My name's Gill, engineman second class." He started to salute but Medici extended his hand and shook Gill's.

"I'm Tom Medici. Any snipe who'll stay out in this dog-shit monsoon at one-thirty in the morning to make sure his machines are working right is okay in my book. Thanks."

Gill laughed. "Well, they're my responsibility. And NILO Jim told me to make sure everything worked right 'cause our passenger would be a sum bitch if things fouled up." They laughed. Gill stowed the AWOL bag forward. A lantern beam played erratically along the dock and fixed at last on the PBR. Jim and Chief Hanson climbed down in full ponchos, carrying their M-16s.

"You guys expecting a firefight at 3 a.m. at 10 miles out in the Gulf of Thailand in an impenetrable monsoon?" Medici said. He and Gill laughed.

"No, but you can never tell. This is the war zone," Jim responded.

"Let's get under way, Gill," Chief Hanson said in a gruff voice.

Gill ignited the engines. They idled throaty-smooth and

responded to the slightest change in throttle. They cast off, used the spotlight to clear the pier, then switched it off so they could read the dim red light of the compass.

"Leave Mui Hanh light to starboard, then steer 286 magnetic as close to 12 knots as you can figure, Gill," Medici said. "That should compensate for deviation as well as the set and drift of the monsoon. The *Garrison County* should show normal running lights. She was instructed to show a white strobe from masthead as she approaches rendezvous. Do we have anything that will flash?"

"Just our flare pistol," Chief Hanson said.

"Chief, I cumshawed a white strobe from a Seawolf," Gill said. "It's on the canopy above your head, strapped to the frame. When we get close we just reach up and flip 'er on."

Medici could see the sailor's wide grin in the dark. "Good thinking, Gill. Let's cruise."

They sailed a wretched sea. The monsoon drove squalls relentlessly from the southwest. Rain flew under the canopy first from port, then from starboard, then, inexplicably, from astern. Medici stood next to Gill and watched him try to steer a true course through a nasty cross-swell they encountered when they rounded Mui Hanh Point. Gill was an experienced helmsman. He quickly computed how much he was driven off course in each direction and eliminated the deviation by rhythmic counter swings in his steering.

"Were you a blue water sailor before river boats, Gill?" Medici asked. He guessed the answer.

"Yessir. A can. The *Fletcher*, DD-784. We all rotated watches. Snipes on the helm, quartermasters in the hole. Never thought it would come in handy like this." It seemed to please Gill that Medici had noticed.

The chief and Jim were trying to nap standing up, wedged against the bulkhead. The cockpit was slick with rainwater and the spume of swells that sloshed aboard. Medici worried about getting aboard the LST in this sea, 13 foot tip to trough, 10-second intervals.

Medici cupped his hands so Gill would hear him. "The trick to boarding in a heavy swell is to keep the boat OFF the side of the ship no matter what. It's the ship that can destroy the boat when the swell grinds it up and down against the steel side."

"Aye, aye. Done it a few times, sir," Gill said.

They slugged on into black-green sea. Jim and the chief looked queasy half an hour out, and Medici didn't feel so good either. The constant hiss of the unsquelched radio wore on them. Suddenly the radio popped and they heard clear as a bell, "Target one, Target one, this is Riptide, Riptide, over." Gill grabbed the handset and answered the LST. Medici looked around. He couldn't see anything except black sea that turned green when light shined on it.

"Target, Riptide. We think we have you on our pathfinder radar, target angle 020, about 5,000 yards. We are showing navigational lights and white masthead strobe."

Medici looked south. If the LST was on course from south to north, the 020 target angle would put the PBR just off their starboard bow. He could see nothing except rain and sea. Gill slowed his engines and turned to port, putting their bow into the swell. They bobbed like a cork at the slower speed.

Medici took the handset from Gill. "Riptide, this is Target. We see nothing. We have come left, head-on into the swell. Do you track our change of course on your radar?" It was entirely possible that the LST was miles away, within radio range, but tracking a fishing boat on radar.

"Target, Riptide. Affirmative. We track your movement. Are you showing lights?"

"Chief, flip on the strobe!" Medici barked. The chief reached up and fumbled. Finally blue-white strobe flashes illuminated the deck and sea around them.

"Riptide, we now show white strobe from canopy. We see nothing yet. Do you see us?"

"Negative, Target."

"Riptide, how fast are you closing us?"

"We have slowed to five knots, Target."

Still nothing. "Riptide, request you show numeral and deck lights. We can't see a goddam thing in this soup."

"Roger, Target. Standby one." They continued to search for the LST. "Target, Riptide. We're not going to get shot out here if we show our lights, are we?"

"Oh, fuck," Medici said, "where the hell have these guys been all the war? In Guam?" He spoke evenly into the handset,

"Riptide, this is Target. Estimate chances of hostile fire at this range from shore to be slim to none. Request you show numeral and deck lights."

"ROGER, Target, WILCO. Lights on now."

They all strained their eyes. On the crest of the seventh wave, Gill saw the LST behind them to port, farther than they expected. Medici informed the ship of the visual bearing. She reduced her headway more, until she barely made steerageway in the quartering sea. Gill turned the PBR and ran safely across the LST's bow so he could approach her from leeward. He wanted the wind shadow and smooth sea on her leeward side. He came round to a course nearly parallel to the ship's, but which closed on her at an oblique angle. They could see exactly how the swell was running along the illuminated hull of the LST, like a high school wave motion experiment.

The deck hands dropped a Jacob's ladder of chain and pipe down the ship's side. Gill steered the PBR alongside and steadied on the ladder. It took minutes for him to synchronize speed with the ship, but when he did, the ladder rose and fell in a straight line next to them. Medici said, "I'll jump to the ladder when we hang at the wave crest. Stay at least two feet off the hull so we don't get in trouble, okay?"

"Will do, sir!" said Gill.

"My bag!" said Medici.

"Don't worry. I'll get it and hand it to you when you're on the ladder," Chief Hanson said.

Medici climbed on the engine cover and held the canopy support. He judged the time between each rise of the swell, said, "Here goes," and stepped to the gunwale while holding the canopy top. At the next crest he locked his eyes on a single rung of the Jacob's ladder, waited to feel the surge solid beneath him and the boat hang motionless, then leaped across three feet of boiling ocean.

The water sucked and frothed, then fell away under him as he flew. He landed hard against the ladder, missed his rung, and grabbed a pipe near the bottom of the ladder. He found himself dangling as the surface of the sea sluiced away below him. He tried to get a foothold against the ship, but the jungle boots would not grip against the wet hull. He saw the water bottom out in the trough, then begin to surge back toward him. Looking over his shoulder, he saw the PBR's stern rising toward him six inches from the ship's hull.

He knew the gunwale would crush him. He lifted his head and shouted to the deck hands holding the ladder chains, "Pull me up quick!" The deck seamen knelt, struggling with the ladder. Medici climbed hand over fist to the next rung while the boat surged under him. A deck hand gave a gargantuan heave to one side of the Jacob's ladder. Medici's legs rose clear as the stern of the PBR crashed against the side of the LST. The impact dumped Jim to the cockpit floor. Gill maneuvered the boat away by reversing the jet drive. He lost only a few inches of fiberglass to the impact.

Medici's feet were on the ladder. He yelled to the boat, "The bag!" Chief Hanson rose to the gunwale to hand it to Medici when someone above yelled, "Don't try it! We'll send down a line." Medici felt relieved. He had little appetite for the acrobatics necessary to transfer the bag.

A line was thrown to the PBR, now five or six feet off the ship's hull. Chief Hanson caught it and elaborately tied it through the handles of Medici's AWOL bag, then shouted, "Haul her up!" Medici watched from the deck as the bag rose five feet, slammed the side of the ship, came loose, then tumbled into the frothy green water.

"Goddam it," Medici said. "One simple fucking bowline would have done the trick." He could see Hanson's face ashen in the bright deck lights. The bag floated momentarily, then started its descent to Davy Jones's locker.

Suddenly Chief Hanson hung over the gunwale, holding his M-16 by the muzzle while trying to hook the AWOL bag with the pistol grip handle. Jim held his legs. "No way!" someone on deck said. The chief bobbed over the side as if he were ducking for apples in the froth between boat and ship. The upsurge engulfed his head and shoulders to his waist. Then he was out of the water. He sputtered, "I got it! I got it!" The swollen AWOL bag emerged on the end of the rifle's handle, leaking seawater from its seams.

The chief tied the line with a proper bowline, and it was hauled aboard ship. Medici stood under a light on deck and waved to the boat crew as it drew away. He opened the bag, drained the warm seawater, entered the superstructure and walked to the bridge.

38

Garrison County

The LST slid undetected through the black night. No lights showed on her exterior, and caged red lamps lighted Medici's way to the bridge. He knew the route by heart from his time on Captain Brown's T at Ha Tien.

He passed the navigator's chart house and entered the bridge, surprised how small and narrow it seemed compared to his old ship *Tulsa*'s. His eyes adjusted to the dark, then fixed on the left corner where he saw the OOD and the quartermaster of the watch clustered at the elevated captain's chair, chatting with the C/O. A bad sign, Medici thought, that the watch standers were not independent from the captain in running the ship. Medici slipped quietly to a point behind the chair, and during a lull in the conversation stepped to the C/O's side and said, "Good morning, Captain. I'm Lieutenant Medici. Naval Intelligence."

"JEE-ZUSS-CHRIST!" the C/O said. He sat bolt upright in his chair. "What'd we do? Drugs?" The OOD and quartermaster withdrew to the far side of the bridge.

"Nothing," said Medici. "I'm here for the ride to Sihanoukville."

"Where the hell did you come from?"

"The PBR that came alongside. I trust you received word from staff in Saigon that I'd be coming?"

"We got some spooky message saying a 'Haitian NILO' would be joining us for the ride. The orders are broad and ambiguous. They say he can come and go as he pleases, do anything he wants."

"Precisely. That's how we write them. By the way, it said 'NILO Ha Tien,' the name of the border post I'm assigned to."

"You have a first name?" Medici noticed the C/O's Boston accent made him sound like Ted Kennedy.

"Tom. And you?"

"Captain. Captain O'Neill."

Fuck you, Medici thought. "Can you give me a bunk, CAPTAIN?" Medici said. "I've been up all night, I'm soaked and have work to do. Also, I need to know where your crypto room is."

"Of course. Just past the chart house here on the 04 level. I assume you have a Top Secret clearance?" Medici nodded. "I'll have the steward give you a stateroom. My X/O is on leave. You can have his. It will give you some privacy for whatever strange things you spooks do while under way. Boats…."

"Aye aye, sir," said the bosun's mate of the watch.

"Buzz the steward and tell him to come get LT Medici, our guest, and put him in the X/O's cabin."

"Aye aye, sir." He rang the intercom.

"If you have time late morning I'd like to meet with you and your ops officer about planning for our arrival in Sihanoukville. We'll want to coordinate plotting and photographing channel buoys, piers, and warehouses. No Americans have been there for seven years, so we don't have much to go on. I'll be going ashore to obtain some information about the port."

"I bet you will," the captain said. "How about 11 o'clock in the wardroom?"

"That's fine. Now if you'll excuse me, I'll go below." He raised his voice so the OOD could hear. "By the way, good station keeping when I boarded. You made a nice lee and kept her steady."

"Thank my OD, LTjg Poe. He's acting X/O and my ops officer." Poe overheard them and looked their way.

"I think I just did," Medici said. They laughed.

A bleary-eyed steward arrived, the top buttons of his white coat undone. Minutes before he had slept soundly.

"Amador, take LT. Medici to the X/O's state room and get him settled in. He'll be our guest for the next few days," O'Neill said.

"Ay'-ay', zirr," said Amador. "Dis way bleas, zirr." He led Medici down the passageway and carried the soggy AWOL bag for him.

"Amador, take me to the armory first," Medici said when they reached the first ladder.

"De armory, zirr? Eess four o'clock in the morning."

"The armory, Amador."

"Ay', zirr."

Amador pointed to Medici's stateroom as they passed. He stopped and flipped on the lights to show that it was neat. Medici took the AWOL bag from him and placed it in the Pullman sink so it would continue to drain. They went down four ladders to the bowels of the ship where the armory was located. Both halves of the steel Dutch door were locked. A sign with balloony cartoon letters said "ARMORY." The white spaces of the paper were covered with hand-drawn color insets of missiles, bombs, projectiles, M-16s, and .45s. A smaller sign below the first said "GM1 Zont, Ship's Armorer." A flower child at sea, Medici thought.

"Okay, Amador. I can find my way back. You can go. Thanks."

Amador looked at Medici with suspicion and hesitated. Then he said, "Ay'-ay', zirr," and left.

Medici banged hard on the door four times. "Open up!" he shouted. He knew an armorer must be on duty 24 hours a day on every Navy ship. He heard stirring, snorts, and mumbling beyond the door. He banged hard twice again then heard shuffling. Keys jangled, the bolt slid, and the top door opened. Medici looked down at the roundest gunners' mate in the Navy. He appeared to be as wide as he was tall, had close-cropped blond hair, and wore the widest expanse of white skivvy shirt imaginable. Medici smiled. He couldn't help liking the guy.

"Good morning, armorer Zont," he said. "I'm LT. Medici of Naval Intelligence. I need a cleaning kit for a 9mm bore, solvent, gun oil, and ammo for a Belgian Browning 9mm pistol."

Zont looked at his watch, then back at Medici. "It's 0415...."

"Zont! I have just come by stagecoach from Saigon, then An Thoi, to join this illustrious ship from a floating cork in the middle of a gulf swept with monsoon rain and wind. I am soaked to the skin, chilled to the bone, salt-encrusted, and fatigued to the edge of pain. But I don't care about that. My personal weapon, the magic feather that has protected me like a talisman in Cambodia, was dropped—kerploush—into the Gulf of Thailand as I risked my life to board *Garrison County*. I wish to clean and protect the Browning immediately so it will continue to function properly as my personal weapon—but more important, so I won't change its karma and my luck! Do you understand the urgency of my request?"

Zont's mouth fell slack until three chubby chins stopped its descent. He said nothing, but he reached down and opened the lower door.

Medici entered. On the back of the upper door were a dozen neatly lettered cards bearing inscriptions such as "Back in five minutes," "Gone to chow," "Head call," "At gun plot." Hanging on the wall behind the door were a meticulously restored Czech AK-47 and a Chinese B-40 rocket launcher. The small ammo crate next to Zont's bunk, his night table, held a two-foot stack of *Weapons Collector* and *Guns and Ammo* magazines. Zont was truly into guns, Medici surmised.

"That Belgian Browning's a fine weapon," Zont said in a low, hoarse voice. He unpadlocked a cabinet. "I'm glad you treat it like a friend. Most officers don't."

"Most officers don't have to rely on it as their only means of protection wherever they go," Medici said. Zont grunted.

"I don't have an exact 9mm bore brush. We don't have any standard issue 9mm weapons in the Navy. But I do have a bronze .38 caliber brush that will do the trick nicely. 9mm is the Euro-version of our .38." He withdrew a brush, cleaning rod, patches, solvent and oil and laid them on the counter.

"I guess that means you don't have any 9mm ammo," Medici said. He frowned.

"I didn't say that, Lieutenant. I said 9mm was not *standard* issue in the Navy." He smiled and reached into the same cabinet and withdrew four stiff brown paper boxes. Each held 50 rounds of "CAL. 9mm, GR. BALL, Made in USA" ammo. He handed them over.

Medici grinned, opened a carton and slid out the inner box, then withdrew a sleek brass cartridge with a polished copper-jacketed slug. It had the shape of a small ICBM. A polished nickel primer cap sat at the center of the casing's base. The bullet was a work of art in itself. "Where'd you get these?" He squealed like a kid on Christmas morning.

"I traded some stuff for them to a CIA guy who came aboard in Nha Trang. Is that where you got the Browning?"

"No. From a friend in Cambodia." Medici dropped the subject.

"How wet is your ammo?" asked Zont.

"It was in the drink for about two minutes. Think it's still good?"

"Might be if it's not the foreign manufactured stuff. Rinse it off with fresh water like you'll do with the pistol, then dry it with a towel and bring it down to me when you can. You can at least use it for practice."

"Thanks, Zont. Sorry to get you up so early," Medici said. He gathered the cleaning gear and ammo.

"That's okay, sir. You might let me take a look at the pistol some time. I'm kind of an aficionado."

"I noticed," Medici said.

39

Repairs

Medici entered the stateroom and closed the door. He went to the sink, took a clean terry cloth towel and laid it on the fold-down desk. He removed the Leica and lenses from the AWOL bag to examine them. They were made of aluminum, salt their worst enemy. He unscrewed the 28mm lens from the camera body, and warm seawater gushed onto the towel. The innards of the camera were already green with corrosion. He inspected the polished metal ledges that held each frame of film in place at precisely the correct focal distance from the lens. They were uneven, covered with chemical salts. He cocked the camera and pushed the shutter release. It made a squishing sound and the shutter did not move. He looked through the 28mm lens. It was fogged. So were the telephoto lenses. "Shit!" he growled.

He gathered all the camera gear together and placed it in the sink, closed the drain and filled the sink with fresh water to cover all the gear. He let fresh water seep in, drained it, then wiped all the exposed surfaces with a washcloth to remove the visible salt and corroded green metal. He dried each piece of gear as well as he could, then laid it on another towel to let evaporation finish the job.

He checked the other items in the ill-fated bag. The film was sealed and perfectly dry; his wash-and-wear civvies were soaked; the Browning was salt stained; the 9mm ammo boxes fell apart at his touch, brass casings tarnished and green. He threw the wet clothes on the floor and placed the pistol on the towel in front of him.

By this time he felt nauseous with fatigue and disappointment. But the Browning had to be cleaned immediately, or he could place no confidence in it. He pushed the knurled button that released the magazine and it popped out with a trickle of seawater. He pressed and slid each of the 12 rounds from the clip, held the pistol in his right hand and drew the slide back with his left until the latch locked open.

The barrel stuck out silvery and obscene from the sleek blue slide. He looked in the chamber to make sure it was empty, then pulled the slide back till it locked for disassembly. He laid the pistol on the towel with its right face up and reached in his shirt for a dog tag, pressing it hard on the protruding nipple of the slide stop pin while jiggling the stop lever from the other side. With a snap it found the release channel and popped out on the towel.

He drew the slide off the pistol, washed the parts with fresh water in the sink, then dried them in the towel. He whipped the pieces through the air to remove any remaining water, then cleaned them with solvent and laid them in order on the white towel. The acrid smell of the solvent made his nausea worse. He belched twice and a nasty aftertaste remained in his mouth. He focused on the pistol nearly in a trance, high from the solvent fumes and stunned with fatigue.

There was a knock at the door and it opened. Amador entered, his eyelids drooping with sleep.

"Lieutenant, I just bont to know if you…." Amador stopped in mid-sentence. He stared at the pistol and bullets on the towel in front of Medici, his eyes opening wide. His mouth hung open.

"It's okay, Amador, don't worry. I'm required to carry this," Medici said. "I'd appreciate it if you could wash these civvies for me. I'll need them in Sihanoukville."

"Anyting you say, zirr." Amador stooped and picked up the wet clothes. His gaze never left the pistol while he backed quickly through the door.

Medici oiled the moving parts and the exposed blue metal, then reassembled the Browning. He loaded both clips with the new ammo Zont had given him and laid the pistol on the upper bunk with the two-dozen film canisters.

His nausea became the unglued, liquid feeling of the onset of gastroenteritis. When he traveled more than 50 kilometers, the change in the ambient bacteria always caused an episode of GI. Now he knew it would run the familiar cycle of nausea, somnolent fatigue, and disabling diarrhea. His recovery time would be about 16 hours if he took the charcoal tablets a Navy medic in Saigon had given him. He simply had to bear it and avoid activity that was strenuous or required concentration. He made a necessary trip to the head, took the charcoal pills, and crawled into the lower bunk with the covers up around his neck against the inescapable chill of the air conditioning. The radium numerals of his watch showed exactly 5 a.m. when he turned out the light.

40

Captain O'Neill

Amador nudged Medici gently on the shoulder. "Zirr, ees den o'glock. I brott you zum brekfess."

Medici sat up on one elbow. On instinct he groped for the Browning under the pillow. It wasn't there. He blinked his eyes twice. Amador backed to the stateroom door, one hand on the knob.

"Where am I?" Medici said in a hoarse voice.

"Chu ess ess *Garrison County*, zirr."

"Right," Medici said. His memory returned. The briefing in Saigon, the flight to An Thoi, the near-disastrous rendezvous with the LST. Panic drained from him and he remembered Amador from the night before. He sat up on the edge of the bunk, groped on the top bunk and felt the icy steel of the Browning directly below the air-conditioning vent. He breathed deeply three times. He smelled the bacon, eggs and coffee that Amador had placed on the fold-down desk. His bowels rolled. He knew time in the head was in store.

"Lieutenant, Captain asgk me to bemind you of meeting at eleben," Amador said, taking his hand off the doorknob.

"Thanks, Amador, I probably would have slept through." Medici laughed and Amador smiled.

"I put your clothes on de top bunk, next to de bullets." He gestured toward the laundry and pistol, and his eyes danced. Medici guessed Amador was warming to the idea of having his own spy to care for.

Medici complimented Amador's quick service and sat down to breakfast when he left. He wolfed his food and started to gulp his coffee but then had second thoughts as his stomach grumbled. He put the cup down. He wrapped a towel around him, grabbed his shaving gear and walked to the shower after an obligatory visit to the commode. He showered, returned to his room and shaved in the small sink.

From the pile of clean laundry he took skivvy shorts, civilian wash-and-wear trousers, and a black turtleneck. The air conditioning chilled him.

He dug into the billow pocket of his salt-encrusted fatigue pants and found the plastic-sheathed map of Cambodia he had made. No one in Saigon had any usable field maps of Cambodia, so he had assembled one, crazy quilt-style, with bits and pieces of maps he'd scrounged from various intelligence shops. It covered the Cambodian coast from the Vietnam border to Thailand. Some panels were full color; others were gray and white photocopies of sole originals. Universal military grid coordinate hash lines crossed them all. He marked agent reports of enemy unit locations with a grease pencil.

At five minutes till eleven he walked to the wardroom. When he entered, he saw only the young LTjg who had stood OOD watch on the bridge.

"I guess it's time for formal introductions," he said. "I'm Tom Medici."

"How do you do, sir? Ahm Jim Poe, acting X/O and ops officer." The jaygee had a baby face and a drawl.

"I'd feel better if you called me Tom," Medici said. He shook Poe's hand.

The wardroom door flew open and the C/O charged in, leading with his jutting jaw. Poe jumped to attention and banged his knee on the wardroom table. Medici sat.

"Morning, Lieutenant. Ahr ahh accommodations suitable?"

"Perfect," said Medici. "Amador attended to everything."

"Good," said O'Neill. "Now let's get down to mission details. I don't know what your mission in Sihanoukville is, and I'm not sure I want to, judging by what Amador saw last night and what my armorer reported. I just want to make it clear I have my mission to do and I would prefer neither of us got in the other's way. Comprenez?"

"Bien entendu," said Medici. "Vous parlez bien Français." *You speak French well,* he lied.

"C'est à cause de ma femme. Elle est parisienne." *It's because my wife's Parisian.*

Medici reached into his pocket and drew out one copy of the blanket orders the Cambodian Shop had written and Captain Ross had signed in Saigon. He handed them to O'Neill who read them:

NILO HA TIEN

"TO WHOM IT MAY CONCERN:

Commander, Naval Forces Vietnam by these orders hereby authorizes their bearer, Lieutenant Thomas N. Medici, USNR, to proceed via any form of military transportation to any destination and to disembark and reembark as he chooses and to carry out his mission orders without explanation."

O'Neill threw the copy on the wardroom table. "I've seen these. Let's get something straight, Lieutenant. I understand the gist of your orders, but I alone am responsible for the safety of my ship and men. I'm not going to let you roam the streets of Sihanoukville, perhaps killing agents or worse, then return to my ship with the Cambodian military or the KGB in hot pursuit. I won't jeopardize my men and ship that way.

"I don't want to be part of an international incident with the politics the way they are in the States right now. Congress would love to find out the Navy's up here engaged in nefarious activities, when all the talk is about our minimal presence in Cambodia. They'd court martial me as a scapegoat so fast I wouldn't know what hit me." He turned and smiled at Poe. "I'm sure my acting X/O Mr. Poe would like to take over my command, but I'm not going to give him the chance. Not that way!"

Poe laughed.

Medici furrowed his brow and looked down at the table. Another by-the-book, cover-your-ass guy, he thought. It's okay for me to take risks to do my mission, but not if the paint gets scratched on his fucking ship. He looked at O'Neill.

"Commander, I'm not going to Sihanoukville to kill anyone. Everyone assumes that's what this business is about because they've seen too many movies. I'm here to collect specific information about maritime operations in the port. I'll need to come and go to accomplish this. I expect you and your crew to give me free rein in port so I can get my job done. If you intend not to, please let me know so we can send a message to the admiral to clear things up," Medici bluffed.

O'Neill shifted in his chair and readjusted his elbows on

the table. "I don't think that will be necessary. Just as long as we understand each other," he said.

Medici didn't trust him. But he really didn't want messages sent to Saigon either, since a compromise of his freedom would likely result by virtue of the staff's unwillingness to ruffle feathers. He would have to keep an eye on the captain. His stomach churned with resentment from having to worry as much about his own people as the enemy.

"Good," Medici said. "Let's get down to details. We're assigned jointly to do a port survey, to include charting the locations of buoys, the channel, warehouses, and the basin entrance. We'll need a beefed-up crew on the bridge to take and record bearings to landmarks we see as we transit the channel and enter the quay basin. Someone will have to call out the exact time as we take bearings, so we can coordinate them and reconstruct their relationship later. Sonar contours would help, but Fathometer™ readings are fine if that's all you can get.

"I'll be busy photographing everything in panorama and with telephoto when I can. That brings up a little problem. My camera swam in the Gulf when I came aboard. It's useless. Does anyone on board have a 35mm with decent lenses that I can borrow?"

Poe looked at the captain, then Medici and said, "I've got a Nikon F I just bought in Japan. It's got a zoom that goes from 28 to 135 mm. Will that do?"

"Fine," Medici said. "I've got plenty of high-resolution film." He turned to O'Neill. "I know LSTs aren't known for speed, but in this case I'd like to bring her in as slowly as you can while maintaining steerageway and a reliable navigation track. The more bearings and photographs we get, the easier it is for the special operations guys back in Saigon to reconstruct the actual layout. Any problem there?"

O'Neill shook his head.

"What plans do you have for the port visit?" Medici asked.

"We have orders to let the civilians off to unload the transmitter and antenna balloon, then to receive a short visit from some Cambodian dignitaries, their Chief of Naval Operations and some aides. A little tour of the ship, cake and coffee, and under way before dark. I'm not staying in this place overnight, Lieutenant. I don't trust the security situation here."

I bet you don't, you pussy, Medici thought.

"I'll be ashore for at least a day doing photography of everything around town. Don't worry about me. When you're ready to get under way, do so, whether I'm here or not. I'll be armed and can get out by boat to Ha Tien or Thailand. Just make sure the port photography film is hand carried by messenger to intelligence staff in Saigon."

"How can we do that?" Poe asked.

"When you pass An Thoi, radio for the NILO there, Jim Thompson, to send a boat or helo out for it. I briefed him before I left. He knows what to do," Medici said. "It'll be real simple."

The C/O looked annoyed. "Simple for you, Lieutenant. We're not used to this spook stuff. We're just an old LST delivering toilet paper and Ding-Dongs to the river rats, and patching up holes in their fiberglass boats. I don't know why, but this stuff makes me nervous." The C/O grimaced, then laughed. "But you're the guy who has to live with it, aren't you? Some job you got."

The C/O was smarter than he appeared, Medici thought. He'd figured out for a fleeting moment what the frustrations of the NILO job were, tried the hat on for a few seconds and didn't like feeling nervous, worrying about personal security, or preparing for the alternative of not completing a mission. The hard part of the job was the tentativeness and fragility of plans.

"The job has its benefits," Medici laughed. Like not having a nervous Nellie C/O like you, he thought.

Poe read his mind, and caught his eye. Wide grins spread over their faces while O'Neill puzzled.

"Guess I'll catch a few more winks if we're through," Medici said. He stood.

O'Neill nodded. "Lieutenant, I'd like you to brief the wardroom on the situation in Cambodia after supper, if you think it would be all right."

"Sure, Captain. My pleasure. I even bring my own map," Medici said. He excused himself.

He walked immediately to the officer's head to release the painful hot fluids from his system. Dehydration made his head ache and throb, leaving him slightly dizzy because of electrolyte depletion. Back in his stateroom he drank water until his stomach bloated, then lay down in the dark for a few hours' fitful sleep.

He dreamt a dream he first had before reaching Vietnam. In jungle fatigues he hid high on a hillside wooded with whispering pines. He trembled with fear. Seventy-five meters below him walked a thousand North Vietnamese regulars in gray uniforms, flat-topped khaki pith helmets, and high-top battle sneakers. The quiet tramp of their unsynchronized steps surged above the moan of the pines.

He awoke soaked in sweat and trembling, held himself tightly until the shaking stopped, then dozed again.

At 4 p.m. he awakened, showered, dressed, tucked his pistol into his pants and went on deck. He heard hammering and sawing and observed sawdust blowing around the main deck. Still shaken by the dream, his unconscious feared that someone was building coffins, as his agents reported the Viet Cong did before an offensive. But he saw the bosun's mates constructing what looked to be a ladder with handrails, in preparation for the visit of Cambodian dignitaries.

He watched them work for a few minutes, then picked up an armful of empty Pepsi cans and walked to the starboard rail. He looked up and a huge barrage balloon—a small blimp—floated on a tether 60 feet above him. The civilians were testing it to make sure it worked, before they installed it to carry the vertical wire antenna for the Radio Phnom Penh transmitter.

He threw a can into the water off the starboard side. The swell was large and the can bobbed, rolled, and fell slowly behind the moving ship. He withdrew the Browning, chambered a round, checked to see the deck was clear around him. He led the can in his sights and gently squeezed the trigger. The round cracked and the hammer and sawing stopped. The can leapt from the water, bottomless, then sank out of sight in a silver flash.

Everyone on deck stared at Medici. He ignored them. He threw the second can and steadied the Browning with both hands and fired. The can scudded along a wave top for few feet like a flying fish and slipped under.

He threw the third can over and holed it but it did not sink. In rapid succession he fired the remaining 10 rounds at the bobbing can, until it was Swiss cheese and the slide locked open on an empty chamber. Medici stared at the water where the can had been. The awesome power of the pistol transfixed him.

Poe interrupted Medici's reverie by booming, "Nice shooting, NILO," from the ship's announcement system on the bridge. The men on deck applauded and Medici smiled, happy the Browning had fired well, then returned to his cabin to clean the pistol before supper.

41

Metcalf

The barrage balloon and shortwave antenna worked fine, Metcalf concluded. He and Burson winched it in after tuning the antenna to the transmitter's output. They secured the balloon on deck and shut the transmitter's weatherproof panel, then returned to their makeshift quarters in the forward bosun's spaces of the LST.

Their orders to the *Garrison County* had specified that "Navy civilian employees Metcalf and Burson" be billeted "in an isolated space" with their "classified equipment." Metcalf brought with him an enormous armory padlock of cold-forged, case-hardened steel to secure the locker door when he and Burson were not inside. It hung huge and silvery from a special hasp welded to support it. Metcalf took the key from around his neck and, after ensuring none of the crew was in sight, opened the watertight door. He and Burson slipped through quickly. Inside they dogged the door and turned on the light. Amid shackles, turnbuckles and spools of wire and rope stood four sea bags, two bearing their stenciled names, two unmarked.

Metcalf noticed the tense expression on Burson's face. "What's the matter, boot, first mission got you scared? This one's a piece of cake. Not like a snatch or anything," Metcalf laughed.

"It's not the mission, Metcalf. The transmitter bit's fine. It's what you're going to do with all that C-4. These Cambodians are supposed to be our allies now. Why the fuck do we have to blow up their warehouses?"

"Not we, wimp—I. You don't have to do a damn thing except get that transmitter on the air and get back to the LST before 4 p.m." Metcalf laughed and pulled a warm Hamm's beer from his sea bag, squeezed it until the tab popped, guzzled foam, then belched. "If you're not finished by then, we're in deep shit. The T has to be away from the wall before 5 p.m. or BOOM!! That's all she wrote, mama."

"Don't worry. I'll be finished. It just doesn't sit right, y'know?"

Metcalf looked at Burson, trying not to betray the depth of contempt he felt. When they returned he would tell their boss that Burson was soft and must be dropped from the Studies and Observations Group.

42

Wardroom

Medici put on clean fatigues and walked to the wardroom when he heard a warped tape recording of a flute playing "The Roast Beef of Old England" over the ship's intercom. The seven ship's officers stood at attention when O'Neill entered and took his seat at the center of the long table. Observing Navy etiquette, they all sat when he did.

Amador served the soup course before anyone spoke. Medici concluded that O'Neill had intimidated his wardroom, judging from the furtive glances between junior officers when the C/O spoke. There was always a fine line between giving young officers independence of thought and speech, and keeping them on a sufficiently tight rein to maintain good discipline. Clearly, for all his intelligence, O'Neill kept them on a tight leash, resolving the independence-discipline dilemma in favor of discipline. Medici knew he would not like to serve in such a wardroom.

After several minutes of pleasantries and small jokes, O'Neill suddenly said in a loud voice, "Gentlemen, if you haven't met him yet, I'd like to introduce LT. Medici, our guest for the next few days. He is temporarily with us for our trip to an undisclosed port in Cambodia, which I now can identify as Sihanoukville."

Pompous ass, Medici thought. Won't even tell his officers where they are going until the evening before, even when Sihanoukville is the only deepwater port in the country.

"He is attached to Naval Intelligence and is in charge of field intelligence gathering in Cambodia, as best I can tell," O'Neill continued. "Mr. Medici has graciously agreed to brief us after supper on affairs in this part of the world." Medici smiled and nodded.

"I suggest you all stick around after dessert," O'Neill said, in case anyone had missed his point. Medici heard throats clear and weight shift in chairs, and he figured the officers were used to the C/O's subtle hints but chafed at his tactlessness.

When they finished dessert Poe took an easel from a closet and set it up so all could see. Medici took this as his cue, gulped a last mouthful of coffee, and walked to the easel. He clipped the patchwork Cambodian map to the easel. The green young officers stopped their chatter and strained to see the colored contours and to read the red and black grease pencil markings.

"Gentlemen, I'm Tom Medici, NILO Ha Tien. That stands for Naval Intelligence Liaison Officer. My formal post is independent duty, and I live with the Army mobile advisory team at Ha Tien, a fishing village and district town on the Vietnam-Cambodia border where it starts at the Gulf of Thailand. Didn't know the Navy had this kind of job, eh? Neither did I." They laughed.

"To give it to you in a nutshell, I'm in charge of all Naval Intelligence field collection in my area, which starts in Vietnam south of Ha Tien and extends northwest along the coastal area of Cambodia clear to the Thai border. I started out interested in the infiltration of Soviet and Chinese weapons through Sihanoukville and Cambodia to the Vietnam border. But political developments have drastically changed my mission. Since Prince Sihanouk was deposed by Sirik Matak and Lon Nol, we've been interested in political intelligence in Phnom Penh as well. A full service spy network, you might say." They all laughed nervously.

"We're headed for Sihanoukville for two reasons. First, to deliver the transmitter equipment you've seen on deck. The second and more important reason from my standpoint is to collect the first port survey intelligence in seven years. You'll all be helping out in some way or another, as I'm sure the captain has told you." Medici smiled at O'Neill, who squirmed. The officers glared at their C/O. He hadn't told them squat, Medici guessed.

"Now, what all's going on up here? What's going on is the country is falling apart, turning to shit. Despite what you hear on the news or read in the *Stars and Stripes*, the new Lon Nol government is unstable and is buttressed mostly by U.S. aid and political support. Cambodia's future is bleak and possibly short. Meanwhile, since Sihanouk was deposed, the North Vietnamese have had a heyday and have relocated to positions far back from the Vietnamese border. These units you see plotted on the map are NVA regimental and larger units. You can see I've reported elements of the 9th NVA Division up here around Sihanoukville for six months. I'm not sure Saigon has accepted it as a fact yet, but I would if I were going to visit the port of Sihanoukville." O'Neill gasped. Medici had neglected to brief him about reports of the 9th NVA Division.

"I'm very pessimistic about Cambodia's ability to survive more than a year, but Dr. Kissinger and his boss hope one year will be long enough to negotiate an acceptable theater-wide withdrawal of American troops. They won't call it that, but that's what it is…."

O'Neill jumped to his feet, his face florid. He stomped to the easel, removed Medici's map and handed it to him. Then he faced the wardroom. "Gentlemen, I want to warn you that most of you are not cleared for what we've heard here tonight—and to keep it strictly confidential. I'm afraid LT. Medici thinks in TOP SECRET. We don't. We just do our job, which in this case is to deliver the transmitter gear to Sihanoukville, entertain some dignitaries, and get the hell out!" He glared at Medici, then strode from the wardroom.

A junior officer let out a slow whistle. "Jeez, Lieutenant, he was really pissed. He always keeps this secret stuff close to his vest. He even withholds information from us when we need it to carry out our mission."

"I gathered that. That's why I took the opportunity to let you guys know what's going on." He looked at the door O'Neill had entered. "Do you think he thinks we're winning the war?" Medici winked and left the wardroom while the officers buzzed.

43

Ralph

Medici returned to the stateroom and examined the X/O's portable typewriter. The key nest was full of dust. He tried a sheet of paper. All the lower case e's and b's left black spots instead of clean white enclosures. But it would have to do.

He reached to the top bunk under the air conditioning duct and took the dry but salty pile of law school applications that he had rescued from the bottom of the wet AWOL bag. He adjusted an application in the typewriter, then began the laborious process of filling it out. No, no relatives had attended this law school. No, no judges in the family. No, no faculty members related. He came to the last page of the application, a blank white sheet which stated simply: "Write an essay of 250-500 words on a subject of concern to you." He rubbed the stubble on his chin hard three times and started typing:

> *"Old Joe Kennedy was right. They should walk down the halls of the State Department and fire every other son of a bitch. They're all a bunch of foreign policy phonies. I've been there, I know," Ralph Lombardi said. I could not disagree with him.*
>
> *Ralph plays a good piano at the Viet-My bar on Saigon's Thai Lap Thanh Street. In his off time, that is. During daylight, he lectures on "American Civilization" at Saigon University, and has for 13 years.*
>
> *Ralph came to Saigon in 1962 on a trip to the Orient calculated to broaden his personal philosophy.*

229

He had just taken a degree at Oxford in foreign affairs after two earlier diplomas from Harvard and Columbia. Not bad for a kid from Brooklyn, he says. His stints with the National Security Council staff and the Council on Foreign Affairs convinced him he needed time off for detached thought, away from the establishment. Ralph sensed something wrong in the American approach to foreign policy. He arrived to identify what the failing was. Saigon in 1962 was a city of 15,000 Frenchwomen, Oriental mystique, an occasional Foreign Legionnaire, and few bungling Americans. It enchanted Ralph. He stayed.

Ralph tells me stories about characters he has known when I sit and listen to him play, whenever I return to Saigon from my post on the Cambodian border.

Ralph continued. "...Cabot Lodge was one of the good ones. He used to come and sit right over there to hear me play. Not just the rinky-dink stuff I do to keep customers, but Malagueña and Rachmaninoff concertos and other pieces hard for the untrained ear to listen to.

"I remember one night back in the beginning, Lodge was here with a bunch of sycophants from his embassy staff. They clung to him like lampreys, each forcefully and earnestly urging on him their solutions to the growing war. After a while he broke free and came to the piano. He looked gray and drawn, like he hadn't had a good night's sleep in weeks. He said to me, 'Ralph, I know you're an expert in foreign affairs and I've heard about your degrees and all that. I'm surrounded by these so-called experts all day long. They each try to tell me what to do about the guerrilla problem and the corruption of Diem's

government. *And none of them are right. Ralph, you play a damn good piano and never try to tell me what to do.... Keep playing, Ralph.' At that, Lodge gave me a little pat on the shoulder and started back toward the group, staring at the floor in front of him as he walked. That was in '62. We killed Diem, and you know how it went after that."*

The Viet-My closes around 2 a.m., and there are always hangers-on. Guys like me from the boonies, tense, exhausted, gaunt and secretly confused by what we saw each day in the field. It occurred to me that I was hanging on just barely when I sloshed the last Martell on the blouse of my musty nine-day cammies.

I threw a pocketful of dirty piastres on the table without counting and got up to leave, then thought to ask Ralph, through a cognac fog, "Why are you here, doing this all these years?"

He turned to me, kept playing, and said, "Because they're mostly phonies, and this is kind of my vigil, y'know?"

"Yeah, I know," I replied sullenly, not really understanding, and walked into the sandalwood-scented night to face the tinny roar of a thousand Honda bikes.

He read the essay over, smiled to himself, placed it in the envelope and sealed it. It was 11:30 p.m. and tomorrow was Sihanoukville. He fell asleep musing about why Ralph Lombardi did what he did.

44

Making Port

At 4 a.m. Medici laid out his civvies. The white shirt was woven so loosely he could see through it. The pants had suffered color alteration from khaki to snot green in the ship's laundry. He had borrowed a pair of plaid civilian skivvy shorts from Poe, so he wouldn't be wearing any olive drab. He made sure he carried no identification, especially the NILO card, removed the laundry labels from each item of clothing, and filled the shirt pocket with black U.S. government ball pens, a grease pencil and a small slide rule he got from a construction engineer he knew in Saigon. He dressed quickly, then looked at himself in the mirror: a doo-wah engineer from the Agency for International Development.

He slid the Browning into the waistband of the trousers, then caught sight of himself again in the mirror. He looked ridiculous, the pistol butt silhouetted against the white shirt. He withdrew it and put it in the AWOL bag. He would have to go ashore unarmed, hoping that the engineer guise would protect him.

He unrolled Xerox copies of the small-scale maps of Sihanoukville pier and warehouse facilities and identified the warehouse corners that he would see when entering the channel from seaward. He marked with a grease pencil those corners and points that would give the most accurate information to update the maps.

He took the maps with him to the bridge. The clock showed 0430. Poe stood OOD watch. O'Neill had not arrived. Poe waved at Medici.

"Good morning, Jim. I'd like your quartermasters to maintain a second plot of bearings on this map in addition to the set on the Naval charts. It would be best to plot the buoys and quay wall entrance on the charts, and the pier, warehouse and landmark locations on these maps. If your guys can do it I'd like synchronized fixes every two minutes, assuming we're proceeding at four or five knots."

Poe studied the Xerox map under the red light of the chart table. Medici noticed that the circles of red grease pencil didn't show up under the red light and recircled them in black.

"I've got an extra quartermaster on watch for that purpose," Poe said. "I've never seen maps as detailed as these. Where'd you get them?"

"Staff in Saigon. I didn't know we had them either. The idea is to verify the pier and warehouse locations for targeting purposes. So they know just what to hit, if we have to do some surgical strikes." They both laughed at the stupid euphemism for bombing. "How do you plan to coordinate fixes?"

"I've synchronized the bridge clocks," Poe said. "I have one quartermaster who'll call out the times as we proceed down the channel, so we all shoot and plot at the same time. He'll announce 'Standby' at five seconds before each two-minute plotting time, then 'Mark—Time 0532,' for example, at each plot time. Sound okay?"

"Fine. Good thinking." Poe impressed Medici. He had his act together.

"Bosun's mate, make sure LT. Medici's awake." O'Neill's voice boomed as he strode onto the darkened bridge.

"I'm here, Captain," Medici shouted back louder, startling O'Neill. It's clear we'll never get along, Medici thought.

"Good morning," O'Neill said. "Have you gotten squared away with Lieutenant Poe?" he asked. He stopped next to them.

"Yessir. Poe's well organized. A good X/O." Medici suspected Poe smiled in the dark.

Poe said, "Captain, I think we should proceed up the fairway toward the channel now. We'll have first light as we pass the first channel buoy."

"Very well. This is the captain. I have the conn. All engines ahead standard. Steer zero four seven true." He checked the plot on the chart table. The ship shuddered and slowly began to gain speed. The swell from the monsoon was broad on their port quarter and the ship rolled and yawed its way toward the flashing channel buoys. The movement steadied as she gained headway. At Poe's direction the quartermasters took practice sights and plotted them until they grew accustomed to the rhythm. They were ready to go.

Medici loaded the camera Poe loaned him with the first 36-frame roll, then set the ASA control. He practiced with the zoom lens until he felt comfortable with its heft and could focus it smoothly with one clean twist past focus, then a tiny counter rotation to exact focus. He laid out another 10 rolls of 36-frame Tri-X on the chart board in front of him, even though he wouldn't have time to shoot more than one or two from the ship as it transited the channel. Through the bridge windows in the half light on deck he saw Metcalf carry two heavy sea bags to the rail, then study the warehouses with binoculars as they passed.

Piers and warehouses at Sihanoukville, Cambodia.

Ships unload at Sihanoukville, 1970.

45

Sihanoukville

The LST rose and fell alongside the quay wall on the surge of the southwest monsoon. The monotonous, slow transit into port allowed the quartermasters to fix the position of the channel buoys, fairway and shoals in order to correct erroneous information on the outdated charts.

Medici photographed the panorama of the quay wall, basin, and warehouse facilities. The old maps erred in orientation, location and number of warehouse buildings and entrances. He would pace off the warehouses later. The basin was empty except for the LST at the quay and a squat, ungainly vessel at anchor named *Kantha Bopha*.

Deck hands lowered the wooden gangway to the surface of the quay wall. Medici judged it insubstantial. A cruiser sailor expected grander things than the small ship, working Navy provided. The main deck of the unladen LST stood high above the wall, and the gangway leaned at a steep angle to the ground. Anyone coming aboard had to climb hand over foot as if going up a stepladder.

The official party arrived. The Cambodian Chief of Naval Operations wore a gray jumpsuit which made it appear that his formidable paunch had been upholstered.

Behind him climbed Claude Bawling, the American Naval Attaché to Phnom Penh, who had been selected over Medici in spite of Lon Nol's request that Medici be appointed. Bawling, a Navy lifer, spoke no French, Vietnamese or Khmer, but he had pull at the Bureau of Personnel.

Medici knew Bawling only from a barrage of irritating messages he sent from Washington during the hectic period of the Cambodian incursion. Bawling wanted to know how to ship his Buick Toronado to Phnom Penh, since his permanent change of station orders allowed him to bring a car. At that time the Mekong was blocked, Phnom Penh was under siege, and Ponchentong airport was under bombardment by the North Vietnamese.

Today Bawling dressed in natty civilian attire: a white short-sleeved shirt, black and red checked polyester pants, and white Corfam loafers. He would appear unobtrusive only on the back streets of Des Moines during a clown's convention, Medici thought.

Behind Bawling, he recognized Son Chea, the port commander of the Cambodian Naval base at Ream, and his lieutenant.

Commander O'Neill waited on deck as the men climbed the gangway. They tried to move with ceremony befitting the first port visit in 10 years of an American Naval vessel to Cambodia. Finally all four were on the ladder, inching up like caterpillars. The ladder lurched and Medici heard the sharp crack of wood. It broke clean in two, dumping the four men to the tarmac. Medici heard their groans from the bow. He started to run to help but then remembered his decision not to reveal his presence to any of the official party, since he shouldn't have come without permission of the ambassador and Naval attaché.

Therefore he sat on a bollard behind the anchor winch and smiled as the men untangled themselves. The chubby CNO had fallen directly on Bawling and knocked the wind out of him. In the melee, Bawling had lost one white plastic loafer overboard. It bobbed toward the bow like a small dory. The crew put over a metal Jacob's ladder and Bawling looked foolish climbing aboard with one shoe.

Medici waited until the party entered the wardroom, then went down the ladder with Poe's camera. At the end of the quay wall he paced off the back walls of the warehouses and photographed them.

He photographed the *Kantha Bopha*. The Cambodian guards on the pier seemed bewildered by his gaping smile and waves. He approached the guards, took their pictures, and got one to photograph him standing next to the other. His antics got them to smile and laugh, exactly what he wanted.

He watched the civilians Metcalf and Burson supervise the unloading of the shortwave transmitter, barrage balloon, and two heavy sea bags into a waiting truck. They stopped to place the sea bags in the empty guard house and padlock it, then drove off the quay toward town.

"Shit. So much for cover," Medici said to himself as he watched a second Jeep pull up to the gangway. His friend, CDR Som Sary, C/O of RCE-311, and Ang Ly Kim, his X/O, saw him and waved. The only thing to do was greet them warmly and pretend he was along for the ride.

"Bonjour. Ici c'est Bangkok, n'est-ce pas?" Medici said. *Good morning. This is Bangkok, isn't it?*

Sary and Kim laughed. "Non, mais la tour de Sihanoukville commence en cinq minutes." *No, but the tour of Sihanoukville starts in five minutes.*

"Quelle bonne surprise," Medici said. *What a nice surprise.* That's it, he thought, the whole fucking mission blown and my time here wasted with these clowns. He smiled enthusiastically, jumped in their Jeep and sped down the pier toward the center of the city.

They took Medici to the Grande Hotel, the showpiece of Sihanoukville, uncompleted and surrounded by a high fence of iron fleurs-de-lis. In front of the hotel, they frolicked and took photos of each other. They rolled slowly through town to an ESSO sign that marked the only gas station in the city. They needed gas, and Medici laughed when he insisted and paid cash for the fuel. He kept the receipt from Sihanoukville Esso, thinking of the superb stories he could tell in Saigon.

They walked together. The Cambodians asked him if he wanted to buy anything. At first he said no, then thought maybe some colorful native sari cloth. He could have shorts made from it that would be a conversation piece back in the world. He chose bright orange material with lurid magenta paisleys, "Cambodian preppie."

They drove south of town to the opulent casino, which had been commissioned, completed, and staffed by Prince Sihanouk, but which had never seen a guest. The staff wore smart, Navy blue skirts or trousers and crisp white shirts.

Medici stopped in front of a dark, short Cambodian woman seated behind the roulette wheel. She had exotic Indian features and the most magnificent breasts Medici had seen in Indochina. He smiled at the girl. She returned the smile, then lowered her head.

The Naval officers laughed and spoke quickly to each other in Khmer, then to the girl, whose eyes and smile widened. Medici asked what was so funny, and Som Sary told him he could go with the girl right now to one of the casino's plush rooms if he wanted. They had told her that Medici was a defender of the new Cambodian republic. Medici stammered a polite refusal to the girl. The girl frowned when Som Sary translated. Medici reached across the table, took her hand and kissed it. She giggled.

After the casino they returned to town. It was midafternoon and Medici again felt frustrated that the touring kept him from his mission, exploring the port, probably what Som Sary had set out to thwart. They were joined by Neal Rea, the port captain. The Cambodes found a sidewalk café, so they sat outside, drank rice wine, then icy cafe au lait. Medici told them he would have to return to the ship soon since they were sailing at 5 p.m.

Neal Rea, a little tipsy, asked Medici what he thought of the port city. Medici told him he was enchanted with the city's beauty and impressed with the port's maritime efficiency. From the little he had seen of it, it was a marvel of Cambodian engineering. Rea laughed.

"The French designed the quay basin, that's why it silts up so fast. If Cambodian engineers had designed it, we would not need the expensive suction dredge to vacuum it. The French charged us a fortune for the dredge *Kantha Bopha*. You probably saw her anchored out in the basin. Her maintenance is expensive, but we have no choice. If she does not dredge, the basin becomes unusable in six weeks' time. Wonderful French engineering, n'est-ce pas?"

They laughed at Rea's diatribe. Medici laughed loudest. He had accomplished his mission by dumb luck thanks to Rea's revelation of the simple way to take out the port of Sihanoukville: sink one small dredge.

NILO in mufti at Sihanoukville Casino with Cambodian Navy LCDR Ang Ly Kim.

46

Saving the Port

They returned to the quay wall just after the truck carrying Metcalf and Burson arrived. Medici saw it stop next to the guardhouse. Metcalf got out, waved the truck on, unlocked and entered the small shed. As Medici passed in the Jeep, he saw Metcalf loading himself up with two heavy sea bags, slinging the strap of each across the opposite shoulder. Som Sary and Ang Ly Kim left Medici at the Jacob's ladder and told him not to fall in the water as Bawling almost had. The Cambodians, still tipsy, laughed hysterically. The Jeep wove down the quay as Medici climbed the boarding ladder.

From the main deck he watched Metcalf struggle to carry the sea bags into the shade of the nearest warehouse to squat and rest. Medici told the OOD to watch where Metcalf went, then ran below to his stateroom.

He threw the camera and film on the bunk, slid the cold Browning into his waistband under his shirt, and ran back to the main deck. He could no longer see Metcalf. When he asked where Metcalf was, the OOD told him Metcalf had forced open and entered a corrugated metal door at the end of the first warehouse.

Medici slid down the Jacob's ladder as the OOD shouted, ordering Medici to stop on the C/O's orders. Medici was not to leave the ship because it would be under way within the hour. Medici said he had one more stop to make on the pier and would be right back. The OOD ran to the ship's telephone.

Medici walked quickly from the ship to the warehouse, wondering where the Cambodian guards had gone. Those at the ship earlier must have been ceremonial. He entered the shade of the overhang, walked the length of the warehouse to the open door, and slid through sideways. He stood still so his eyes could adjust to the dim light. From deep in the warehouse he heard scraping noises and

241

the clang of heavy, hollow metal.

His eyes adjusted to the light. Rows of pallets stacked high with wooden crates extended the length of the warehouse. Those closest to him were stenciled with Russian Cyrillic characters, but he could read "82MM:HE," high-explosive 82mm mortar rounds. The next row's crates had the same characters but read "108MM:HE," either artillery or mortar rounds, Medici could not tell.

So this was it, the "Sihanoukville connection" his agents had reported. Tons of ammunition delivered by the Soviets and Chinese to aid the North Vietnamese war, now in the possession of the Lon Nol government. His pulse quickened.

The hollow scraping came again, more muffled. He slipped out of his leather shoes and stood in his socks on the cool cement floor, crouched behind the first row of pallets and withdrew the Browning from his shirt. He held it tight between his legs to muffle the noise, then slowly chambered a round and cocked the pistol. Holding the pistol in front of him with both hands, he crept down the darkest aisle of pallets, peeking around each corner when he approached a cross-aisle.

The scraping noise grew louder. When peeking around the fifth cross aisle he saw Metcalf's sweating face above a pyramid of cases of high-explosive mortar bombs. An acrid chemical smell hung in the air. On the floor he saw dozens of green canvas wrappers that appeared to be peeled from foot-long candy bars. Medici knew they were torn from C-4 plastique. The tops of two compressed gas bottles with valves and hoses hooked to them poked above the shell cases. Medici watched Metcalf turn the valves. They hissed and Medici smelled nitrogen.

Metcalf backed out of the pyramid, closed it up with six more cases of mortar bombs, and draped it with two heavy rubberized tarps. Vapor clouds of cold nitrogen gas leaked from the edges of the ponchos until Metcalf taped the seams. Metcalf drew a small aluminum box from his pocket and picked up a spool of wire that ran into the cases. He unrolled the wire to its full length as he crept backward. He split the two wires apart at the end, then stripped the insulation with his teeth and secured the wires to two terminals on the aluminum box. Medici watched him turn a knob that looked like the dial on a kitchen timer, then set the box down. It started to tick.

"What the hell are you doing?" Medici said to Metcalf's back. His voice cracked. He held the Browning shakily in front of him. His hands felt weak and slippery with sweat.

Metcalf froze but did not turn. He rotated his head slowly to the left until he could see Medici out of one eye. "Hey, hey, Lieutenant. We really should get out of here. This fuckin' place'll be history in 30 minutes. We're supposed to be getting under way right now. Why the pistol? We're on the same side."

"What are you doing?" Medici shouted. The strength returned to his pistol hand.

"What does it look like I'm doing! I'm going to blow these fucking warehouses with nitrogen-enhanced plastique in a cluster of high-explosive mortar bombs. This warehouse will go and the concussion will touch off the other that is full of ordnance. There's enough ammo here to supply the NVA for 14 months if Lon Nol decides to sell it to them, or if they take it themselves. That's why we got to blow it." Metcalf's eyes darted from side to side past Medici.

"Why wasn't I informed of this?"

"No one was, not even the captain of the LST, which we gotta' make sure gets out of here before this thing blows. Capisce?" Metcalf pleaded.

"Why the hell do you want to blow their only deepwater port right now? This may be the only place they can receive food and weapons from us. The White House already sent them 2,000 rifles. Why would we want to blow the place at the same time...." Medici's mouth hung open and his eyes narrowed. "Because this plan didn't come from the White House, did it?"

Metcalf's eyes went cold and the mock friendliness disappeared. "This was authorized by Studies and Observations Group in Saigon working with Naval staff. That's all I can tell you."

Medici's mind raced. All he could think of was Commander Holland who would not, could not send him into the midst of this insanity if he had known about it. He would not have sent the LST but would have flown in the transmitter. No, Holland would not have sent Medici without telling him about his plan. Holland didn't know. No one knew except Studies and Observations Group. It was their plan.

"Cut the wire, Metcalf."

"What! Are you crazy, Lieutenant? I've got my orders…."

"Cut the fucking wire now!" Medici's voice echoed along the metal walls of the warehouse.

"Okay, okay," Metcalf said. He bent to the wire and unsheathed his K-Bar knife. He grasped the wire as Medici turned toward the sound of shouting at the far end of the warehouse.

In a split second, Metcalf exploded into action. He whipped his right leg out, pivoted on the ball of his left foot, and spun toward Medici. His right arm arced in a sidearm pitch as he hurled the heavy K-Bar at Medici's torso.

Medici saw only a blur as he turned toward Metcalf. He fell to his right like a dead weight. The knife's heavy handle crashed into his forehead above the eye and stunned him as he fell. Metcalf leaped at him, howling like an animal, fingers extended like cat's claws. Medici heard his pistol fire one round as Metcalf crashed down on him, crushing him to the floor. The last thing he heard before lights out was Poe yelling, "They're here! They're over here!"

47

The Sihanoukville Inquiry

[Author's note:

There are sparse materials in diaries or U.S. Naval messages about what followed the Sihanoukville incident. What is known is that LCDR O'Neill brought LT. Medici back to Saigon in hack—ship's house arrest—and insisted a formal Naval Board of Inquiry be convened to consider whether criminal charges under the UCMJ should be brought against LT. Medici.

The proceedings, including LT. Medici's pretrial meetings with counsel, took place in the "Cambodian Shop" of Naval Headquarters in Saigon. While not describing the proceedings, LT. Medici did provide a detailed description of the Cambodian Shop in a letter home:

> The Cambodian Shop is located in a room on the third floor of a former French colonial administration building adjacent to the French Embassy compound. Through the open double bank of windows I can see the French tricouleur flag on its pole at their embassy next door.
> The room is rectangular, 20 by 40 feet. The door into the room from the stairwell is a large, black steel plate with a heavy sliding bolt, and it clanks and slams heavily with a metallic ring whenever it is opened and closed, sort of like a medieval dungeon.
> The walls of the room are covered with blackboard size maps, framed with varnished wood, some covered in a light blue cloth, others with the cloth drawn back to reveal parts of Cambodia's coast and border with Vietnam, infiltration routes marked with thin red or blue tape lines. A six-foot-square enlargement of a chart on an easel behind the witness chair depicts the port facilities of Sihanoukville, Cambodia,

including the quay wall, basin, deepwater pier, and two warehouses in red at the junction of the quay wall and pier. It also shows the outline of the *USS Garrison County*, alongside the pier on the outside wall, near the warehouses.

A single wood table covered in green baize sits on a foot-high platform with a chair behind it for the Board of Inquiry officer.

To the left and right of the table are two smaller rosewood counsel tables set at oblique angles to the larger one, me and my counsel Mr. Carlson on the left, and prosecuting officer Mr. Breuner and prosecuting witness Metcalf on the right. In a corner is a small table with a red, secure military telephone.

A hardwood witness chair with arms and back of curving wood spokes is on the platform next to the big table. The platform is new white pine, obviously thrown together quickly for my Inquiry.

A souvenir flag of Prince Sihanouk's recently deposed Cambodian monarchy hangs sloppily from one wall, and next to it hangs a poster-sized photograph of the smiling Prince, with a hand-lettered sign under it saying, "BYE-BYE SNOOKIE. March 18, 1970."

Three tall, four-drawer military file cabinets with vertical, steel locking bars welded to the front stand against the wall of the room to the right of the black steel door. The cabinets bear large red and white diagonal striped posters with block letters announcing "SECRET," "TOP SECRET," and "SPECIAL COMPARTMENTALIZED INTELLIGENCE." A small wood table and chair sit in front of the cabinets, at which the Yeoman sits tape-recording the proceedings. A Casablanca ceiling fan turns slowly. The room is sweltering hot.

Medici writes nothing more of this time in his diaries or letters, but in 2003, under a Freedom of Information Act request, the author obtained the transcripts of most of the tapes of the SECRET inquiry, including the yeoman reporter's meticulous parenthetical notes, all of which follow.]

48

Pre-Inquiry Counseling Session

CARLSON
(LT. Medici's defense counsel)
(Menacingly)
So the only person you've shot face-to-face in this war is Gunner's mate Metcalf, an American sailor!
(Shakes his head)

CARLSON
Nice shootin', Tex!
(Carlson stands up straight, intense)

CARLSON
What disturbs me, Lieutenant, is this: Not only do you think you're smarter than these special warfare guys, but you seem firmly convinced you're morally superior to them. You don't dirty your hands with violent "wet" operations in Cambodia, but you go nuts when Metcalf tries to carry out HIS orders and destroy the warehouses at Sihanoukville…
(Thrusts at Medici with his forefinger on each "YOU")

CARLSON
…because no one informed YOU, and YOU disagreed with the idea.
(Carlson turns his back to Medici, with a slight limp steps away from the desk and stares through the window)

CARLSON
You knew exactly what you were doing when you went to Ha Tien up on the border — two gold stripes and glory, and only an accidental chance of injury. You dash in and out of Cambodia, get shot at once in a while for credibility, publicize it all in your glib intelligence reports, and make yourself a hero. Low risk, high return.
    (Carlson turns sharply to Medici, glaring with disdain)

CARLSON
Well sorry, Lieutenant. That's not what war's about. You're fighting a dilettante war, without getting your shoes dirty.
    (Carlson picks up his briefcase and starts
    to walk out of the room. Says over his shoulder)

CARLSON
Next time, Lieutenant, shoot the bad guys.
    (Medici jumps to his feet.)

MEDICI
Does that mean you won't defend me in the inquiry?

CARLSON
(Snorts)
I think not.

MEDICI
(Medici goes after Carlson, spins him around by the shoulder)

CARLSON
(Carlson drops the briefcase, braces as if to fight,

NILO HA TIEN

then lowers his arms to his side
as Medici retreats a half step.)

MEDICI

Listen, Commander. Hear me out. You're not far wrong on my motives for going to Ha Tien in the first place. But consider this: The job changes the man. I was scared to death when I got there — thought I'd be shot by a sniper as I jumped off the helo. But I got my bearings, then realized that the only way I could do my job and get intelligence was to cross the border into Cambodia and see for myself. No one will write me orders to cross the border, because it's illegal, so I just do it by hook and crook.

I go with sailors who park their junks on the riverbank and shop in the market at the Cambodian village of Ton Hon. We walk in and plant electronic sensors on the same paths the North Vietnamese use at night to smuggle weapons across the border.

I cajole inexperienced helo pilots to fly a few kilometers across the border to see what goes on in the North Vietnamese ammo dumps, on the trails and the roads. I go up along the coast in Cambodian ships and in Vietnamese fishing junks at night to see what I can of light signals between the gun runners.

And when I can't get a ride, I just walk in or get flown in one way by my helo pilot buddies, so I can do recon—alone, with a lousy pistol tucked in my belt. My pal Frank Brown says I'm the fucking Johnny Appleseed of Cambodia! Even the special ops guys only go in under doctrine, with a trained squad of linguists carrying weapons and radios and with helos standing by.
  (Carlson, attentive, walks back to the table and leans against it. Medici remains standing.)

CARLSON

Go on, Lieutenant.

MEDICI

I can't get any support or security, or even ask for it, because the whole damn mission is illegal. It violates international law, Cambodian neutrality, and our own Rules of Engagement!
 (Medici sits down, looking dejected.)

MEDICI

It's my show and my risk all right—entirely mine. Staffers in Saigon won't look me in the eye when they tell me they can't help me if I continue my solo trips into Cambodia and get caught. Then they always wink and say, "But keep up the good work."
 (Medici shakes his head slowly, looking at the tabletop.)

MEDICI

Do you know how isolated that makes me feel? I've got the enemy in front and this wishy-washy staff behind me. At least the special ops guys know their people will make an effort to rescue them if the squad's in trouble. I don't have shit to back me up. I AM my own security. Yet I keep doing it—because it's MY job.

CARLSON
(Nods sympathetically.)

MEDICI
(Quietly)
You're right. I don't get into firefights every day with platoons of North Vietnamese. It's not what I'm paid to do. But I never know what's out there waiting for me. It's unimaginable risk each time I go, and my nerves show it. I haven't slept more than a few hours a night for months.
 (Medici straightens up, meets Carlson's gaze,
  speaks with conviction and energy.)

NILO HA TIEN

MEDICI
But damn it, Commander, I do it. I've made myself responsible for knowing what goes on in my part of Cambodia. And you've got to believe this: Metcalf had to be stopped from blowing the warehouses in Sihanoukville. Their destruction would have been a disaster in every way. I'm sorry he was wounded, but he had to be stopped.

CARLSON
(With hands in pockets, moves a few steps, then turns, with a flicker of a smile across his face.)
You really go into Cambodia without support or security?

MEDICI
(Nods once)

CARLSON
Lieutenant, you're a lot crazier than you look. I think you'll need help.
(Carlson picks up briefcase.)

MEDICI
You'll defend me?

CARLSON
Yes—it's my job.

49

Inquiry - First Session

SIHANOUKVILLE INQUIRY ROSTER:
CAPT **LARKIN**, USN, Presiding Officer of Board
LT COLONEL, **BREUNER**, USMC, Prosecuting JAG Officer
LCDR **CARLSON** USN, JAG, defending officer (for LT. Medici)
LT **MEDICI**, USNR, NILO Ha Tien, Target Defendant/Witness
LCDR **O'NEILL**, USN, C/O USS Garrison County, Witness
GMG2 **METCALF**, USN, NAVSPECWARGRU, Witness
LT(JG) **KELLY**, USNR, NAVSPECWARGRU, Witness
YN1 SMITH, Recording **YEOMAN**

LARKIN (Presiding Officer)
(Taps gavel)

This Board of Inquiry on matters occurring in Sihanoukville, Cambodia, on or about June 6, 1970, will come to order. I apologize to counsel for the heat, but due to the sensitive nature of these proceedings and the secrecy of this room itself, it was necessary to remove the broken air conditioner to an Army repair shop. You'll notice we have no reporter—we couldn't find one with adequate security clearance—so the yeoman will tape-record the proceedings and transcribe them later. You all are aware this room, the Navy's Cambodian Intelligence Shop, formally does not exist on the table of organization, but because of its photo and map facilities relating to Sihanoukville, and its secret location, it serves as an appropriate venue for these classified proceedings. So bear with me and the heat, gentlemen.

Now, I understand this Board is to focus on events that occurred during a naval mission to Sihanoukville during June 1970—about five weeks ago.

NILO HA TIEN
Colonel Breuner, is the judge advocate ready to proceed?

BREUNER (Prosecuting Officer)
(stands, remains standing)
Ready, your honor.

LARKIN
Commander Carlson, ready for Lieutenant Medici?

CARLSON (Medici's Defense Counsel)
(Stands)
Ready, your honor.
(Sits)

BREUNER
May it please the court, on behalf of Commander, Military Assistance Command, Vietnam, I request this Board at its conclusion to issue charges under the Uniform Code of Military Justice against Lieutenant Medici, in summary:

First, three Article 92 charges:

1. For disobeying on June 6, 1970, LCDR O'Neill's direct order not to leave *USS Garrison County* while in Sihanoukville, Cambodia;

2. For interfering on June 6, 1970, with the Studies and Observations Group—SOG's—direct orders to petty officer Metcalf to destroy two warehouses containing Communist weapons at the port of Sihanoukville, Cambodia, by physically injuring petty officer Metcalf by gunshot wound;

3. For disobeying on March 29, 1970, a direct Presidential Order not to supply weapons or ammunition to Cambodian forces...

CARLSON

Objection to the two June 6th specifications, your honor. First, under the definitions of SOPA—senior officer present afloat—we believe that Lieutenant-Commander O'Neill was not Lieutenant Medici's SOPA on June 6th, and we move to strike that allegation. Second, we move to strike the phrase "and physically injuring by gunshot wound." The court is aware there exist no assault or battery charges in the UCMJ. If an enlisted man strikes an officer, it may be an Article 91 charge of Insubordinate Conduct. No similar charge exists if an officer strikes or injures an enlisted man.

LARKIN

(Frowns, nods head)

On the SOPA questions, I will consider those definitions as an affirmative defense during my deliberations. On the second point, counsel correctly states the code, and that portion of the specification which states "and physically injured by gunshot wound" will be stricken, leaving the requested charge of interfering with the execution of a lawful order.

LARKIN

But to forewarn you, Commander Carlson, I have decided to hear all testimony related to the shooting incident, so save your objections.

(Turns to Breuner)

Any further charges you wish me to consider, Colonel?

BREUNER

Yes, your honor. The specifications relating to the delivery of American ammunition to the Cambodians on March 29, and interfering on June 6 with the destruction of the Sihanoukville warehouses that contained tons of Communist ammunition, each constitutes an Article 104 violation—aiding the enemy.

NILO HA TIEN

CARLSON
(Medici and Carlson look at each other, stunned;
Larkin frowns, looks at them, then back at Breuner)

CARLSON
Objection your honor! Aiding the enemy Article 104 charges can carry the death penalty! There has been no notice to defense counsel that Col. Breuner would request such charges. I request more time to prepare on behalf of LT. Medici.

LARKIN
Calm down, Commander. These requests for charges, while very serious, are only requests, and all charges should be considered here.

CARLSON
Then I will request the Board to consider Article 91 insubordination charges against petty officer Metcalf for assaulting LT. Medici, his senior officer present in the warehouses at Sihanoukville.

LARKIN
They will be considered. And you are pushing it, counsel.

LARKIN
Any other charges the Judge Advocate wishes the Board to consider at conclusion?

BREUNER
Yes, your honor. One Article 88 charge—Contempt Toward Civil Officials—to wit, that on or about March 29, 1970, when warned that

HL Serra
transferring American ammunition to Cambodian forces violated a direct Presidential Order, Lieutenant Medici, serving as NILO Ha Tien, stated "Fuck Nixon and his Kraut."

(Medici hides his eyes with his hand, then turns to Carlson and shrugs. Carlson stifles a smile, shakes his head once)

LARKIN
Any MORE charges, Colonel?

BREUNER
(Shakes his head)
No, your honor.

LARKIN
Very well. Call your first witness.

BREUNER
Lieutenant Commander O'Neill, commanding officer *USS Garrison County* LST-972.

YEOMAN
(Holds Bible, leads O'Neill to stand)

O'NEILL
(Takes oath while standing)

YEOMAN
Do you solemnly swear that the testimony you are about to give shall be the truth, the whole truth, and nothing but the truth, so help you

NILO HA TIEN

God?

O'NEILL

I do.

(Sits)

BREUNER

Your full name and duty station, sir?

O'NEILL

Lieutenant-commander Robert J. O'Neill, commanding officer *USS Garrison* County LST-972.

BREUNER

To what command was *Garrison County* attached on June 6, 1970—about five weeks ago?

O'NEILL

We were attached temporary additional duty to Commander Naval Forces Vietnam on June 1, 1970, and taken away from our naval support activities in the western Pacific by special orders from CINCPACFLT.

BREUNER

What were those support duties?

O'NEILL

Carrying supplies from Guam to naval facilities in Saigon and Danang. These orders forced us to change our scheduled return to Guam, transit the Saigon River to the Naval facility at Nha Be, pick

HL Serra

up a 10 kilowatt shortwave transmitter, barrage balloon, antenna, and two civilian technicians, and deliver them to Sihanoukville, Cambodia on June 6, 1970.

BREUNER

Did you know why?

O'NEILL

Well, not from the orders. But at Nha Be the scuttlebutt was that the North Vietnamese Army had overrun the Lon Nol government's Radio Phnom Penh transmitter site in Cambodia and knocked it off the air. Since we were new allies with the Cambodes from the time Lon Nol deposed Prince Sihanouk in March, the transmitter we carried was to get the government radio back on the air to let the Cambodian people and foreign press know Lon Nol was still in control. The transmitter had a long wire antenna held aloft by a big barrage balloon. Pretty clever setup, actually. Two civilian technicians were sent along to install it and get it working during our 12 hours in Sihanoukville.

BREUNER

Was petty officer Metcalf one of the two "civilian" technicians sent with the shortwave transmitter and listed on your orders?

O'NEILL

Yes. He was in civilian clothes, and I thought he and his partner were civilians.

BREUNER

Did *Garrison County* take the transmitter and men to Sihanoukville?

NILO HA TIEN

O'NEILL

Yes...Sihanoukville is the only deepwater port in Cambodia. The Gulf of Thailand is very shallow—60 feet at its deepest—and half the year the monsoon blows from the southwest with a long fetch up the Gulf that causes a huge swell, sometimes a 12- to 20-foot rise and fall against the quay wall at Sihanoukville. My LST is shallow draft when unladen, so they figured I could get in, unload the transmitter easily enough even with the swell, and get out the same day. We didn't want any international incidents or embarrassing photos in TIME Magazine, what with all the political upset at home about invading Cambodia—Kent State and all. We heard the Cambodes had dredged a basin behind the seawall and we hoped it would provide an offloading site protected from the swell. Turns out we had to park outside the basin, near the warehouses.

(Points offhandedly at the chart behind him)

BREUNER

Sounds pretty straightforward a mission.

O'NEILL

That part was. Until the spook came aboard.

BREUNER

Are you referring to LIEUTENANT Medici—NILO Ha Tien?

O'NEILL

(Sits up straight. Glares at Medici.)

Yes, sir. On the way up the Gulf of Thailand we receive this FLASH TOP SECRET message from Admiral Zumwalt ordering *Garrison County* to rendezvous at 0300 on June 4 with a river patrol boat off

HL Serra
Phu Quoc Island to embark Lieutenant Medici, NILO Ha Tien, for transit to Sihanoukville.

BREUNER
For what purpose?

O'NEILL
Damned if I knew!

(Larkin smiles)

O'NEILL
His written orders, when he presented them, were James Bond gobbledygook, ambiguous—go and come as he pleases; embark and disembark when he wants; don't question him about his activities—like that.

BREUNER
Did the orders pose a mission problem for you?

O'NEILL
Well, I was damned nervous about getting in and out of Sihanoukville without incident, toot sweet. I didn't want some spook mucking it up. Everyone knows Sihanoukville was the main port for Communist weapons coming into Cambodia to be infiltrated across the border into Vietnam. The press was watching it like a hawk, and there had to be a lot of bad guys there. So I wanted this to be a clean, in-and-out deal, with no complications. In at first light, out before dusk.

BREUNER
Did Lieutenant Medici cause you any problems?

NILO Ha Tien

O'NEILL

You bet he did! From the get-go. We rendezvoused at three in the morning in a driving monsoon with 12-foot swells. His patrol boat is bobbing like a cork, even loses a gunwale rail scraping our side. Lieutenant Medici does some acrobatics to get aboard. Someone drops his bag in the Gulf and we have to fish it out in that foul weather. I'm on the bridge and the NILO—that's what they call him—appears on the bridge like a ghost and scares me half to death telling me he's from Naval Intelligence. I'm thinking one of my men is smuggling drugs or something. And he was in US jungle greens, but wearing this strange Cambodian naval beret.
(Sniffs.)
I thought it an affectation myself.

O'NEILL

Then the NILO insists on waking my armorer at four in the morning to get a gun-cleaning kit and 9mm bullets, 'cause his pistolo got soaked in warm seawater. Then he stays up, meticulously cleaning the pistol and camera gear. My steward and armorer told me this.

CARLSON
(Carlson and Breuner speak over each other re: objections and response)

CARLSON
Objection. Hearsay.

BREUNER
Reports received in the line of duty through the chain of command by Captain O'Neill are not hearsay as to his state of mind in which he gave the orders Lieutenant Medici violated.

LARKIN
Overruled. Continue, Lieutenant-commander.

O'NEILL
(Agitated)

Next morning the NILO briefs me and the Exec on his mission, which requires my ship and crew to do a port survey, locate buoys, piers, warehouses, and take soundings on the way into the harbor, because we've had no port information on Sihanoukville for seven years. Suddenly our simple job got a lot more complicated.

O'NEILL
(Sits up straight. Regains composure.)

But we didn't complain. Orders are orders, and the mission made sense.

BREUNER
Did Lieutenant Medici cause any discipline or order problems while on *Garrison County*?

O'NEILL
Problems? You bet! The afternoon after he came aboard I was in my sea cabin and heard gunfire. I was about to send the ship to general quarters. We're 50 miles from Cambodia's coast. There's nothing on radar and the lookouts had reported no small boats nearby. I ran out to the bridge and there's the NILO on deck, shooting Pepsi cans off wave tops with his pistol. And on the bridge my Exec Mr. Poe's grinning like a cat, announcing over the ship's loudspeakers, "Nice shootin', NILO." I'm furious because we have doctrine for the use of small arms aboard ship, and Lieutenant Medici doesn't ask, just starts shooting.

NILO HA TIEN

BREUNER
Okay, captain, but did this violate any order Lieutenant Medici was aware of?

O'NEILL
No. But it made me even more concerned that his mission in Sihanoukville was to shoot someone, which would cause a nasty incident, maybe get us detained there indefinitely, or my ship fired upon. I didn't like it. Don't forget, mission orders aside, my first responsibility is the safety of my ship and crew.

BREUNER
Did you ever ask Lieutenant Medici exactly what his mission was?

O'NEILL
No. He wasn't very approachable. He was very direct and businesslike —curt—around me. And I guess I really didn't want to know if he was up to no good. I just didn't want my ship hazarded or my crew harmed.

BREUNER
You didn't get along well with Lieutenant Medici, did you?

O'NEILL
(Embarrassed.)
You could say that—but mission is mission, and I don't let things like personalities affect my orders.

BREUNER
Any other incidents before Sihanoukville?

O'NEILL
The wardroom briefing. I asked Lieutenant Medici to brief my officers and me on the situation in Cambodia. Lieutenant Medici had spoken to Mr. Poe, and Mr. Poe informed me that Medici was sort of "Our Man in Cambodia," and very knowledgable about what was going on.
(Shakes his head)

O'NEILL
Boy, what a mistake letting him brief us was!

BREUNER
Why?

O'NEILL
After dinner, I asked him to begin. He whips out this crazy-quilt map of Cambodia and puts it up on an easel. It's got North Vietnamese Army and Khmer Rouge units identified in grease pencil all over it, with reported troop strengths. I mean, this was TOP SECRET stuff.
(With excitement)
To look at the map, you'd think Cambodia was being overrun by North Vietnamese troops! Then, Lieutenant Medici proceeds to tell us Cambodia is quote "turning to shit" now that the North Vietnamese are on the move because Lon Nol joined our side. And that Cambodia's future is quote "bleak and possibly short." That's what he said!

MEDICI
(Looks sideways at Carlson with a sheepish, apologetic expression.)

NILO HA TIEN

O'NEILL

Worst of all, he points out that units of the 9th North Vietnamese Division—a heavy weapons division—have been reported operating in the vicinity of Sihanoukville!

BREUNER

Did his briefing cause you a mission problem?

O'NEILL

No. A morale problem.
    (Shifts in chair)

O'NEILL

I was sure my young officers were upset and nervous at the prospect of encountering an enemy heavy weapons division in what was supposed to be a cakewalk. I didn't want them jittery when we entered Sihanoukville the next morning—the first American ship there in years.

BREUNER

What did you do?

O'NEILL
    (Shifts again in chair.)
I pulled Lieutenant Medici's map off the easel, told him that was enough briefing, and left the wardroom.

BREUNER

Any other incidents?

O'NEILL

Finally, when we made Sihanoukville and were alongside the quay wall, I asked Lieutenant Medici to join me to greet our official guests who came to receive the transmitter—the Cambodian Chief of Naval Operations and our new American naval attaché from Phnom Penh. Lieutenant Medici tells me he can't participate, because he is here without permission of our diplomatic mission and it would be impossible to explain his presence. So he sat forward out of sight as the dignitaries came aboard, then snuck off the ship for whatever spook stuff he was up to—in violation of my first order to him.

BREUNER

What was that?

O'NEILL

I told him I didn't think he should go ashore in Sihanoukville.

BREUNER

Was that an order?

O'NEILL

On my ship, when I tell an officer I THINK he shouldn't do something—that's an order!

BREUNER

What did Lieutenant Medici say?

O'NEILL

He told me I had a copy of his written orders from Admiral Zumwalt, that to stay aboard would prevent his mission, and that he was going ashore. Then he tells me, "Don't wait up for me, Captain. I can get back on my own. If I'm not here by 1700, just get under way without me." And he left the ship as I've described.

BREUNER

But he did return to the ship, didn't he?

O'NEILL

He did, I'm informed, about 1630 in the afternoon. I left explicit orders with the officer of the deck, that if Lieutenant Medici returned, he was to be kept aboard. Period. No ifs, ands, or buts. The OOD said Lieutenant Medici appeared agitated when he came aboard and asked him to keep an eye on petty officer Metcalf who was down at the end of the pier. Lieutenant Medici darted below and came back on deck with his pistol tucked in his belt. He asked where Metcalf had gone, and the OOD told him Metcalf had carried some seabags into the closest warehouse. The OOD insisted that Lieutenant Medici stay aboard on my orders, but Lieutenant Medici ran past him, slid down the Jacob's ladder, walked quickly to the warehouse and went inside. I was called by the OOD and was on deck by then, and I sent Lieutenant jaygee Poe and some armed men to the warehouse to bring Lieutenant Medici back aboard. Just after Mr. Poe disappeared into the warehouse, I heard a single gunshot, and Mr. Poe came out and called for our ship's medic to treat Metcalf. I was furious but anxious to get under way before dark. After he was given first aid, my men carried Metcalf back aboard, and I put Lieutenant Medici in hack—he could not leave his stateroom—for the trip back to Saigon. Petty officer Metcalf was MEDEVACed to hospital by helo, and I personally escorted Lieutenant Medici back to Naval headquarters in Saigon and tried to file charges against him on the spot, but I had to settle for this Board of Inquiry.

BREUNER

Am I correct that the Article 92 charges you **wish the** Board to

O'NEILL
consider arise specifically from Lieutenant Medici's failure to obey your order not leave *Garrison County* while in Sihanoukville?

O'NEILL
Yes, but more specifically the second unequivocal order not to leave the ship after he returned around 1630. If Lieutenant Medici hadn't gone ashore to snoop Metcalf, none of this would have happened....
(points to Metcalf)
And this young sailor would not have been severely wounded trying to carry out his orders.

BREUNER
I have no further questions of this witness, your honor.

LARKIN
Cross-examination, Commander Carlson?

CARLSON
(stands)
Just briefly your honor. Lieutenant-commander O'Neill, if Lieutenant Medici hadn't gone ashore and stopped Metcalf, the warehouses and much of the pier at Sihanoukville would have been destroyed, wouldn't they?

O'NEILL
I suppose so. I have since learned their destruction was petty officer Metcalf's undisclosed mission.

CARLSON
Might that event have hazarded *Garrison County* and its crew?

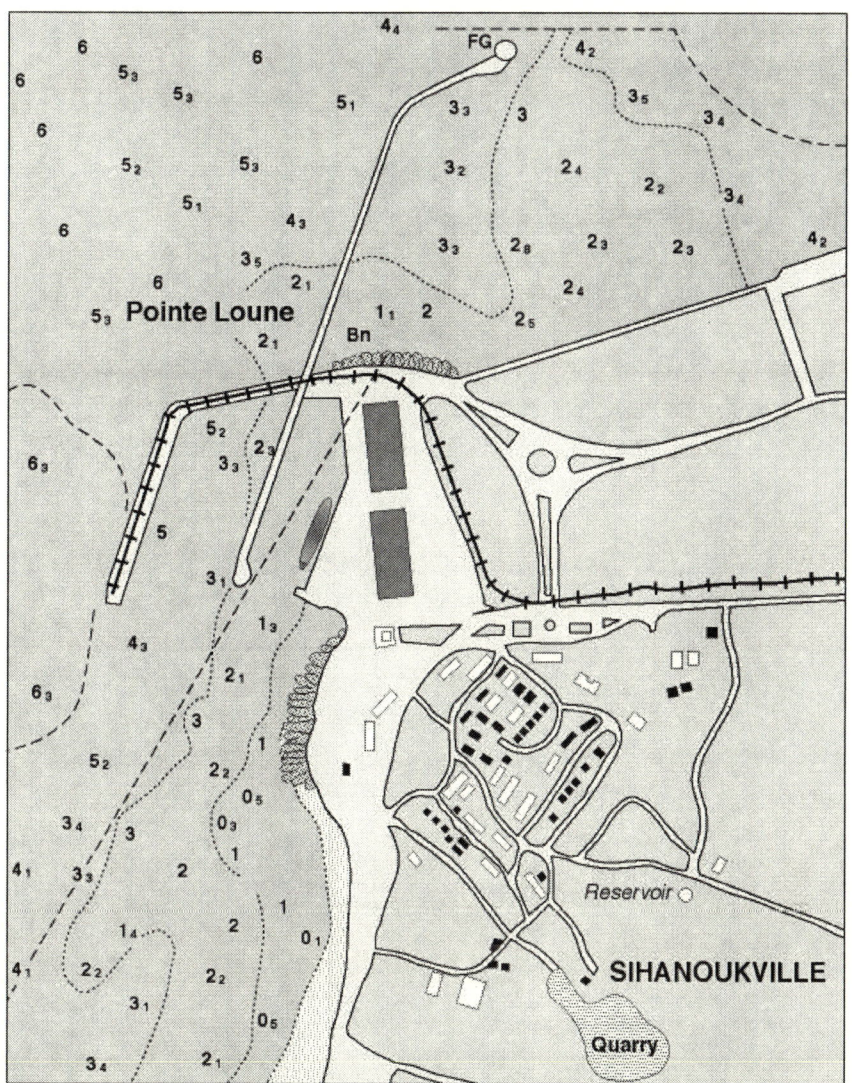

O'NEILL

Well, Metcalf said he set the timer to blow the warehouses after we were under way, so I don't think there could have been any real hazard....

CARLSON

Do you know for sure? Have you investigated how much ordnance

HL Serra
was in the warehouse, how big the explosion would be, how reliable the timer was, and how long Metcalf set it for?

O'NEILL
Well, no.... I don't know for sure.

CARLSON
Take a look at the exhibit, Lieutenant-commander. Your ship was pretty close to those warehouses, wasn't it?

O'NEILL
(Looks at chart exhibit, waffles)
Well...perhaps it's not to scale....

CARLSON
But you are still sure "None of this would have happened" if Lieutenant Medici had stayed aboard at 1630?

O'NEILL
Yes, I'm certain.

CARLSON
Just a couple more things: Did Lieutenant Medici's briefing make your young officers or YOU nervous about the North Vietnamese units around Sihanoukville?

O'NEILL
(Sputtering)
Why, what do you mean "Make me nervous?" I've—

NILO HA TIEN

BREUNER
Objection, your honor. Argumentative and badgering the witness!

LARKIN
Sustained.

CARLSON
Withdrawn. Commander, did you know Lieutenant Medici, at 24, is the youngest full Lieutenant in the Navy?

O'NEILL
I may have heard something like that from Mr. Poe. He and Medici were chummy.

CARLSON
Did Lieutenant Medici irritate you because he was a brash, highly competent up-and-comer, and you had already been passed over for commander?

O'NEILL
(Astonished, livid, sputters)

BREUNER
OBJECTION, your honor! This is irrelevant, argumentative, and badgering to Lieutenant-commander O'Neill.

LARKIN
(Sharply)
I agree, Colonel. Commander Carlson, I'm instructing you to treat

HL Serra
this witness with the respect due a naval officer.

CARLSON
Aye-aye, Captain. I'd like to reserve the right to recall this witness later.

LARKIN
(Still mad)
Very well. This witness is excused.
    (O'Neill leaves stand)

LARKIN
Colonel Breuner, call your next witness.

BREUNER
Gunner's Mate First Class Richard Metcalf.

METCALF
(Hobbles to stand on crutches, sits)

YEOMAN
(Holds out Bible)
Do you solemnly swear to tell the truth, the whole truth, and nothing but the truth, so help you God?

METCALF
I do.

NILO Ha Tien

BREUNER

Please state your full name and duty station.

METCALF

Gunner's mate First Class Richard Metcalf, 057-22-0555, United States Navy.

BREUNER

Petty officer Metcalf, what is your present command?

METCALF

SEAL Team One, CTF 77.7.9.1, DET Bravo. Attached temporary additional duty to Naval Special Warfare Group, Commander Naval Forces Vietnam, at Nha Be.

BREUNER

Who do you work for?

METCALF

That depends—
(Grins nervously)
We are attached directly to Admiral Zumwalt's Staff, but our missions can be assigned from a variety of sources through our task force commander, the SEAL boss at Nha Be.

BREUNER

How did you come to be on *USS Garrison County* on June 5th and 6th, 1970?

METCALF

Two men from our detachment were selected to assist setting up a

HL Serra

new shortwave transmitter for the Lon Nol government in Cambodia, our new—(Metcalf smirks) "ally."

METCALF

The North Vietnamese units around the Cambodian capital had blown up the main transmitter of Radio Phnom Penh—knocked it off the air—when they surrounded Phnom Penh. Our job was to set up a portable shortwave transmitter, generator, and antenna at the port of Sihanoukville so the Lon Nol guys could broadcast their daily propaganda to the people of Cambodia AND the foreign press. To let everyone know Lon Nol was still in control—despite the stranglehold the North Vietnamese Army had on Cambodia.

BREUNER

You are quite knowledgable about politics and the military situation in Cambodia—

METCALF

That's one of my jobs—political officer for DET Bravo. I'm supposed to keep up on military and political developments in any area in which we operate.

BREUNER

How do you do that?

METCALF

Well, I read all the Army and Navy message traffic dealing with action reports, political reports, and intelligence reports. I also get translations of broadcasts from enemy propaganda radio in the area.

NILO HA TIEN

BREUNER
(Looks askance at Medici)
Sounds like you are thoroughly prepared for YOUR job, petty officer Metcalf. By the way, what is your job?

METCALF
I am weapons and explosives specialist for DET Bravo.

BREUNER
Did you receive specialized training in these areas?

METCALF
Yes. Navy B School for weapons, and I am EOD-qualified—Explosive Ordinance Disposal—I can handle all types of explosives.

BREUNER
Any other training?

METCALF
(Looks at Breuner with surprise for an instant,
then continues, a little cocky)
Of course. All SEALs are UDT-qualified before SEAL training. We go through an arduous training period of 18 months at the Amphib Base in Coronado. Physical training, weapons specialist training, language training, political training, covert operations training—like that!

BREUNER
(Paces behind counsel table, then stops and focuses intently on
Metcalf, lowering his voice—serious)
Was there a second part to your mission in Sihanoukville?

                    METCALF

Yes, sir.

                    BREUNER

What was that?

                    METCALF
           (Looks at Medici with disapproval)
To destroy the two warehouses at the foot of the pier—

                    METCALF
(Points with one crutch at warehouses in red on the large map of
              the port on the easel behind him)
—if they contained Communist weapons. That's exactly what Lieutenant Kelly told me during the mission briefing.

                    BREUNER

How were you to accomplish this part of your mission?

                    METCALF

First, I had to be sure the weapons were in there. And they were. I peeked through holes in the metal buildings on our way out to deliver the transmitter gear in the morning—

                    BREUNER

Of June sixth?

                    METCALF

of June sixth—and saw rows of crates of Russian and Chinese

NILO HA TIEN

weapons stacked high in both buildings. We had to hustle to get the long wire antenna and generator set up during daylight, and we accomplished it because we had rehearsed it several times in Nha Be. I alone was assigned the warehouse mission, so I had to deal with it AFTER we set up the transmitter. We finished with the set up around 1500, and I asked the Cambodes to drive us back to the ship since we were to get under way as soon as we completed the installation. I had left all my explosives gear in locked sea bags at the guard shack on the pier, telling them it was stuff for the transmitter. After we returned to *Garrison County* the Cambode guards left, and I quietly entered warehouse one—
(points with crutch to it on harbor map—closest to *Garrison County*)

METCALF
—and carried my explosives gear inside—it was heavy with the nitrogen bottles and all.

BREUNER
Nitrogen?

METCALF
Yes. It was a nitrogen-enhanced weapon that the Teams had experimented with at Dam Neck, Virginia. If you detonate regular C-4 plastique in a nitrogen-enhanced environment, you get an explosion about 10-15 times more powerful. For field use, all we had to do was make a teepee with a couple of ponchos, set the C-4 charges inside it with nitrogen gas saturating the interior of the teepee—then BOOM—

METCALF
(Laughs nervously)
—Bye-bye warehouses and weapons.

BREUNER
How far did you get before Lieutenant Medici interfered?

CARLSON
Objection—leading. Calls for a legal conclusion that Lieutenant Medici "interfered."

LARKIN
Sustained. Colonel, please keep to the facts, I'll draw the conclusions.

BREUNER
Certainly, your honor.

BREUNER
(to Metcalf)
Did you install the explosives inside the warehouse?

METCALF
Yes. I got into the first warehouse by breaking the hasp. I carried the seabags to the middle of the warehouse—in the middle of the weapons crates—and proceeded to build a hollow pyramid with crates of artillery shells. I stripped the C-4 plastique explosive bars, set detonation cord around them, and connected them all to the timer wire. Then I wrapped the pyramid of crates with the ponchos, sealed them good and tight, and taped the seams. I opened the nitrogen tanks to ooze gas into the teepee nice and slow. There was plenty of gas to keep it saturated for awhile, while the timer was running.

NILO HA TIEN

BREUNER

Then what happened?

METCALF

I was setting the timer, when I hear from behind me someone say in a pretty high voice, "What the hell are you doing?"

BREUNER

Who said that?

METCALF

I turned my head slowly and saw—
                    (points to Medici, voice rises)
THAT Lieutenant pointing a pistol at me!

BREUNER

Were you surprised?

METCALF

I was shocked! First, all I could think was that the Cambodes had caught me—then I couldn't believe one of my own Navy guys was pointing a weapon at me!

BREUNER

Then what happened?

METCALF

He starts some kind of discourse with me about "What am I doing? Why blow the warehouses? No one told HIM what the plan was," like that. Then he says something about the White House sending 2,000 rifles to Cambodia, why would they want to blow up these

279

                             BREUNER
What did you do?

                             METCALF
The lieutenant was obviously confused—and uninformed. I told him the mission was authorized by the Studies and Observations Group—SOG. That's all I could say, I was so astonished. Then he looked really confused.

                             BREUNER
What happened next?

                             METCALF
He told me to cut the wire.

                             BREUNER
From the timer to the explosives?

                             METCALF
Yes. Then he screamed, "Cut the fucking wire now!"

                             BREUNER
What did you do?

                             METCALF
             (Sits up straight in the chair, very formal)
I determined that Lieutenant Medici was an impediment to my mission, and had to be dealt with.

NILO HA TIEN
BREUNER

How did you do that?

METCALF
(Clears his throat)

I was kneeling on one knee. I nodded twice to him, as if to say 'OK,' and unsheathed my big K-Bar knife as if to cut the timer wire. Then there was shouting from the end of the warehouse. Lieutenant Medici was distracted, so I hurled my knife at him. It hit his forehead, and he fell. As I leapt to disarm him, he discharged the pistol—
(Squirms in his chair and looks disdainfully at Medici)
—and by dumb luck hit me in the leg. I was on him where he had fallen to the floor. Next thing I know the ship's exec, Lieutenant Jaygee Poe, and several armed sailors are pulling us apart, calling for the medic and carrying me out—I lost a lot of blood.

BREUNER

Were the warehouses destroyed?

METCALF
(Lowers his eyes; quietly)

No. The ship's armorer told me he disarmed the explosives, disassembled the whole thing, restacked the cases of artillery shells, and threw all the C-4 and nitrogen bottles off the pier. Kinda' cleaned up after me.

BREUNER

Do you believe Lieutenant Medici physically interfered with your carrying out your lawful orders?

CARLSON

Objection—leading, calls for a legal conclusion.

LARKIN
Sustained.

BREUNER
Did Lieutenant Medici physically interfere with your mission to destroy the warehouses?

METCALF
Yes. He screwed the whole deal up.

BREUNER
To your knowledge, did your inability to carry out your mission orders result in any aid or benefit to North Vietnamese forces in Cambodia?

METCALF
I believe so, sir. We have received reports that weapons from the warehouse were removed at night by trucks in the two weeks following June 6th to undisclosed locations in the vicinity of the Cambodia-Vietnam border. Presumably for infiltration into Vietnam or use by North Vietnamese forces along the border.

CARLSON
Objection: "Presumably" and what follows are pure speculation. Move to strike.

LARKIN
Sustained and stricken.

NILO Ha Tien

BREUNER

Nothing further, your honor.

LARKIN

Cross-examination, Commander Carlson?

CARLSON

Yes, your honor.

CARLSON
(Walks slowly to within a few feet of Metcalf)
Petty officer Metcalf, do you speak or read French?

METCALF

No, sir.

CARLSON

Khmer?

METCALF

No, sir.

CARLSON

Vietnamese?

METCALF

Yes, sir. Southern dialect.

CARLSON
Were you sent to school to learn Vietnamese?

METCALF
Yes, sir. Monterrey Defense Language Institute for a year.

CARLSON
Did they also teach Khmer there, if you know?

METCALF
I don't think they did, sir. I understand it's mostly a spoken language and not completely written the way Vietnamese is.

CARLSON
Not written into transliterated English characters, like Vietnamese is?

METCALF
I'm not completely sure, sir, but I think it's in Sanskrit type characters.

CARLSON
Very good—it is Sanskrit-based.

BREUNER
(Stands)
Objection, your honor. This entire line of questioning is irrelevant to the events of June sixth.

NILO Ha Tien

LARKIN

Response, commander?

CARLSON

If the court will indulge me, it is very relevant to Gunner's Mate Metcalf's understanding of events in Cambodia on that day, and the soundness of his orders countermanded by a senior officer present, Lieutenant Medici.

LARKIN

Very well, proceed.

CARLSON

Petty officer Metcalf, can someone trained in Vietnamese understand spoken Khmer?

METCALF

Generally not, sir. The languages come from different cultural and ethnic bases.

CARLSON

What languages did your Cambodian Navy and Army contacts speak in Sihanoukville?

METCALF

Khmer or French to each other, a tiny bit of Vietnamese, and pidgin English to us.

CARLSON

Do you know why they speak French?

METCALF

I believe because all their formal military training was done by the French, in Cambodia and at the French naval and military academies, right up through the 1960s.

CARLSON

You spoke of reading action, political, and intelligence reports from Army and Navy traffic, and broadcasts of enemy propaganda in the area—

METCALF

Yes, sir—

CARLSON

Any of those reports in Khmer, French or Vietnamese?

METCALF

No, sir. They're all in English.

CARLSON

I meant the sources—any of the sources from Khmer, French or Vietnamese language reports?

METCALF
(Hesitates)
Well, I assume some must be, where else would they get that stuff?

CARLSON

Who is "they," Metcalf?

METCALF
Well, the intelligence reporters.

CARLSON
Do you know who these reporters are? Explicitly what their sources are?

METCALF
Well, no sir, they are just reported on the daily message traffic boards. But I do know when we do missions in Vietnam there are generally identified sources from our military intel networks.

CARLSON
From NILOs around Vietnam?

METCALF
In the case of Navy Intel, yes. For the Army it's from the 5-2-5 Military Intelligence Group and Special Forces Teams in the field—generally tactical stuff—unit locations, weapons, maybe reporting the general mission objectives of the units.

CARLSON
Do you regularly review any CIA information or reports in keeping yourself informed?

METCALF
No. That's civilian authority under the U.S. Embassy's control. I'm sure they communicate daily with the military intelligence guys.

CARLSON
Do you know as a fact they do that?

METCALF
Not as a fact, no sir.

CARLSON
Are you sure you were as well-informed as you could be about conditions in Cambodia during your June 6, 1970, mission?

METCALF
(Authoritatively)
YES SIR.

CARLSON
What were the enemy units around Sihanoukville on June sixth?

METCALF
Probably small VC or KR units under cover in town—not enough to pose a serious threat to our mission to set up the shortwave transmitter.

CARLSON
Probably?

METCALF
I was sure enough to require only our own personal weapons and a small Cambodian Army squad for our physical security.

NILO HA TIEN

CARLSON

How about pier and port security for the ship?

METCALF

Commander O'Neill was concerned about his ship, as he should be, but we knew the piers were guarded lightly during the day and usually not at all at night.

CARLSON

From what source?

METCALF

Navy Intel.

CARLSON

From NILO Ha Tien—Lieutenant Medici's reports?

METCALF
(Caught unaware)

Including NILO reports—yes. I don't know if they were NILO Ha Tien—Lieutenant Medici's reports or not.

CARLSON

But you can't say they weren't, correct?

METCALF

Correct.

CARLSON
What did you know about the political situation in Cambodia on June sixth?

METCALF
Well, as I said before, I knew the General Lon Nol government was reportedly on our side after the overthrow of Prince Sihanouk in March. They were our allies for the moment.

CARLSON
Did you think that alliance might change?

METCALF
Of course! I think it was Henry Kissinger who called Cambodia a third-rate, piss-ant country that wasn't going to dictate foreign policy to the U.S. SOG thought Lon Nol could fall any day. We knew there were North Vietnamese Army heavy weapons units holding the capital, Phnom Penh, under siege—that's why they needed the alternate transmitter site in Sihanoukville. You wouldn't know day-to-day what would happen in Cambodia.

CARLSON
Is that how the decision was made by SOG to destroy the warehouses at Sihanoukville?

METCALF
The decision? I'm not sure about how the decision was made, I just follow my orders.

CARLSON
Orders from whom?

METCALF
Like I said before... (Shifts weight in chair) ...it depends.

CARLSON
In this case, petty officer Metcalf, who ordered you to prepare for and execute a covert mission to destroy the warehouses and pier in Sihanoukville on June 6, 1970?

METCALF
(Pauses, looks at Larkin)
Do I have to answer that sir?

LARKIN
(Nods yes)
Yes.

METCALF
Lieutenant Kelly, my Naval Special Warfare Group DET Bravo executive officer. He said it had been determined in consultation with SOG, the Studies and Operations Group.

CARLSON
Did you have written orders to destroy the warehouses?

METCALF
(Looks startled)
Negative, sir. I've never received written orders for any of our missions during two tours in Vietnam.

CARLSON
Nor for missions in Cambodia, correct?

METCALF
Correct. Sir, these are TOP SECRET missions and we can't risk Team or DET security by having written mission orders floating around that could be compromised to the enemy by our
(Makes quotation marks in the air with his fingers)
"allies."

CARLSON
But the gist of your mission was to destroy the warehouses and pier because these new Cambodian allies could flip any day and start aiding Communist forces again—correct?

METCALF
Basically.

CARLSON
Did you discuss at any time the effect that the loss of the port—the only deepwater port in Cambodia—would have on the stability of the flimsy Lon Nol government—our ally?

METCALF
Loss of the port? We were only going to blow the warehouses—

CARLSON
With a nitrogen-enhanced weapon powerful enough to set off the explosives in the second warehouse!

NILO HA TIEN

METCALF

Yes.

CARLSON

You have EOD and nitrogen weapon training. Was there any doubt in your mind that the pier and quay wall would be destroyed in the process?

METCALF

Well, we looked at the location of the warehouses on charts and agent photos. It looked like they were far enough inland to spare the jetties and quay wall. Of course, once an ammo dump goes up, you can't tell what will happen....

CARLSON

Point out the warehouses on the chart, please.

METCALF
(Points with crutch)

CARLSON

Those are big warehouses, aren't they?

METCALF

Yes, sir—longer than a football field and a third as wide. You could fit two *Garrison County*s in each of them.

CARLSON

And where was *Garrison County*?

293

                    METCALF
              (Points with crutch)

                    CARLSON
Seems pretty close, about half a ship length, correct?

                    METCALF
About.

                    CARLSON
But your original mission plan assumed *Garrison County* would be moored in the inner harbor, considerably farther away from the warehouses than where she actually moored, correct?

                    METCALF
         (Considers the harbor map, then quietly)
Correct.

                    CARLSON
What about damage to *Garrison County*?

                    METCALF
I thought we could get her out of there quickly before the explosion.

                    CARLSON
You started the explosives timer around 1630, correct?

NILO HA TIEN

METCALF

Yes.

CARLSON

For a 30-minute delay time?

METCALF

Yes.

CARLSON

Did you ask the Commanding Officer of *Garrison County* if he could get his ship under way that fast?

METCALF

No, the mission was TOP SECRET. I just assumed he could.

CARLSON

So the possibility of destroying the pier at Sihanoukville and causing damage to *Garrison County* was at least generally discussed in preparation for your mission?

METCALF

Very generally. Our objective was to ensure those Communist weapons never got back into circulation to Communist forces in Cambodia—no matter what the political situation.

CARLSON

Petty officer Metcalf, were you aware on June sixth that the Cambodian government had asked the United States to supply 2,000 M-2 carbine rifles to its marine battalions besieged by the North

HL SERRA
Vietnamese Army in the hills around Kep province, Cambodia?

METCALF
(Looks puzzled)
No, sir.

CARLSON
Hypothetically, if this request for rifles existed and you knew about it, would it have changed your thinking about destroying the weapons in the warehouses at Sihanoukville?

METCALF
I don't know—I can't answer that. That's a possibility I never discussed with anyone—if it's true.
(Pauses)
But I can tell you that we usually like to supply our formal allies with our own weapons, not the enemy's. That way if the allies decide to play footsie with enemy units and sell the weapons to them, we know right away when it's our stuff they're shooting at us—it sounds different. If we supply them with enemy weaponry—AK-47s and the like—we never know where they came from, or if our allies are supplying them to the bad guys. So request for rifles or not, the warehouses still would better have been destroyed.

CARLSON
With whom did you discuss the possible consequences of your mission to destroy the warehouses at Sihanoukville?

METCALF
Lieutenant Kelly.

NILO HA TIEN

CARLSON
Anyone else?

METCALF
No. He told me he had discussed it with his liaison at SOG, so everything was okay, and we should blow up the warehouses regardless of any collateral damage it might cause.

CARLSON
You said Phnom Penh was under siege by North Vietnamese Army forces: the airport was closed, correct?

METCALF
Yes.

CARLSON
Even boat shipments of fuel, food, and ammunition were stopped on the Mekong River for a time, correct?

METCALF
Yes.

CARLSON
With the port of Sihanoukville out of order, Cambodia would be a dead duck from the standpoint of supply and logistics, correct?

METCALF
I—I don't know, sir. That's not my area of expertise.

HL Serra
                    CARLSON
Is it Lieutenant Kelly's area of expertise?

                    METCALF
I'm not sure, sir. We just knew the mission had been OK'd by SOG.

                    CARLSON
Through Lieutenant Kelly, correct?

                    METCALF
Yes.

                    CARLSON
What is his full name and rank?

                    METCALF
Lieutenant
                         (shifts in his chair)
junior grade
                    (everyone turns to look at Metcalf —
                    Kelly is only a Lieutenant jaygee!)
William C. Kelly, USNR, SEAL Team One, DET Bravo executive officer.

                    CARLSON
He's only a jaygee!

                    METCALF
Yes, sir.

NILO HA TIEN

CARLSON
(Pauses to let the astonishing fact sink in with Larkin, who keeps his eyes on Metcalf. Carlson walks back and forth behind counsel table for a few seconds, then turns to Metcalf)
One more thing: Did Lieutenant Medici give you a direct order to stop your mission to blow the warehouses?

METCALF
Sir, when an officer points a cocked 9mm pistol at me and shouts, "Cut the fucking wire!"—that's a direct order in my book.
(Metcalf, Larkin, counsel and Medici all laugh at this)

CARLSON
(Still smiling)
Nothing further of this witness, your honor.

LARKIN
Very well, commander. Redirect Colonel Breuner?

BREUNER
(Stands)
Petty officer Metcalf, is there any doubt in your mind what your covert mission orders were in Sihanoukville on June 6th?

METCALF
No, sir: blow the warehouses on the pier if they contained Communist weapons.

BREUNER
Did you accomplish that mission?

                    METCALF
No, sir.

                    BREUNER
Why?

                    METCALF
Because Lieutenant Medici interfered.

                    BREUNER
(Paces a few steps, stands behind Medici, then asks Metcalf)
What's the prognosis on your leg, son?

                    METCALF
It's a deep wound and healing slowly. Fortunately Lieutenant Medici missed the bone, but the doc says I'm out of field operations for good—
                    (Turns and glares at Medici)
—SOG or SEAL.

                    BREUNER
No further questions.

                    LARKIN
Colonel Breuner, your next witness?

                    BREUNER
No further witnesses, your honor. Judge Advocate rests.

NILO Ha Tien

LARKIN
Commander Carlson, your first witness.

CARLSON
Lieutenant Thomas N. Medici.

YEOMAN
(Yeoman leads Medici to stand, swears him with Bible)
Do you solemnly swear that the testimony you are about to give shall be the truth, the whole truth, and nothing but the truth, so help you God?

MEDICI
I do. (Sits)

CARLSON
Your full name?

MEDICI
Thomas N. Medici, Lieutenant, USNR, 7-2-8-4-7-1.

CARLSON
Your billet?

MEDICI
NILO Ha Tien: Naval Intelligence Liaison Officer—direct member of Admiral Zumwalt's Naval Forces Vietnam staff. I report directly to Admiral Zumwalt and his Chief of Staff for Intelligence.

CARLSON
Are you on independent Naval duty?

MEDICI
Yes, sir. I have my own communications call signs and independent billet description.

CARLSON
What does that mean, Lieutenant?

MEDICI
It means I'm a completely independent duty station with a complement of one—me—just like a ship is a completely independent unit.

CARLSON
What's a NILO?

MEDICI
NILOs perform independent field intelligence collection and analysis, both with their own eyes and ears and through reports of their field agents. We also coordinate intelligence efforts—"liaise"—with our Vietnamese and American military and civilian counterparts in the intelligence community.

CARLSON
Such as?

MEDICI
I attend a daily DIOCC meeting in Ha Tien with the Vietnamese

NILO HA TIEN

District Chief, the local Regional Force commander, the local Chief of National Police, the local Vietnamese Navy NILO.

CARLSON

Do you do any original intelligence collection work?

MEDICI

Yes, sir. I manage a Naval spy network of agents called Collection Team 5—CT-5. I receive and process their reports through a principal interpreter—the net handler. This network has been expanded during my time in Ha Tien to cover the Vietnam-Cambodia border from the Gulf of Thailand to the Bassac River, and north along the Cambodian coast all the way to Thailand.

CARLSON

Where is Ha Tien? Can you point it out on the map?

MEDICI

(Points to Ha Tien on large map of Indo-China)
Smack-dab on the Vietnam-Cambodia border where it hits the Gulf of Thailand. We are WAAAY out there. Kind of the Barstow of Vietnam.

CARLSON

Do you have any direct access to any other original intelligence reports?

MEDICI

Yes. I board with Frank Brown, an Army warrant officer who runs the 5-2-5 Military Intelligence Group outpost in Ha Tien. He and I are very good friends and colleagues. We share a lot of original intel

HL Serra

product and work on new collection schemes and tasking for our agents. We also devise collection missions where I do the collection personally—whereever I need to go.

CARLSON

I thought your area of operations was the Ha Tien area in Vietnam?

MEDICI

It was—is. I try daily to brief whatever American patrol boats are in the area about any specific threats that our agents uncover, before the boats go on night ambush.

CARLSON

Where do they patrol?

MEDICI
(Points on the map)

The Vinh Te Canal along the Vietnam-Cambodia border, and the Rach Giang Thanh River connecting it to the Gulf. We are in the area the North Vietnamese Army calls its Military Region 3—where all the weapons and ammunition for the Mekong Delta come into Vietnam from Cambodia. The patrol boats' job is to intercept those weapons shipments.

CARLSON

Has your job changed at all since you've been NILO Ha Tien—since the beginning of 1970?

MEDICI

Yes, a lot. My collection efforts have gone from local to more broadly strategic—where the stuff is landed, stored, shipped, and infiltrated

NILO HA TIEN
through Cambodia into Vietnam.

CARLSON
Precisely to stop this infiltration is why we conducted an invasion—excuse me—"incursion" into Cambodia in April of this year, correct?

MEDICI
Yes, sir. We tried to mop up the Communist supply depots along the Cambodian side of the border—the "sanctuaries." You'll recall that former head of state Prince Sihanouk professed Cambodian neutrality, while looking the other way from North Vietnamese Army supply activities on the border with Vietnam.

CARLSON
What do you mean your job changed to focus more on "strategic" intelligence?

MEDICI
Political intelligence. For instance, Frank Brown recruited as an agent the Recording Secretary of the new Cambodian Cabinet.
(Larkin, Breuner, mouths open, stare in disbelief.)

LARKIN
I order everyone here to treat this information as TOP SECRET SPECIAL INTELLIGENCE, and not repeat it to anyone outside this room. The agent's life may depend on it.

MEDICI
Not necessary, Captain. He was killed at the end of May. I saw him get it.

LARKIN
I still don't want the information repeated outside this room. Continue, Lieutenant.

MEDICI
We were the first to hear and report that Prince Sihanouk was ousted as head of state by his cousin, the parliamentary leader, Sirik Matak, and replaced by the government of the Lon brothers— Lon Nol and Lon Non.

CARLSON
Why is political intelligence so important from Cambodia?

MEDICI
Because the new Lon Nol government has stopped Communist weapons shipments into Sihanoukville. Certain Cambodian Generals —including Lon Nol and Lon Non—used to receive half the weapons that were imported into Sihanoukville to sell to whomever they wanted. That was the bribe necessary so the other half could be shipped down to the border into Vietnam for the Viet Cong and North Vietnamese Army units there.

MEDICI
(Medici sits straight up.)

The point is, that traffic has stopped completely in the last three months due to the goodwill of this new, shaky Cambodian regime— and possibly some payments from the CIA. To their credit, the Lon brothers have resisted all inducements by the Communists to resume shipments—resisted the offer of bigger bribes; resisted the offer by the Chinese to ensure that the popular Prince Sihanouk "has a plane crash"—their words, not mine—while in China under asylum, in order to eliminate popular resistance to the new Lon regime. And they are now resisting—barely—North Vietnamese efforts to capture Phnom Penh by closing the airport, blockading the Mekong, destroying Radio Phnom Penh, and cutting off petroleum imports to the country.

MEDICI
(Turns to Larkin)
This is one shaky but steadfast government. Its survival means the enemy units in the delta will die a slow death of attrition from the weapons cutoff. That's why ensuring the survival of Cambodia—and this government—is so important.

CARLSON
How do you know all this?

MEDICI
From my agents, from 5-2-5 Military Intelligence agents, and discussions with intel staff in Saigon. And from Khmer, Vietnamese, and French language intel agent reports.

CARLSON
Any input from civilian agencies?

MEDICI
I speak periodically with the CIA regional chief—one way: he asks, I report. Never anything from them. We heard that they have no agents in Cambodia, so have to debrief refugees coming across the border at Ha Tien, and steal what intel they can from us.

CARLSON
Why do you speak with them if they offer nothing?

MEDICI

Because I was ordered to by the U.S. Ambassador! Our Cambodian intelligence was so good—or the CIA had so little—that I was ordered to limit distribution of my reports only to the CIA station chief, to General Abrams, Admiral Zumwalt, and the White House Situation Room. I had to cut out my zone boss, and it pissed him off and got me in trouble.

CARLSON

Are you consulted by anyone on Cambodian matters?

MEDICI

All the time. I'm jokingly called "Our man in Cambodia." Civilian, Army, and Navy Intelligence brass come up to Ha Tien regularly for briefings or for me to be their tour guide in border Cambodia. That's how I met John Paul Vann….

BREUNER

I object, your honor. This discussion is irrelevant to what Lieutenant Medici did on June 6th.

CARLSON

Not at all, your honor. I'm painting the picture of what the senior officer present in the warehouses—Lieutenant Medici—knew at the time of the incident that compelled him to act as he did.

LARKIN

I agree with Colonel Breuner that this testimony seems to be getting far afield, but upon Commander Carlson's offer of its relevance, I'm inclined to let the witness continue—but not until we take a break.
(Looks around)

LARKIN
It's too damn hot in here. I'll see how the techs are doing with the air conditioner. Recess for 10 minutes, gentlemen.
(Raps his gavel; Larkin leaves)
(O'Neill, Breuner, Carlson, Medici and Metcalf in room)

O'NEILL
(Walks up to Medici)
Don't think you're going to get away with this, Lieutenant. You goddam reserves come into the Navy with your outrageous conduct and ideas....

CARLSON
(Steps in front of O'Neill, face-to-face.)
That's enough, Lieutenant-commander. I ask you as a gentleman to restrain your remarks and leave him alone. Your lawyer will have his chance at him on cross-examination.

O'NEILL
(O'Neill gives one last contemptuous look at Medici, then faces Carlson, starts to say something, then walks away briskly and mutters.)
Slick bastard!

MEDICI
(Hangdog look, head down, when Breuner is gone.)
Is Breuner going to rip me on cross-examination?

CARLSON
I don't know. He's seen all your service reports and claims to have

HL Serra

talked to the people you worked with. He's very thorough. I hope you've been candid with me about any other boo-boos you made up there.

MEDICI
(Sits up, nervous)

Do you think he's talked to Redkin—about the mortar ammunition?

CARLSON

I don't know. I've been unable to contact Redkin. They said he was out on patrol.

MEDICI

Is Larkin getting the point?

CARLSON
(Looks blankly at the empty dais.)

I hope so.

(Goes out steel door.)

YEOMAN
(Approaches Medici)

Excuse me, Mr. Medici. The intel boss asked me to make sure you still want to be considered for deep selection by the Lieutenant-Commander Promotion Board. It meets in Washington next week, and we'll need to assemble all your fitness reports and certificates for all your medals if you still want to be considered.

MEDICI

Yes, I still want to be considered by the Lieutenant-Commander

NILO HA TIEN

Board. Please have them put the package together.

YEOMAN

But the boss thought, with the Inquiry and all, you might want to wait.

MEDICI
(Explodes)
Goddammit, Yeoman! What part of "yes" don't you understand?

YEOMAN
(Backing away)

Aye-aye, sir.

MEDICI
(Turns, finds himself looking at Metcalf who sits in a chair with crutches on table. He and Metcalf try to avoid each other's stare, then look directly at each other, Medici vacant, Metcalf with anger.)

METCALF
(Metcalf tries to stand, falters on his wounded leg and falls back into chair, defeated by pain. Then he raises one crutch and smashes it on the counsel table with a resounding crack.)

METCALF

You bastard!

MEDICI
(Hangs head down.)

50

Inquiry - Second Session

(Medici on stand. Carlson continues questioning. Larkin, Breuner, Metcalf and Yeoman seated at tables)

CARLSON
Lieutenant, do you speak any languages?

MEDICI
English, French, Vietnamese, southern dialect.

CARLSON
In what language are your field agent reports from your network?

MEDICI
French—written on rice paper by the principal interpreter, the man who recruits the agents, pays them, and solicits weekly information, then delivers the reports to me. I also receive reports from the Vietnamese NILO of Vietnamese and Khmer agents—those are translated into French.

CARLSON
How can you understand these reports?

MEDICI
Commander, I'm fluent in French, that's why I was sent to Ha Tien.

NILO HA TIEN
I'm an honors graduate of Princeton in Politics, with a minor in French. Almost all the Cambodes were either educated in French at local lycées, or in France, or used French in dealings with the old colonial government. I'm quite good at the language.

CARLSON
How do you judge that?

MEDICI
Well, I'm good enough that I was able to negotiate the weapons deal with the Cambodian Navy for their Marine battalions at Kep. I got a medal for it!

CARLSON
Tell us about that.

MEDICI
A Cambodian Navy corvette sailed into Vietnamese waters off Ha Tien in April and signaled our LST to send an interpreter. Captain Brown of *USS Whitfield County* called me on the radio and asked me to come talk to them. I rode out on a patrol boat to the Cambodian ship. I was received cordially by Captain Som Sary, and I instructed our boat to leave, that I would be okay.

CARLSON
This was before we knew the Cambodians had decided to switch sides, correct?

MEDICI
Yes—but I had been in Cambodia before and I trusted the people. I trusted Som Sary. We spoke, finally, in French for four hours, and

he made the official request from Lon Nol for 3,000 M-2 carbines from the U.S. to save their Marine battalions surrounded by North Vietnamese units at Kep, Cambodia, about eight miles north of the Vietnam border. They were desperate. We knew the North Vietnamese had begun to capture the border areas of Cambodia to continue their weapons shipments regardless of whose side the new government took.

CARLSON

What did you do?

MEDICI

I returned to Captain Brown's ship, sent a TOP SECRET FLASH message to Saigon with the request, and waited—and waited. Finally Som Sary had to get under way back to the Cambodian Naval base at Ream near Sihanoukville and said he would return in two days. I heard nothing back from Saigon for two days, then just a short message from intel staff saying, "Everything A-OK," nothing else. Som Sary came back, I went aboard and reported Saigon's response. Som Sary just smiled and said, "Okay, je le comprends. C'est okay." He then took me on a tour of the Cambodian coast on his ship for a few days. I did some recon and found their maps and charts—old French jobs—to be inaccurate. We returned to An Thoi, I got off and Som Sary steamed back to Cambodia. And I didn't see him again—until Sihanoukville.

(Larkin turns and looks at Medici, puzzled.)

CARLSON

What about the 3,000 rifles?

MEDICI

I didn't know what happened, since no one reported back to me. But when I flew to Phu Quoc Island to catch the *Garrison County*

NILO Ha Tien

for this mission, there was a big black Air Force CONEX container by the airstrip. I asked the NILO there what that was, and he said, "I'm not sure. Probably an installment of the rifles the CIA has been delivering to Cambodia by Air America."

BREUNER

Objection, hearsay.

CARLSON

Your honor, offered for LIEUTENANT Medici's state of mind when he did what followed. May I continue?

LARKIN

Yes, let's see where you're going with this.

CARLSON

What did you do next, Lieutenant?

MEDICI

I examined the CONEX container, which was heavily sealed. Stenciled in new paint on its side was "Carbines, M-2, 500 each." I concluded that the CIA had made good on the delivery of the weapons.
(Larkin, Breuner, Metcalf now all listening, rapt.)

CARLSON

(Pauses, walks back and forth behind counsel table, then stops)
OK, Lieutenant. And you did all the negotiations with the Cambodians in French language, as well as your agent reports being in French?

HL Serra
MEDICI
Yes.

CARLSON
Now, what precisely was *your* mission to Sihanoukville on June 6th, 1970?

MEDICI
To conduct a port survey using personnel of *Garrison County*, and to ascertain HOW to take out the port of Sihanoukville IF we had to.

LARKIN
(Larkin looks puzzled.)
Not to destroy the port, Lieutenant?

MEDICI
No sir, not then. As I was trying to say before, these negotiations were going on with the Cambodes. The new government had stopped the enemy weapons shipments into Sihanoukville, and we were doing all we could to shore up the government against the all-out attack by the North Vietnamese—which began as soon as they knew the weapons shipments had stopped. The Mekong was blockaded on and off for supplies to Phnom Penh—Ponchetong airport was closed to air traffic—all they had left was the Port of Sihanoukville. We knew Cambodia might fall, and then we might have to destroy the port. But until that happened we HAD to keep the port open as a last means of supply. We had plans laid to run truck convoys from the port up Route 2 to Phnom Penh. It would be difficult and dangerous but a last resort to save the new government. That's why I was sent to obtain information on the port. And that's the intellectual reason I knew something was out of whack when I saw what Metcalf was attempting to do.

CARLSON
You said "intellectual reason." Was there another reason?

MEDICI
Yes—intuitive. Commander Holland, my boss in Saigon, would have told me about the SOG plan to blow the warehouses. I believed to a certainty he would never have led me into a mission with that kind of risk without informing me, regardless of its security classification. What's more, he never would send me on a merely academic mission. If he knew the port was to be blown, why send me to find out how to do it?

CARLSON
Any other reason?

MEDICI
USS Garrison County. They wouldn't risk that ship and those men so close to the explosion of a major ammo dump without making sure the ship was well clear in plenty of time. That's how we do things in N-2.

LARKIN
(Larkin makes a note.)

CARLSON
(Carlson walks around behind the counsel table
to let the last answer sink in, then continues)
Lieutenant, did you accomplish your mission to Sihanoukville?

MEDICI
Yes, but barely.

HL Serra
CARLSON
What do you mean?

MEDICI
We accomplished the port survey part fine on the way in, photographed the piers, warehouses, quay wall, sounded the channel, precisely plotted the location of all navigational marks.

MEDICI
(Clears his throat, shifts in his chair.)

This is where it really starts to sound goofy. I went ashore shortly after the dignitaries were received on *Garrison County* when we berthed that morning. I waited for a taxi at the foot of the piers in my civilian clothes, with a camera, but without a weapon. I was trying to be a tourist best I could, for a Caucasian wandering around Sihanoukville. Then who of all people drives by, but Captain Som Sary of the Cambodian Naval ship—the guy I had negotiated the weapons deal with. He's in a Navy Jeep with his Exec. I'm devastated—my mission is blown—they know who I am and likely why I'm there. In a flash I get paranoid, calculating how they knew I would be there, were they setting me up, like that.

They see me and are all smiles, shouts and waves. They stop and ask me if I need a ride, where am I going? I say just around town, a little "tourisme," some "photographie." They say "Bon! We will take you—a friend of Cambodia."

I try to beg off, but they graciously insist I come with them. I get in. They drive me all around the port and city, take me to eat, to see the hotel and casino, take photos at all the tourist spots. More food, more drink. I think my mission is sunk. We buy batik material so I can have some cool Cambodian Bermuda shorts. I buy them gas at the ESSO station. We have a jolly good time, and I've concluded they probably don't want to kill me, because of the weapons deal.
(Clears his throat, shifts his weight in chair)

MEDICI

We end the afternoon at a cafe overlooking the new walled harbor—the one built by the French to protect berthed ships from the dangerous swell of the southwest monsoon. There's an odd craft anchored in the harbor that we watch. The port captain of Sihanoukville joins us at our table. Som Sary tells him what a friend of Cambodia I am. I ask what the funny little ship is. He says a French suction dredge that breaks down constantly. A gift to Cambodia to protect the harbor from currents that silt it up so fast it must be dredged each week or the harbor would be rendered useless in only six weeks! French engineering! Aye yie yie!

(Medici sits up, looks at the Board and smiles.)

MEDICI

BINGO! There it was, at the end of my tourist day, the elegant answer of how to take out the port: sink the dredge and the harbor will silt up and become useless.

(Larkin smiles, but shakes his head.)

CARLSON

So your mission was accomplished. What did you do then?

MEDICI

They drop me off at *Garrison County*. I find Metcalf gone and in the warehouses. I get my Browning—I just know something's not right—run down to the warehouses, and I find him there ready to explode them. All this goes through my mind about saving the new Cambodian government and about Commander Holland not putting me in this predicament.

HL Serra
MEDICI
(Looks directly at Metcalf.)
I yelled at Metcalf to cut the wire—then the shouting in the warehouse, Metcalf threw something, hit my head, and was on top of me—and the pistol went off.
(Deflates, looks at Larkin with a far-away, spent look,
then speaks quietly, with humility)
It seems incredible to me as I relate it here today.

CARLSON
Do you know what, if anything, happened to the weapons in those warehouses SINCE June sixth?

MEDICI
Yes. My agent reported—
(Looks at Metcalf)
in French—
(Turns back to Larkin.)
that they were all trucked out over 12 nights to Governor Um Samuth's palace in Bokor Province in the Elephant Mountains southeast of Sihanoukville, where they are under constant guard by Lon Nol's Cambodian Army. He counted the trucks and saw the cases being removed from the warehouses — and one night rode with the trucks to Bokor.
(Medici reaches into his pocket and pulls out a rice paper report
with French writing on it.)
I have the report right here.

BREUNER
Objection—hearsay.

CARLSON
Business records exception. Lieutenant Medici's agent reports are

NILO Ha Tien
business records maintained in the normal course of business—intelligence collection for Naval staff.

LARKIN
Overruled.

CARLSON
Forces of the government friendly to U.S. efforts, Lieutenant? That is, not the North Vietnamese or Khmer Rouge?

MEDICI
Yes. The Cambodes moved them inland to Bokor where they would be less exposed to—let me translate—
    (Reads *sotto voce* in French from rice paper report)

MEDICI
"... *operations de cowboy pour les détruire par les unites secrètes du gouvernement des États-Unis*"—
    (Looks up at Carlson, in full voice)

MEDICI
—where they would be less exposed to "Cowboy operations to destroy them by secret units of the U.S. government."—their words, not mine.

LARKIN
    (Shakes his head in exasperation)
Goddam French never left this place.

CARLSON
Your honor, could we take a short break?

LARKIN
Yes. Do you have more questions for Lieutenant Medici?

CARLSON
I think I can finish quickly with him after the break, your honor.

LARKIN
Colonel Breuner, are you ready to cross-examine Lieutenant Medici when we resume?

BREUNER
Yes, your honor—READY!

LARKIN
(Taps gavel)
We'll take a 15-minute recess.
(Larkin, Breuner and Metcalf leave room.)

MEDICI
Breuner didn't put on any evidence of the violation of the Presidential Order about no ammunition to the Cambodes—does that mean he dropped it?

CARLSON
Maybe, but he's smart. I think he's saving it for your cross-examination. To help him with his other charges.

MEDICI
(Medici stands up from witness chair, stretches and smiles at Carlson. Steps down.)

NILO HA TIEN

CARLSON
What are you smiling at Lieutenant? You look like the Cheshire cat.

MEDICI
We got my story out, didn't we?

CARLSON
Yes, but I'm not sure Larkin looks at it the same way you do. All this agent report bullshit, your trips into Cambodia with these Naval officers—illegal and in violation of neutrality—and who knows what the Cambodes motives are? You live in a different world than line officers.

MEDICI
(Incensed, full of hubris.)
I AM a line officer, Commander. I'm doing this job because I asked for it, and it needs to be done with some finesse, not just blowing shit up all the time. I was a gunfire director officer on *USS Tulsa*. I blew stuff up all the time with her 6-inch guns. You may think this is a fruitcake job. But it's real, and it makes a difference.

CARLSON
(Turning to leave room.)
Let's hope Larkin thinks so.
(Carlson leaves room.
Yeoman approaches Medici, hesitant)

YEOMAN
Lieutenant, Intel boss sent this note about the Lieutenant-commander Promotion Board....

MEDICI
Dammit, man! YES! I want my files in front of that Board next week! I could become the youngest Lieutenant-commander in the Navy's history….

YEOMAN
Sir, you just need to sign this file release form. That's all I meant.

MEDICI
(Glares at Yeoman, grabs papers, scribbles signature, slaps pen on the papers, and walks off.)

51

Inquiry—Third Session

(Larkin, Carlson, Metcalf seated, Medici on witness stand being cross-examined by Breuner, standing.)

BREUNER
Lieutenant, what's an order to you?

MEDICI
Sir?

BREUNER
What is a military order to you? Define it.

MEDICI
When a superior officer in my chain of command directs me to do or not do something, I obey.

BREUNER
Well, what about your standing orders from N-2, the staff, and Admiral Zumwalt. Do you obey them?

MEDICI
Yes, sir.

HL Serra

BREUNER
When they order you not to go into Cambodia by yourself....

MEDICI
(Squirms in chair.)
They never really ORDER me NOT to go.

BREUNER
Have you ever discussed directly with Commander Holland, or the Chief of Staff for Intel, or Admiral Zumwalt your forays into Cambodia, and their views about your actions?

MEDICI
(Looks at Carlson)

MEDICI
Not directly.

BREUNER
Indirectly?

MEDICI
(Looks at Carlson for guidance; Carlson just sits there calmly.)
I guess so.

BREUNER
You GUESS so?
(Picks up a folder of message reports.)

NILO Ha Tien

BREUNER

You have sent reports of your forays into Cambodia—before the Sihanoukville mission—to Naval Intel staff and others, correct?

MEDICI

Yes.

BREUNER

Cambodia was a neutral country in this war when you went to Ha Tien in February 1970, correct?

MEDICI

Well, technically....

BREUNER

What do our Rules of Engagement say about entering Cambodian territory or shooting into Cambodia?

MEDICI

That we are not permitted on Cambodian territory unless we are first shot at from Cambodia, then we may enter Cambodia and shoot back in hot pursuit.

BREUNER

The "Hot Pursuit" exception, right?

MEDICI

Yes. But we know Cambodia was not really neutral, because Prince Sihanouk turned a blind eye to the North Vietnamese shipping weapons into Vietnam across the border, and in fact we knew

HL SERRA
Communist weapons were being brought into Sihanoukville by the shipload for transport into Vietnam.

BREUNER
Something of a dilemma, right?

MEDICI
Of course. But we need to know what's going on in Cambodia—so I go in.

BREUNER
So that dilemma is your justification for illegal entries into Cambodia in violation of the Rules of Engagement?

CARLSON
Objection. Question states a legal conclusion, that any particular entry into Cambodia violated the Rules of Engagement.

LARKIN
Sustained—Colonel, please limit your questions to specifics.

CARLSON
It's also irrelevant to what happened on June sixth.

BREUNER
But not to this officer's state of mind about what his ACTUAL orders are, and WHETHER he obeys them.

NILO HA TIEN

LARKIN
(Looks peevishly at Medici.)
You may continue this line of questioning about specifics, if you have them, Colonel.

BREUNER
Lieutenant Medici, you admit that you have entered Cambodia numerous times since February 1970, correct?

MEDICI
(Very quietly)
Yes.

BREUNER
Did anyone on Naval staff ever discuss with you your expeditions into Cambodia?

MEDICI
They might have.

BREUNER
Did Captain Ross, your Chief of Staff for Intelligence, ever discuss these expeditions with you?

MEDICI
Yes.

BREUNER
Did he not tell you they were illegal, and that if you were caught there, the Navy would have to disavow you and your mission?

MEDICI
What I remember is that he said my expeditions were "cheeky." He says stuff like that.

BREUNER
Did he warn you of consequences of getting caught?

MEDICI
I think so—but he also said he was pleased at the original intel I was getting from those trips.

BREUNER
How about Commander Holland, your mentor at N-2. Didn't he warn you what you were doing was illegal?

MEDICI
(Flushed at mention of Commander Holland)
I didn't take it as a lecture on the legality of what I do. I took it as his sincere personal concern for my safety, and staff's inability to help me if I got caught.

BREUNER
So you never saw those warnings as ORDERS not to go into Cambodia?

MEDICI
No. They were NOT orders. They were cautions.

NILO HA TIEN

BREUNER

Let me ask you some specifics, Lieutenant.

BREUNER

(Opens file, picks up one sheet and reads.)

Did you on February 18, 1970, debark River Patrol Boat 14 of River Division Five, with Lieutenant jaygee Marks as officer in charge, on the Cambodian side of the Giang Thanh River at the border, and walk armed into the Cambodian hamlet of Ton Hon?

MEDICI

I don't remember the exact date. But yes, I did.

BREUNER

Did you have orders to go into Ton Hon?

MEDICI

I was tasked to see how much diesel fuel was for sale there in the market—we suspected that over 50 percent of the diesel we supplied to the South Vietnamese is sold on the black market at the border and ends up in enemy hands. So I guess in a way I was ordered to find out about the diesel, and the only way to do it firsthand was to go in. Since we were there, we laid sensors on the way out along the trails the Red Star Transportation Battalion used to cross the river at night.

BREUNER

But no direct orders from N-2 or anyone else, correct?

MEDICI

Correct.

BREUNER
(Takes another sheet of paper from the file and reads.)
Did you in early March 1970 call in Naval gunfire from the U.S. Coast Guard cutter *Kodiak* onto Nui Dai Dung mountain on the Cambodian border?

MEDICI
(Squirms)
Yes, but there had been enemy trucks transporting weapons in and around the mountain, and we never could reach them with the four deuce mortar at Ha Tien. The cutter was shallow draft and could get in close enough to shoot them up.

BREUNER
Did not some of the rounds go long over Dai Dung into Cambodia?

MEDICI
Probably.

BREUNER
Were you under orders to shoot into Cambodia?

MEDICI
No.

BREUNER
Was the action in hot pursuit?

MEDICI
No.

NILO HA TIEN

BREUNER
(Takes another sheet from folder)
Lieutenant, do you know Warrant Officer third Stan Zablocki?

MEDICI
Yes.

BREUNER
Did you not organize with him a "Navy Fire Team" to man an 81mm mortar at points around the Ha Tien peninsula?

MEDICI
Yes, we did. To have some land-based naval firepower so we wouldn't have to rely on the Army in emergencies.

BREUNER
Was there such an emergency on March 12, 1970, when you and your fire team set up near Thach Dong Regional Force outpost and placed mortar fire on the slopes of Nui Dai Dung mountain?

MEDICI
Well, it was—kind of. The North Vietnamese Army had been moving weapons around the back of the mountain, which would all end up in Vietnam and be used against us. We tried to shake them up at night.

BREUNER
On the Vietnam or Cambodian side of the mountain?

MEDICI

Well, probably both.

BREUNER

In hot pursuit?

MEDICI

Not exactly.

BREUNER

What happened to you on the 13th of March?

MEDICI

I don't remember.

BREUNER

You don't remember the combat action for which you were awarded a Bronze Star?

MEDICI
(Sheepish)

Oh, that day. We drove up to the border to see what damage we had done with the mortar the day before. We had seen secondary explosions and wanted to see what we hit. Frank Brown drove out with me during the afternoon. Before we got to the border…
(Sits up, excited.)
…the North Vietnamese on Dai Dung started mortaring us! We spent the afternoon and evening in a ditch. The major declared it a "Tac-E"—tactical emergency—and we had all kinds of aircraft up from Canh Tho bombing the bejeesus out of Dai Dung. I acted as forward observer till the real ones got there to continue the bombing.

NILO HA TIEN

BREUNER

All in hot pursuit, correct?

MEDICI

Yeah, I guess that was actual hot pursuit of fire from Cambodia.

BREUNER

And how long did it continue?

MEDICI

Umm…about two weeks, day and night. There was little left of the North Vietnamese caves on either side of Die Young when the bombing ended.

BREUNER

And all based on your unsolicited fire into Cambodia, in violation of the Rules of Engagement on March 12, correct?

MEDICI

I guess you could look at it that way.

BREUNER

Were you proud of that, Lieutenant?

MEDICI

Proud? No.
    (Grins gleefully.)
But the weapons infiltration stopped at Ha Tien, and we sure slept a lot better at night from then on!
  (Larkin and Carlson stifle snickers, Breuner looks peeved)

BREUNER
(Takes another sheet of paper and reads.)
Do you know Gunner's mate Second Class Redkin?

MEDICI
(Looks at Carlson, shrinks into witness chair.)
Yes, he runs the armory for the river division at Ha Tien.

BREUNER
He is responsible for all the Navy's weapons and ammunition stored in Ha Tien, correct?

MEDICI
Yes.

BREUNER
Do you remember obtaining from Redkin six cases of 60 mike-mike mortar ammunition—two high explosive, two white phosphorous, and two air burst—on March 28, 1970?

MEDICI
I'm not sure of the date or amounts.

BREUNER
(Holds up green canvas-covered Navy logbook.)
Would it refresh your recollection to see Redkin's detailed armorer's log regarding the date and details?

NILO HA TIEN

MEDICI
No. I assume Redkin's entry is correct.

BREUNER
What did you tell Redkin the mortar shells were for?

MEDICI
A special operation we were doing next day.

BREUNER
In fact, didn't you provide that ammunition to the Cambodian District Chief of Kampong Trach district along the border?

MEDICI
That was the purpose of getting the shells. But I don't know for sure that they got to him.

BREUNER
(Takes another sheet from file)
Do you remember an Air America helo pilot named Ned Anderson?

MEDICI
Uhhh, was he the guy who flew the stuff into Kampong Trach?

BREUNER
That's the guy.

HL Serra

MEDICI
Yes, I loaded the six cases into an Air America helo for direct delivery—I was told—to the Kampong Trach District Chief.

BREUNER
Did not Anderson remind you that giving ammo to the Cambodes violated a Presidential Order?

MEDICI
(Nervously.)

Ahh, maybe....

BREUNER
To which you responded with the "Fuck Nixon and his Kraut" remark?

MEDICI
(Meekly.)

Yeah.

BREUNER
And this happened on or about March 29, 1970?

MEDICI
(Dejected)

Yes, the day after I got the ammo from Redkin.

BREUNER
(Takes out a Naval message)

Lieutenant Medici, do you remember receiving this ALL

NILO Ha Tien

COMMANDS message to your communications address on or about March 20, 1970, nine days before this ammo transfer?
(Flips a copy to Carlson, hands one toLARKIN,
shows original to Medici)

MEDICI
(Dejected, reads message cursorily, but knows what it is)
I think so.

BREUNER

Please read it out loud.

MEDICI
(Mumbles.)
From Commander in Chief, blah-blah-blah....

BREUNER

Out loud, Lieutenant!

MEDICI
(Sits up, reads louder.)
It's from "CINC—Commander in Chief—the President—to ALL COMMANDS Vietnam. Dated March 20, 1970, and it requires us to "NOT, repeat NOT, provide ammunition or weapons to Cambodian forces during this critical period of review of Cambodian-U.S. relations."

BREUNER

Were you aware of this message before you caused the mortar shells to be provided to the Kampong Trach District Chief?

HL Serra
CARLSON
Objection. I must assert the Lieutenant's Fifth Amendment privilege against self-incrimination.

LARKIN
I believe he has waived the privilege, commander, by taking the stand.

CARLSON
Then I also object because the line of questioning is irrelevant—Colonel Breuner put on no evidence of the violation of the Presidential Order in his case in chief. I therefore move to dismiss that charge.

LARKIN
That motion was appropriate at the close of Colonel Breuner's case.

CARLSON
I could have made the motion your honor, but I assumed Colonel Breuner had abandoned the charge. I would have advised Lieutenant Medici differently if I had known Colonel Breuner had intended to question him about it. So my position is that you should either grant the dismissal of that charge, and rule Colonel Breuner's questions on it irrelevant, or permit the question, and allow me to advise my client of his Fifth Amendment rights on this specific issue.

LARKIN
Well, I'm inclined to allow the question, and the Privilege is personal. Do you wish to assert it Lieutenant Medici?

MEDICI
(Looks at Carlson, looks down)

NILO HA TIEN
No, your honor, I do not assert it.

CARLSON
Your honor, may I have a moment to counsel my client?

MEDICI
Commander, I'm okay. I want to get the facts out.
    (Turns to LARKIN, looks unburdened)
Sir, the North Vietnamese were overrunning Kampong Trach District in the days immediately after Prince Sihanouk was deposed, in order to capture that part of the border to continue their weapons movement into Vietnam. The district chief was an ally of ours for years. He reported regularly on North Vietnamese weapons crossing at the border in his district, at great personal risk. He had virtually no local troops or weapons, or ammunition—a few rifles and a 60 millimeter mortar tube. We thought the least we could do was send him some ammo to defend himself until Dr. Kissinger got off his butt and decided what to do about Cambodia after his "critical period of review,"—which was actually Kissinger's vacation! Don't forget, we didn't invade the border sanctuaries in Cambodia until April 30th, almost six weeks after Sihanouk was deposed—a long six weeks.
    (Turns to Breuner)
I heard the mortar shells helped the District Chief hold off the North Vietnamese units till then.

CARLSON
    (On his feet, upset by Medici's confessional rambling)
Your honor, may we take a break?

LARKIN
Yes, 10 minutes.
    (Larkin, Breuner, Metcalf leave. Carlson stares at Medici)

MEDICI
(Rocking back and forth in chair catatonically, singing to himself, to the tune of "Shortenin' Bread")

MEDICI
Momma's little NILO gonna' Portsmouth, Portsmouth,
Momma's little NILO gonna' Portsmouth shed.
Momma's little NILO gonna' Portsmouth, Portsmouth,
Momma's little NILO gonna' end up dead!

CARLSON
What the hell are you doing? Breuner put on no evidence of this charge, and you spill it all out! We discussed this possibility, and I told you to hold up what you were saying if you heard me raise the Fifth Amendment Privilege—so I would have a chance to counsel you.

MEDICI
The hell with it. I did it, I knew it was wrong, and I even joked about it. And I would do it *again* to save one of our guys. That's my war, commander, whether you and the Board like it or not!

CARLSON
(Shakes his head, walks slowly to the door, turns)
You are one stubborn bastard, Lieutenant!

MEDICI
(Laughs)
Now everyone agrees on at least one thing—I'm a bastard!
(Shakes his head)

52

Inquiry—Fourth Session

(Larkin, Carlson, Metcalf seated, Medici on witness stand, Breuner standing)

CARLSON
(Stands, speaks to Larkin)

Your honor, for the record, I'm going to renew my motion that the Judge Advocate's request for a specification on the charge that Lieutenant Medici violated a direct Presidential Order be stricken. Colonel Breuner put on no evidence of it in his case in chief, and I could have asked for a dismissal when Colonel Breuner rested his case. But in the interests of getting the facts out in this very unusual matter, I didn't make that motion. I think you can see I had no opportunity to counsel Lieutenant Medici on his Fifth Amendment rights before he tried to waive them on the stand. So under the circumstances I now move to strike that charge, and all Lieutenant Medici's testimony supporting it.

LARKIN

I see your point, Commander, but I do believe that testimony was relevant to Lieutenant Medici's state of mind when he did what he did in Sihanoukville on June sixth. The testimony will stand, but I will consider the legal validity of that charge, and of Lieutenant Medici's testimony and Fifth Amendment rights during my deliberations.

LARKIN
(Turns to Breuner)
Colonel Breuner, you may continue.

BREUNER
Lieutenant, let's get back to orders. You're an intelligence officer with an intelligence designator, correct?

MEDICI
No. I am an unrestricted surface line officer serving in an intelligence billet.

BREUNER
(Puzzled)
You don't have an intelligence designator?

MEDICI
No sir, unrestricted surface line, a ship driver—ultimately able to take command at sea, and any other operational job the Navy gives me.

BREUNER
Do you do line operations in Ha Tien—patrols, ambushes, and the like?

MEDICI
Yes, occasionally with the Army advisors I'm stationed with—with the SEALs and our patrol boats. But my main job is intelligence collection.

NILO HA TIEN

BREUNER
What is your chain of command in Ha Tien?

MEDICI
Intelligence staff and Admiral Zumwalt—a specific shore command—that's it. Unless of course there is a SOPA—senior officer present afloat—in specific operations who will be calling the shots.

BREUNER
Is there a SOPA in Ha Tien?

MEDICI
I've never thought of that. The river division commander Lieutenant Hayward would probably be—but I don't know if he's senior to me. When on the boats, I follow the knowledgable boat commander's instructions—even if he's an Ensign or a third-class bosun's mate. He knows more about the boats than I do.

BREUNER
(Incredulous)
Are you saying you might be SOPA at Ha Tien?

MEDICI
I guess I might be—it depends on Lieutenant Hayward's seniority.

BREUNER
You live with the Army Advisory Team in Ha Tien, correct?

HL Serra
MEDICI
Correct.

BREUNER
Does the team's senior officer—a major—give you orders?

MEDICI
No. Only about issues of our physical security on the hill—bunker, defense, and evacuation drills and such. I just live there with them.

BREUNER
So you really don't take orders from anyone.

MEDICI
Intelligence staff and Admiral Zumwalt, a specific shore command. My written orders say I can come and go as I please without interference, and that I need not explain my actions to anyone. Lieutenant-commander O'Neill didn't understand that in Sihanoukville.

BREUNER
But wasn't he SOPA to you for operations on his own ship?

MEDICI
Yes, while on board, but I told him not to wait for me, to get under way when he was ready. To come and go in Sihanoukville, I was NOT under Lieutenant-commander O'Neill's operational control.

BREUNER
(Exasperated)

NILO HA TIEN
Lieutenant—do you take anyone's orders in this war?

MEDICI
Intelligence staff, Admiral Zumwalt, and SOPA—only if operations require.

BREUNER
(With oomph and frustration)
Lieutenant, it sounds like you think you must obey only the orders you choose. Maybe YOU'RE the cowboy in Ha Tien!

CARLSON
Objection. Badgering the witness and argumentative. Move to strike!

LARKIN
Sustained and stricken. Any more questions, Colonel?

BREUNER
(Throws up his arms. Looks through papers
trying to regain his composure.)
One moment please, your honor. Lieutenant, why did you get your pistol before going to the warehouse around 1630 on June 6th?

MEDICI
Just a hunch that something was wrong down at the warehouses. I have a lot of experience being unarmed in strange places—when in doubt, I take the pistol.

BREUNER
Was the pistol loaded?

MEDICI

Yes.

BREUNER

Cocked?

MEDICI

Not till I was in the warehouse and saw what Metcalf was doing.

BREUNER

Did you aim the pistol at Metcalf?

MEDICI

Yes, I held it with both hands—I was shaking a little.

BREUNER

Was your finger on the trigger as you held the pistol aimed at Metcalf?

MEDICI

Yes—but I didn't remember pulling the trigger. He hit me in the head with the knife, then was on me like a ton of bricks. All I remember was the shock of hearing the pistol discharge.

BREUNER

Lieutenant, do you admit you shot Metcalf in the leg during the scuffle?

MEDICI
I really don't remember shooting…just the crack of the shot when he was on me.

BREUNER
(Shakes his head)
Nothing further, your honor.

LARKIN
Redirect, commander?

CARLSON
(Looks cautiously at Medici, shakes his head no)
No, your honor.

LARKIN
Any more witnesses, commander?

CARLSON
Yes, Lieutenant jaygee William C. Kelly, SEAL Team One, DET Bravo.

KELLY
(Kelly comes in steel door.)

YEOMAN
Do you solemnly swear that the testimony you are about to give will be the truth, the whole truth, and nothing but the truth, so help you God?

KELLY
I do.

CARLSON
Please state your full name and duty station.

KELLY
Lieutenant jaygee William C. Kelly, 7-3-0-9-9-9, executive officer, SEAL Team One, DET Bravo.

CARLSON
You are qualified as a SEAL, Lieutenant?

KELLY
Yes, sir.

CARLSON
How long have you been Executive Officer?

KELLY
Two months. I was spot promoted to the Exec job, for which I volunteered.

CARLSON
How many combat missions have you had in Vietnam?

KELLY
Two, in my first six weeks in-country.

NILO Ha Tien

CARLSON
And then you became Exec?

KELLY
Yes. Our Exec was MEDEVACed after being wounded on a mission earlier this year.

CARLSON
How old are you, Mr. Kelly?

KELLY
Twenty-two, sir.

CARLSON
What are your duties as Exec of DET Bravo?

KELLY
I am responsible for readiness of our DET—personnel, weapons and supplies, and mission scheduling.

CARLSON
How are missions scheduled?

KELLY
In two ways: First, directly with Admiral Zumwalt's staff through the Special Warfare Group commander. Second, by special assignments from SOG, with whom we maintain direct liaison.

HL Serra
CARLSON
Who is the direct liaison person from DET Bravo to SOG?

KELLY
Technically, our commanding officer, but he has delegated that duty to me.

CARLSON
So you are DET Bravo's direct contact with SOG for special assignment scheduling of SEAL personnel?

KELLY
Yes.

CARLSON
Did you direct petty officer Metcalf to destroy the warehouses at Sihanoukville on June 6th, 1970, if they contained Communist weapons?

KELLY
(Shifts weight in chair)
I'm not at liberty to say, commander.

CARLSON
Please answer the question, Lieutenant.

KELLY
I'm not at liberty to testify regarding any SOG missions, sir.

NILO Ha Tien

CARLSON
(To Larkin)
Would the Board please direct the Lieutenant jaygee to answer?

LARKIN
Yes. Answer the question, Lieutenant jaygee Kelly.

KELLY
I am not at liberty to answer, sir.

LARKIN
Son, I will hold you in contempt of this Board if you don't answer.

KELLY
Sir, I am not at liberty to answer any questions about SOG missions
(Kelly pulls scrap of paper out of pocket and reads)
—per National Security Council Directive 68-009.

CARLSON
Lieutenant jaygee Kelly, who is your contact at SOG regarding special assignment missions for DET Bravo personnel?

KELLY
I'm not at liberty to say, sir.

CARLSON
In planning Metcalf's Sihanoukville mission, did you discuss with your contact at SOG the consequences of the mission to the new Cambodian government? Or to *USS Garrison County* and its crew?

KELLY

I'm not at liberty to say, Commander. Please understand that these are my standing orders regarding all matters related to SOG.

LARKIN

We will take a short recess, gentlemen. Lieutenant jaygee Kelly, please remain so I can speak with you privately, and so we can call your commanding officer on the secure phone while the others are outside.

> (All rise and leave room through steel door,
> except Larkin and Kelly who stand at
> a secure red phone in corner. Kelly dials.)

53

Inquiry—Fifth Session

(All seated. Kelly off the witness stand.)

LARKIN
(Perturbed and unsettled.)
Gentlemen, I'm afraid I must excuse Lieutenant jaygee Kelly as a witness. What he said about his orders is correct, and we would need a National Security Tribunal order to compel him to testify about his involvement in any SOG derived operations.

CARLSON
(Confers intensely with Medici)

LARKIN
Commander Carlson, any more witnesses?

CARLSON
Recall Lieutenant-commander O'Neill.
(O'Neill comes in steel door, takes stand.)

CARLSON
Remember, commander, you are still under oath.

HL Serra

O'NEILL

Yes.

CARLSON

You told us earlier that you had not considered the consequences to *Garrison County* and her crew if Metcalf's mission to blow up the warehouses succeeded, correct?

O'NEILL

Yes. I didn't know about the mission till after Metcalf was shot.

CARLSON

Why did you order your ship's armorer, Gunner's mate second class Zont, to dismantle the explosives rigged by Metcalf in the warehouse?

O'NEILL

I didn't.

CARLSON

Who did?

O'NEILL

My acting Exec, Lieutenant jaygee Poe, exceeding his authority, I might add. Zont was one of the party Poe took to the warehouse. When they broke up the fight between Lieutenant Medici and Metcalf, Poe told Zont to dismantle everything ASAP, put the warehouse back in order, and chuck everything off the pier, while they brought Metcalf and Medici back to the ship.

NILO HA TIEN
CARLSON
Then Lieutenant jaygee Poe saved your ship, correct?

O'NEILL
That's not the way I looked at it. I gave him a letter of reprimand when I realized he had acted on his own initiative without asking me, and that Zont's dismantling assisted in disrupting Metcalf's mission.

CARLSON
(With disbelief)
Are you out of your mind, commander? Poe saved your ship and your crew from death or injury!

BREUNER
Objection! Argumentative!

LARKIN
Sustained.

O'NEILL
(Looks smugly at Carlson)
Depends how you look at it.

CARLSON
(Shakes his head)
Nothing further of this witness your honor.

LARKIN
Any cross, Colonel Breuner?

BREUNER
(Gazes at O'Neill, contemplatively, then turns to Larkin)
I don't think so, your honor.

O'NEILL
(Leaves witness stand for his seat)

MEDICI
(Stands)
I have something to say, your honor.

CARLSON
(Jumps to his feet, keeps Medici seated
with hand on his shoulder)
Your honor, I think my client has said quite enough.

LARKIN
Let him speak, commander. The evidence is closed.

CARLSON
(Grabs Medici's arm, whispers loud)
Watch yourself, mister!

MEDICI
(Stands, faces Larkin and Metcalf from counsel table)
There's something I need to say. I've found it hard to defend my job and my conduct at Ha Tien and Sihanoukville. Everything is so complicated—the war, Rules of Engagement, Cambodia, neutrality, chain of command, conflicting orders and missions, and their consequences. I want the Board to know three things directly and unequivocally from me:

NILO HA TIEN

First, I am a sensible and patriotic officer. My job has left me privy to secrets and contradictions and dilemmas I never would have chosen to explore on my own. I'm doing the best job I can as NILO Ha Tien, in fact, NILO Cambodia, at physical risk to myself, and now it appears even legal risk and risk of my career in the Navy. All because I tried to do the best job I could in dealing with the dicey Cambodian situation.

Second, I want the Board and Gunner's mate Metcalf to know how immeasurably sorry I am that he was wounded in the melee at Sihanoukville. I have heard that his career as a SEAL is over because of it. It keeps me awake at night thinking about the fact that I harmed a fellow sailor. I'm not a killer—I'm a collection guy.

Finally—after all that said—to a CERTAINTY in my mind, the warehouses and pier at Sihanoukville should not have been destroyed at that time because of their importance to the survival of Cambodia. I do not waiver in that assessment.

     (Medici sits down)

LARKIN

Very well.
   (Looks to Breuner and Carlson)

LARKIN

If you gentlemen are ready to summarize—briefly—I can begin my deliberations this afternoon, and we'll all plan to reconvene here...
  (Looks at his calendar, turns back to Breuner and Carlson)
...three days hence. Summation, gentlemen?

  [Transcript of summation arguments water damaged and unreadable.]

54

Inquiry—Sixth (Final) Session

(All seated)

LARKIN

Gentlemen, this has been a hard inquiry and harder deliberation. We've all been exposed to aspects of this war that are classified beyond imagination, but worse, are contradictory and embarrassing and have demonstrated the cross-purposes of our elaborate intelligence establishment, especially its covert operations. What we've seen shows us this is no way to run a railroad—but that really is for my recommendations to the Commander of Naval Forces here, to the Chiefs of Naval Operations and Intelligence and their counterparts at MACV.

I've listened carefully to the far-ranging testimony I've purposely allowed to help us all fairly grasp these matters. The principal witnesses are young, dedicated and patriotic officer and petty officer, and our Navy is proud of them both for their service.

Nonetheless, cross-purposes of our secret intelligence programs have caused serious physical injury to petty officer Metcalf, probably ending his operational career, and have called into question the methods of Lieutenant Medici in his unbridled intelligence collection efforts, with the possibility of his Naval career also ending, should charges be brought and proved.

I considered these matters carefully for nearly three days before deciding what to do. The linchpin of my decision is the bedrock tradition of independence of command in the United States Navy,

NILO HA TIEN
(Looks at Breuner)
and I include the Marine Corps, Colonel. As compared to the land-based services, the Navy—because its assets were far-flung and out of touch with central command much of the time—had to vest its commanders, junior officers, and petty officers, absolute discretion to assess the on-scene situation and act immediately, in accordance with their best judgment.

This tradition began in the British Navy when it covered the known world, whose admiralty could only give squadron commanders general orders, such as—
(Reads from paper)
"Interdict French shipping on the Spanish Main"—for a cruise that might last four years. Gentlemen, our service's tradition is—the buck stops with the on-scene commander. He has to have the big picture, know the mosaic of background details, and act boldly and quickly when confronted with unusual situations.

At Sihanoukville on June sixth, there was a confluence of events that in my judgment could not be perfectly resolved by any man there.

Lieutenant-commander O'Neill—a careful commanding officer—was, unfortunately, not privy to any of the background events that brought Lieutenant Medici and petty officer Metcalf to Sihanoukville with their own specific covert missions. Under the circumstances he acted very conservatively—and cannot really be faulted for it—in disliking Lieutenant Medici's conduct while on board *Garrison County*.

Of course, Lieutenant-commander O'Neill knew nothing of Lieutenant Medici's covert collection mission to seek ways to disable the port, nor petty officer Metcalf's covert mission to destroy the warehouses. Because he was uninformed about their mission orders or the political background of our dealings with Cambodia, he could NOT be considered Senior Officer Present—SOPA—on the ground at Sihanoukville.

Sections 0929 and 0930 of Navy Regulations on SOPA support my view, in excluding from a SOPA's command, quote "…such units as may be assigned to shore commands by competent authority…" unquote—as Lieutenant Medici and petty officer Metcalf were here, on Admiral Zumwalt's and SOG's orders.

As relates to Lieutenant-commander O'Neill ordering Lieutenant Medici to stay aboard his ship, Section 0907 directs SOPA—quote — "NOT to divert a command from an operation or duty assigned by another authority unless the public interest demands" — unquote. 0907 leaves unresolved SOPA's authority to divert a subordinate whose orders are not to be disclosed, and both men's covert orders here were undisclosed.

Properly, as commanding officer, Lieutenant-commander O'Neill gave orders he believed would protect his ship and crew, without knowledge of the two underlying missions. On that count, I conclude that his order to Lieutenant Medici to remain aboard *Garrison County* when he returned to the ship at 1630, in light of Lieutenant-commander O'Neill's lack of information and in light of Lieutenant Medici's written freedom-of-movement and non-disclosure orders from his shore command, CANNOT be considered a lawful order to Lieutenant Medici, and Lieutenant Medici's disobeyal of it should not result in Article 92 charges against him.

CARLSON
(Carlson smiles and lays his hand on Medici's arm)

LARKIN
(Looks directly at O'Neill)

Also, after careful consideration, I strongly recommend that Lieutenant-commander O'Neill reconsider his letter of reprimand to his Exec, Lieutenant jaygee Poe, and instead consider a decoration for that young officer's quick thinking, which likely saved *Garrison County*, its crew and the lives of petty officer Metcalf and Lieutenant Medici. I ask you, Lieutenant-commander, to report back to me personally within 60 days on what action you have taken on this recommendation.

(Turns to Medici)

Similarly, on the issue of lawful orders, Lieutenant Medici CANNOT be subject to an Article 92 charge for interfering with petty officer Metcalf's unwritten and unproven mission orders. There is frankly doubt in my mind, after hearing Mr. Kelly's testimony—or lack of it—of the lawfulness of petty officer Metcalf's mission orders, from SOG or from whomever transmitted. Even if the mission were considered technically lawful, the evidence has shown it might not have been well thought out as to impact on the fragile new Cambodian government, and as to the clear potential danger to Lieutenant-commander O'Neill's ship and men, who were unwitting and uninformed accomplices. We'll never know, but the SOG planners may have been inadequately informed, and their mission folly.

I think Lieutenant Medici thought quickly in the fog of war, evaluated his course of action rationally and intelligently, and, as Senior Officer Present on the pier at Sihanoukville, he properly ordered petty officer Metcalf to desist.

Petty officer Metcalf, a trained operative, responded second nature to the threat he perceived Lieutenant Medici posed to his mission, and we cannot fault him, now or in future proceedings, for doing all in his power to complete his mission. I would remind Lieutenant Medici that despite his initiative, if the men from *Garrison County* had not arrived when they did, both he and petty officer Metcalf might be dead, the warehouses at Sihanoukville destroyed, and perhaps the fragile new government fallen.

On the Article 92 charges related to ammunition sent to Cambodia in violation of a direct Presidential Order, Colonel Breuner, I don't think it fair to use the Lieutenant's own testimony against him, when he admitted the facts on the stand in a flurry without proper consultation with his lawyer about his Fifth Amendment privilege against self-incrimination, and you put on no evidence of the charges in your case in chief. And frankly, in Lieutenant Medici's case, the six cases of mortar ammunition he sent to help save a loyal agent doesn't seem untoward, and in fact seems like the American thing to do.

Further, I completely reject the Judge Advocate's request for Article 104 charges of aiding the enemy—the furthest thing from the minds of these two brave young men on the pier at Sihanoukville.
(Looks at Breuner)
The Article 88 charges, disrespecting civilian authority—probably based on a thoughtless, salty epithet—are absurd, and no charges will be filed.
(Sits up; turns stern face to Medici)
However, Lieutenant, a good man has been injured and it is clear from the testimony that you have a record, in your short time as NILO Ha Tien, of pushing the gray areas to their limits by conscious calculation. A Presidential Order, young man, is a Presidential Order, extenuating circumstances or not. You might care to remember in your Naval career—if it goes further—that General MacArthur was fired by his Commander-in-Chief, Harry Truman, for just such insubordination in Korea, regardless of extenuating circumstances. The chain of command and discipline to obey orders mean something in this Navy and under our Constitution.

I caution you, Lieutenant, during the rest of your tour at Ha Tien, to reflect upon the calculated rule-bending that characterized your first six months and almost cost a fellow sailor his life. And to remind you, I will draft a Letter of Caution for your service jacket, focusing on your tendency toward recklessness.
(Looks at Breuner)
Colonel, anything else?

BREUNER

No, your honor.

LARKIN

NILO HA TIEN
Commander?

CARLSON
No, your honor.

LARKIN
Very well, these proceedings are concluded. No charges are recommended to be filed against Lieutenant Medici or petty officer Metcalf, and a Letter of Caution will be drafted by the Board for placement in Lieutenant Medici's file.
(Taps gavel, rises and leaves.)
(Breuner helps Metcalf to his feet, stares and shakes his head at Medici; all exit except Medici and Carlson.)

CARLSON
You happy? You beat the rap.

MEDICI
Happy? No. I'm the youngest lieutenant in the Navy. What do you think that Letter of Caution is going to do to my chances for promotion at the Lieutenant-Commander Selection Board, or for command?

CARLSON
(Startled, cannot believe Medici's audacity.)
Promotion? Command? Are you kidding, Lieutenant? You may have beat the filing of criminal charges, but you'll never have a command, I'll tell you that.
(Pauses.)
Do you think this is some kind of game? You did what you did, and it came to this Board's attention. You may have saved the flakey Cambodian government for a while, but you ruined two careers,

HL Serra

Metcalf's AND yours. At least you don't have a gunshot wound to show for it.
    (Stands up straight, salutes Medici.)
I wish you a fair wind and a following sea, Lieutenant. At least I kept you out of Portsmouth brig!
    (Carlson turns and walks out door.)

MEDICI
(Stands gaping at Carlson.)
But commander, you don't understand. You can't understand….
    [Tape ends here.]

55

Homecoming

The team-house hill looked small and brown from the air. Medici had flown the approach to Phao Dai dozens of times, and though he now considered it his home, it had never looked more insignificant. He saw that porch space had been added to the Junkies' hooch. Their last-stand sand bag bunker had collapsed from the weight of monsoon rain. The parade ground was deserted except for the major's shiny Jeep and Medici's, covered with muddy dust.

As the helo made its approach to the lonely pad at the foot of the hill, Medici realized the ammi barges and patrol boats were gone. Not a trace of the River Division remained. He looked seaward as they descended and saw that Captain Brown's LST was gone. Seven weeks' absence from Ha Tien and "Vietnamization"—the turnover of the war and its facilities to the South Vietnamese—had run a virulent course and denuded Phao Dai of the signs of American presence. Medici felt lonely before the helo touched down.

He smiled wanly at the Army helo pilot and waved acknowledgment for the ride home. The chopper was out over the Gulf of Thailand before he was halfway up the hill. It seemed unusually quiet, the patio empty of beer drinkers though it was almost noon. The team house shimmered through the rising heat of midday. The spring of the screen door screeched as he opened it.

The radio room was empty. His gray Navy sideband radio had been moved from its center console spot to a useless position a foot off the floor. New green Army radio gear filled its place.

From behind him, an effeminate southern voice said, "Haaay, NILO. We'd given you up for daid! You back to stay with us or you goin' down to the new Navy base with your squid buddies?" Medici turned and looked at lanky Sgt. Cassel, who had arrived to relieve the team supply sergeant the day Medici left for Sihanoukville.

"Where's Sergeant Dodge? And the major?" he snapped at Cassel.

"Take it easy, NILO. Dodge left for the States three weeks ago. The major's in Can Tho for new instructions on team mission during the turnover. I'm in charge until he returns," Cassel said. He spoke with a slowness meant to underscore the dignity of his new position. "If you're going to stay with us, I'll have my new communications guy move out of your room. We really didn't think you were coming back."

"I'll be staying, so get him out. Did the River Division move down to the new base in town?"

"Yessuh. Not only the River Division but the Junkies and everyone else. We called it the squid evacuation," Cassel laughed hysterically. "We figured you'd want to go with your Navy buddies, but of course that's up to you."

"Where's Frank Brown?" Medici asked nervously. The missing faces made him feel like his roots had been torn up. As crummy as Phao Dai was, it still was his only fixed point of reference in a world of uncertainty. The absence of his friends unnerved him.

"Frank left eight days ago for the States. His tour was up. He was upset that he couldn't see you before he left, especially since you were gone so long. And we didn't know, y'know, if you were killed or something…"

"Your sentiment is overwhelming," Medici glared.

"…but he left a letter for you. I'll get it," Cassel said. He double-timed to his bedroom.

Great, Medici thought. The Navy's gone, Frank's gone, and this dipshit has become house mother. Fuck it. Only three months left.

He took the sealed, taped letter from Cassel. "Did I get any other mail?"

"Now that you mention it, I think ya'll did," Cassel said coquettishly.

"Get it," Medici said. He opened Frank's letter, and a cassette tape fell out with it. The letter read:

NILO Ha Tien

"Dear NILO,

"By the time you read this, and I'm confident that you will despite the scuttlebutt about your demise in Cambodia, I'll be back in the world. I actually thought about extending another three months so we could finish our tours together and keep up our good work. But you know how wives are about these tours, not much flexibility even after 15 years of Army marriage. To be honest, NILO, I kept thinking about the guys that get greased accidentally after extending their tours or on their last run to the border and such. I guess my intuition told me it was time to get out.

"The hill has really changed in an unbelievably short time. Bob Dodge left and took with him all his Johnny Cash tapes and, more important, his good spirits. The Rube DEROSed and took his guitar, but he left the enclosed cassette tape for you. I think you will enjoy it.

"This new guy Cassel is a weak entry and treats the team house as his own, as if he's den mother or something. I'm afraid the war as we knew it is over. The chicken shit is starting to catch up even on the Cambodian border.

"The Navy left, lock, stock and barrel when the new VN Navy base was finished in town. Even the Junkies went down under orders, but only after vocal protest to Saigon. They had grown fond of our funky hill. Fortunately, Hayward has become senior naval advisor for Ha Tien, so you and he are the top brass here for the Navy now. Congrats, Lieutenant!

"The new base has a secure teletype communication facility, a gift from your friend Commander Lane in Saigon. Said he was a good buddy of yours during weapons training at Camp Pendleton where you 'helped the old codger out' (those were his words). The bad news is, we're now required to keep our secret message traffic securely locked in a safe, which you'll find in your office. The LST has been relieved of communications responsibilities and is no longer on station but visits here occasionally. The Seawolf helos are permanently stationed across the river at the Special Forces

camp at To Chau and we seldom see them anymore.

"Hayward said that since you were on independent duty, you could stay up here on the hill or take a room down at the new base. He's even saving you an 'office' there. Think it over before you decide, but I think you'll find a certain ambiance missing from the hill under Mother Cassel's regime with everyone gone.

"Unfortunately, Carlos has been assigned to take over my net as well as his Special Forces agents. I know how you feel about working with him and the lack of confidence he inspires, but please try to make do for the sake of the mission. Try to work with him, NILO.

"I'm really sorry we didn't get to see each other before my DEROS, but that's the nature of the game, eh, Double-Oh One Double-Oh? I just wanted to say that I'm really glad we had the chance to work together out here. I've been doing this stuff for a long time, but your enthusiasm and smarts made it possible for us to do a damn good job. And of course, our friendship made this shit-bad year tolerable and at times even fun. (Except for that mortaring nonsense!) I've enclosed a card with my home address and telephone number in Illinois. Please send me yours. I hope we get together after this is all over."

> Regards,
> Frank

Medici felt numb. Frank's leaving without a trace hit him like a truck, as if Frank were writing from the grave.

He got up and walked around the team room, impatient. He spied a cassette player on one of the tables and popped in Rube's tape. It was the Rube, strumming his guitar, singing in his best Johnny Cash bass a variant of Johnny's song "Wanted Man":

Wanted man in Nooey Die Young,
Wanted man in Kampog Trach,
Wanted man in ville Tuk Meas,
Wanted man in old Chau Doc.

NILO HA TIEN

If you ever see me coming and if you know who I am,
Don't you breathe it to nobody
'cause the NILO's on the lamb!

Be safe, NILO. What a wild year! The Rube.

Medici belly laughed. That Rube was great.

"NILO...NILO." Cassel was speaking to him from what seemed like miles away. "Here's your other mail." He left another letter and a large manila envelope on the table in front of Medici.

The large envelope bore the legend "Commander, Naval Forces Vietnam, Judge Advocate General, Official Business" in the upper left-hand corner. Medici knew what it was. He held it and felt its heft before opening it.

The sheaf of documents was neatly typed on very white heavy bond paper, the whitest he had seen in months. He flipped quickly to the last page and his eyes found the words "NO CHARGES TO BE BROUGHT." He let out a long breath, settled in the chair, and read the Findings and Opinion of the Board of Inquiry from start to finish.

There were suggestions that Medici had been quick on the trigger with Metcalf, but that on independent duty as a NILO, he had to act quickly on his best judgment. Such action was the very essence of independent authority, so important a part of Naval tradition.

In fact, the report concluded, Medici's judgment had probably been correct, that to permit the destruction of Sihanoukville's warehouses would have seriously damaged U.S. relations with the new Cambodian republic, and that the Studies and Operations Group's decision to accomplish that destruction may not have been authorized. It had been unfortunate that Metcalf had been seriously wounded in the leg, but due to Metcalf's size and hand-to-hand combat training, in light of Medici's appropriate decision to stop him, he had no choice once Metcalf attacked. But Medici would receive a Letter of Caution in his service record for his sometimes reckless behavior at the border as NILO.

Medici put the papers on the table. The tension of the last weeks drained from him. He didn't feel good about what happened in Sihanoukville, but at least he felt vindicated. He could still visualize catching Metcalf red-handed in the warehouse, and it made the hair stand up on the back of his neck. But he felt sorry that he had wounded Metcalf.

Medici looked at the other envelope halfheartedly. It was from his administrative boss, the Fourth Coastal Zone Intelligence Officer. The Walrus had written on his personal stationary:

> "Tom:
>
> "I wanted to write and explain to you about something that is transpiring. You remember that Joel Feiner met an untimely end at Seafloat a while back. We haven't replaced him yet, and those guys really need a NILO with guts down there. Intelligence staff in Saigon is screaming that he should be replaced immediately and have asked me for recommendations since Seafloat is in my Zone.
>
> "Tom, all here and on the staff in Saigon agree you are without a doubt the best NILO we have. I am not unmindful of the expertise you have developed on Cambodia and shared with all agencies, nor of the fact that you only have three months left in-country. However, the needs of the Navy come first, so I've recommended you to staff to replace Joel. The admiral will make the final decision himself, since Seafloat is so important to him.
>
> "I hope you understand my dilemma, and the reason for my decision. You are my best NILO. Keep up the good work."
>
> *Regards,*
> *LCDR Plover*

Medici stared straight ahead at the pea-green wall. "Fuck it. I'm not going to Seafloat. I'll simply deny my orders," he said precisely.

An inauspicious homecoming, he thought.

56

Dep

Dinner that evening seemed strange to Medici. The crowd was pure Army, Medici the only Navy man present. The "Rube," Medici's guitar-playing Army pal, had also gone home. Medici knew casually maybe two of the 12 young enlisted soldiers who ran the Army's microwave telephone facility, plus the major, who had returned, and Cassel. The crowd, formerly animated and talkative at meals, was oddly subdued and inhibited. It was as if the major was the unassertive father and Cassel the stern mother of the group, and a smothering conspiracy existed between the two to reassert traditional Army discipline over the young soldiers now that the rowdy Navy was gone.

It made Medici edgy. The Ba spoke to no one as she served the tables. She nodded curtly at Medici without her gaping, beaming smile and said quietly, "*Chao, Dai-Uy*," a cool reception for a close friend after six weeks' absence. He felt as if he were a ghost watching the scene.

No one asked him about his mission to Sihanoukville, what he did or what he saw. Whenever he had returned to the hill before, his adventures were items of immediate curiosity and conversation. He felt the present scene was like the movie *Invasion of the Bodysnatchers,* where the humans had assumed robotic personalities after their bodies were taken over by alien beings. It spooked him.

Toward the end of dinner Cassel got up to open the screen door to let in Dep, the hill's rat-eating dog, after she scratched persistently. Medici was shocked. For years, a baseline sanitary rule of the team house was that all pets remained outside the team room during meals. Dep, although a personality, was mangy and flea-ridden.

Medici spoke. "Sergeant Cassel, one of our team house rules is that no pets are allowed in at mealtime," he said solemnly. He looked to the major for support. The major looked down at his food.

Cassel, at the next table, didn't turn. He kept feeding Dep scraps from his plate as she frolicked and jumped and begged. Her paws scratched the table, and she spilled food. The young soldiers at Cassel's table sat stone-faced.

"NIIIILO," Cassel drawled, "lots of things have changed since you left us. Dep's our mascot here. She's mah pride and joy, aren't ya, babe?" he said to Dep. He teased her with another fatty scrap. Her paw knocked one soldier's plate to the floor where it spilled meat and gravy, which Dep attacked.

"Sergeant, get the dog out of the team room," Medici said in a rage. "It's mealtime."

Cassel laughed as Dep devoured the soldier's food from the bricks. "See, NILO, she helps us with cleanup detail!" He laughed again and watched the dog eat with no intention of putting her out.

Medici said nothing—but stared coldly at Cassel for 10 seconds. Cassel did not meet his gaze. He kept laughing at Dep's antics. The two soldiers who knew Medici slid back from the table. The rest sensed the tension and remained quiet.

Medici rose and walked to his bedroom. He took the Browning pistol from the shelf, walked back into the team room, and stood next to Cassel with Dep in front of him. He calmly drew back the slide on the Browning and heard the round seat and the slide return with an icy metallic noise.

Then he held the cocked gun at Dep's head and said quietly to Cassel, "Sergeant, remove the dog or I'll kill it."

Cassel looked straight into Medici's cold stare for a heartbeat. The smile left his face. He squirmed in his seat, brought a shaking hand toward his face, and whined, near tears, "But NILO, you're being unreas—"

"NOW!" Medici bellowed. Two more soldiers slid away from the table.

Cassel pushed his chair back and it fell over. He babbled, then started to sob. He picked up the slobbering Dep, carried her to the porch, then hooked the screen door. Still trembling, he walked through the team room to his bedroom.

Medici put the pistol on safe, sat down with it on his lap, and finished his dinner while the soldiers whispered.

57

Em Chou

Medici tried to call Province to tell the Walrus he would not go to Seafloat, but his sideband radio didn't work. Sgt. Cassel told him that since there was a radio Medici could use at the new Navy base, he'd assumed Medici would not need this one, so he had disconnected it. Now the transmitter would not tune up, no matter how Medici adjusted it. All he could do was climb the water tower and check the antenna.

The tower's plywood floors hung from wooden posts and held a dozen water barrels. The sun heated the drums during the day, and they could take warm showers in the afternoon. The searing heat took Medici's breath as he climbed. Waves shimmered off the corrugated metal roof of the team house like a huge stove top. He felt the rickety tower sway as he neared the top where his antenna extended from the tallest post.

He paused and looked around and perspired. The brutal sun made him squint, but the perspective from the tower surprised him. The hilltop looked small and the buildings close together. Before Sihanoukville he thought the hill formidable. Now it seemed inconsequential.

His sweat started to evaporate and cooled him. He looked across the parade ground at the Junkies' stucco hooch. It looked like an old Mexican cantina with a flat roof and wooden posts supporting the tin porch cover.

Medici sat in the shade of a water barrel. He began to enjoy the bird's-eye view of the hill from this secret perch. He could watch without being seen, the ultimate spy sensation.

He made himself comfortable, thinking about the junk advisors that lived in the hooch until the move to the new base. A ragtag bunch in camouflage uniforms, long hair, sideburns and mustaches, the Junkies hung hammocks inside the hooch as they did aboard the Vietnamese junks they rode. The hooch doubled as their armory. He remembered it full of ammunition and grenades they carried on patrol. He smiled when he remembered how they papered the walls from floor to ceiling with *Playboy* centerfolds.

Medici and Frank had planned to move into the hooch and make it their spook house after the Junkies moved to the new base. They thought it ideal for their big maps, aerial photographs and radios, and the major was pleased with the prospect of getting the midnight meetings and radio squeals out of his team house. Delays had postponed the opening of the new base, Medici went to Sihanoukville, and Frank finished his tour. The move never happened even though the Junkies moved out.

Medici reached up and splashed a handful of water on his head from the barrel. The dribbling water made him remember Westy Westland, the Junkie who showered naked under a leaking barrel when they first filled them up. He laughed. A six-foot-five basketball star, Westy led the Americans in their games against the team from the local Vietnamese Catholic school. Man-for-man, the Americans were eight inches taller, but the Vietnamese drubbed them regularly.

Medici liked Westy because of his compassion. In Saigon Westy befriended Em Chou, a nine-year-old street orphan. He wangled transportation for him to Ha Tien where the boy lived with the Junkies, and Westy became his surrogate father. In Saigon the boy had been a streetwise thief. But after six months in Ha Tien, he softened and became a child again. The rural atmosphere, Westy's nurturing, and the fact that Em Chou didn't have to worry where his next meal came from calmed him and gave him stability. Yet Em Chou cried every time Westy went on junk patrol, unnerved by the possibility that he might not come back.

Westy had survived the patrols. The problem came when the Junkies moved to the new base. Because of security regulations, Vietnamese civilians, including Em Chou and the amahs, were not permitted to dwell on base. So Em Chou stayed in the Junkie hooch with chubby, slow Co Hoan, the laundress. Westy visited the hill to see Em Chou as often as he could, but Em Chou reacted predictably. The tough little street fighter had his emotions wrenched before, and he endured the separation by withdrawing. Medici urged Westy to find a foster home in town for Em Chou, but the patrol schedule prevented Westy from making the arrangements.

Medici wondered why he was reminiscing so much. He guessed he was heat giddy. In a fog of nostalgia he gazed down at the Junkie hooch from the tower and puzzled as plump Co Hoan burst out of the screen door and ran across the empty parade ground, moaning. Her movement made no sense, until the windows and doors blew out.

Medici felt the concussion first through the wood deck. Then the blast wave smacked his face and forced the air from his lungs. Thick gray smoke billowed from the windows and doors. At the blast, Co Hoan fell to the ground, howled and pounded the dust with her fists.

Medici gripped the sloshing water drum. If this were a sapper attack on the compound he was dead without a weapon. What a way to get it, after all he'd survived. He crouched behind the drum to hide himself.

Men shouted in Vietnamese, then ran across the dirt oval. Militiamen strode from their building, eyes puffy with sleep, M-16s at their hips. They squatted next to Co Hoan, rifles aimed at the smoke-filled hooch. Medici heard her sob, "Em Chou! Em Chou!" and he understood immediately.

The militiamen entered the hooch, waving away clouds of greasy smoke with their shirts. A sole cry of anguish rang from inside and confirmed Medici's fears. Two militiamen carried out a smoldering poncho liner with a small torso in it.

The major ran out of the team house with his interpreter. They spoke quickly to the militiamen, looked inside the hooch and walked back to the team house. Medici heard the major crank the field telephone and shout to be heard.

Weak, Medici climbed down from the tower and walked to the door of the hooch. The smell of burnt flesh overwhelmed the smell of cordite. The *Playboy* centerfolds not blasted or burned from the wall were spattered with tiny red bits of meat. Em Chou's mattress smoldered, a large hole blown through it. Medici saw chunks of flesh and gristle strewn about the room. A single melancholy brown eye stared at Medici from where it lay on the pillow of the second bed.

He walked back to the team house as the Junkies arrived in

their Jeep. Westy leaped out and ran to the hooch. Medici heard "OH FUCKING GOD" echo over the hill. Other Junkies led Westy, near catatonic, to the team house. The major found brandy and poured him a full glass. They laid Westy down on a bunk and watched over him until sunset, when they took him back to the new base.

Medici had stopped next to the major as they brought Westy in. Without being asked, the major whispered, "Co Hoan said there was a case of concussion grenades under Em Chou's bed. He found it and took one out, playing soldier with it. She told him to stop, that it wasn't funny, but he grinned at her and pretended to pull the pin. It came out accidentally, and he dropped it on the bunk and stared at it. She ran, hysterical, and it blew as she crossed the parade ground. A terrible accident...."

"Accident!" Medici glared at the major in disbelief, then shook his head and went to get a brandy for himself.

58

DIOCC

The morning after Em Chou died, Medici spoke to no one at breakfast and refused to return the major's pleasantries. Cassel, who would no longer enter the team room when Medici was there, hovered in the hall, waiting for him to leave so he could eat. Medici glared at Cassel as he passed him when he went to his room to get the pistol and the notepad he took to the DIOCC, the district intelligence briefing. He had not attended the DIOCC for seven weeks during his mission to Sihanoukville and its aftermath. Now with Em Chou's death and the sour homecoming, he hoped to lose himself in routine.

He walked across the parade ground to his interpreter Anh Duc's hooch. "Duc Ay." *Hey, Duc*, he called. No one answered. He heard sobbing, knocked, and entered the small room. Co Hoan, their laundress, sat cross-legged on Duc's bed, tears falling down her cheeks. Her pupils were as big as coins. Stoned.

"Duc o dau?" *Where is Duc*, Medici asked.

"Em Chou—dam ma…." She started to sob again.

Medici didn't understand, and didn't want to talk to the woman in this condition, so he left. He knew Em Chou's death weighed on them all like a heavy gravity, perturbing their individual orbits. But he didn't want to get involved in solace. He wanted to work.

He drove his Jeep down the hill in the white glare of morning, which worsened a headache he had not been aware of. At the bottom of the hill he stopped and Father Ninh, the town's Catholic priest, passed in white funerary robes leading a procession of 15 people. Behind him were two Vietnamese altar boys Em Chou's age. One carried a staff and cross, the other a gold incense burner on a chain. A squad of four Navy men in neat camouflage uniforms, junk advisors, followed solemnly, bearing on their shoulders a small magenta coffin that glowed like an ember in the morning sun. Behind them was the sole rear guard, Westy, too tall to carry one corner of the coffin with the shorter Junkies. Behind Westy were Duc, several Vietnamese that worked on the hill, and a few Navy river sailors.

The priest recited some Latin. Medici recognized only a few words from his altar boy days: "...omnipotens deus...mortus...." *Almighty God...dead.* The procession entered the tiny graveyard at the foot of the hill. Medici had passed it a hundred times but always looked away. Now he saw a miniature Boot Hill with tilted wooden crosses. It dawned on him that it was the paupers' graveyard for Ha Tien.

Medici let the procession pass in front of him through a tumbledown gate in the concertina wire that protected the graveyard from God knew what. The procession passed within 10 feet of the Jeep. No one looked at him. He felt increasing anxiety in the pit of his stomach, as he glimpsed the fresh mound of saffron earth next to Em Chou's grave.

Finally he put the Jeep in gear and rolled forward when the last mourner passed, then drove quietly along the dirt track until it joined the tarmac road to town. There he jam-shifted and tore past terrified Vietnamese women and children to the District Chief's office, where he skidded to a stop in the dust, flipped the ignition off, and ran up the stairs while the Jeep dieseled to a halt.

He was late. The meeting had already started. The District Chief, Thieu Ta Cuu, smiled and with ceremony offered him his own seat while the head White Mouse—Chief of National Police—droned on with his briefing: "Fifty Viet Cong of the 101st VC regiment came to Xa Xia pagoda and informed the presiding monk that Xa Xia hamlet was to be taxed by the Provisional Revolutionary Government as its own territory since it is now a controlled sector of the Cambodian-Vietnamese border...We must undertake efforts to eliminate the brazen Communist aggressors...."

Medici looked at his counterpart, the Vietnamese NILO, LT. Lang. Lang twirled the eraser end of a yellow pencil in his ear, withdrew an obscene lump of earwax, wiped it on the table's edge and reinserted the eraser. Thieu Ta Cuu sat with his pig-face aimed at the ceiling, lips pursed in feigned concentration. His hands were clasped comfortably around his pot belly, which protruded like a small melon under his camouflage jump suit. Medici felt a wave of revulsion that made him wince.

"This is the same fucking bullshit you were reporting when I left six weeks ago," he shouted at the Chief of Police. "Have you captured any of these Viet Cong? Have you set an ambush for them? Have you used Phoenix or SEALs to snatch their leaders?"

The ashen chief understood his tone perfectly.

Medici stood and leaned menacingly across the table, grabbed the pencil from Lang's hand and threw it across the room where it left a wax spot on the stucco wall.

"And you, Lang, have you ever ridden with your Vietnamese patrol boats? You sit on your ass here or in your house diddling your wife, while your Naval compatriots are maimed or killed on the river. Do you feel proud of your actions in your country's war?"

Lang raised a trembling, long-fingered hand to his forehead.

"Jesus fucking Christ! Don't any of you care?" Medici shouted. He looked around and saw only stoics, who averted their eyes to avoid acknowledging his outburst. He searched each man's face for a flicker of conscience, anything, and found nothing.

Medici turned, said, "Good day" in a low voice to the District Chief and left. He jumped in the Jeep and sped back to the hill, trying without success to keep his eyes from the little hump of earth that marked Em Chou's grave.

Ready to explode, jittery and jumpy, he knew he had to shoot or drink, and didn't trust himself to shoot with people around. He entered the team house at a gallop, grabbed a bottle, and was stone drunk by noon.

59

Changes

That rotten bastard Kenck, Medici thought as he read the teletype message on the morning of Kenck's arrival. He set me up in Sihanoukville. Then he thought, maybe Kenck hadn't known about the SOG operation and Metcalf...no, no fucking way. Metcalf had testified about "tacit approval" from the Naval staff in Saigon during Medici's Board of Inquiry. Metcalf's superior had stonewalled, refusing to identify the person who gave him the mission orders, and Kenck was never called as a witness.

But Rick Reffe had once told Medici that all special warfare ops in Cambodia were filtered through Kenck's Cambodian Shop to ensure that they would not prejudice any secret collection missions there. So the zitty bastard Kenck had risked Medici, the LST, and fledgling relations with Cambodia for one stupid operation. Today Kenck was coming out to the border, after things had quieted down and were safe, "to review entire border collection situation, for purpose of reassigning CT-5 collection assets to CB shop for direct administration."

Medici fumed. Now that he had extended his agent network from Vietnam all the way up the Cambodian coast to the Thai border, fat Kenck would emasculate the Ha Tien NILO post. The coward wouldn't even administer it from the border where he might get shot at or overrun. Medici guessed Kenck would run it from his foul Saigon office filled with porn and sexual appliances. He shuddered.

Then fear crept into his bowels. If they took his collection activities away, there would remain only liaison duties that any untrained bozo could perform. Medici would no longer be indispensable at the border. And now that Admiral Zumwalt had gone back to Washington to become CNO, Medici had less confidence about his own untouchable status with staff.

He felt a stinging pain in his stomach as his mind made an

inductive leap: SEAFLOAT! Kenck's severing Medici's Cambodian connection would make him the candidate certain to replace Joel, the NILO killed at Seafloat. Diabolical. Two months left and he'd be sent to a place where he could not expand intelligence collection efforts, only fly low in helos and get shot at looking for moving ambush units. Or sit bored on the ammi barges and get rocketed and shot at, with Friday steak and lobster dinners the only consolation. Great. If he went, at least he'd get a Purple Heart.

For the first time in-country, Medici felt boxed. After thinking about it, he decided he could not deny his orders to Seafloat. He could go to Saigon to talk to the intelligence staff, but that wouldn't help. Captain Ross wouldn't intervene for him; he would rather reassign a field agent to Seafloat than appear the bastard by transferring someone from staff. Because of the ground rules of their understanding, Medici could not seek Commander Holland's intercession. If the Navy needed Medici at Seafloat, he would have to go.

Kenck gets the last laugh, he thought. Why is it that the manipulative cowards in the back room always get what they want, simply because they're near the seat of power? The poor field bastards who took risks daily and didn't whimper got it in the shorts, the disposable fodder of every war. He understood now how the term REMF—"rear echelon motherfucker"—came to be the grunt's description of staffers.

60

Kenck at the Border

Medici met Kenck at the helo pad. Kenck wore bright new lieutenant tracks on his wash khakis, with a piss-cutter hat and glossy black Corfam shoes. He carried a brand new CAR-15, a shortened assault version of the M-16. He wore two huge bandoleros of ammunition clips, 20 in all, cinched over an old-style, metal-plate flak jacket. In his hands he carried an olive drab helmet and a small overnight bag. Medici wore plaid madras shorts without a belt, a black turtleneck and thongs.

Medici laughed. "You expecting World War III today?" he said. The chopper lifted off and they started up the hill.

Kenck flushed. "Well, you never know—here at the border...."

They climbed the hill in silence. Kenck labored under the weight of his load. Medici relieved him of the light assault rifle, ostensibly to help, in fact to examine it. He had heard these CAR-15s existed, but he never saw new gear at the border. By the time they reached the team room, Kenck sweated like a pig.

"You can put your gear in the end room on the left. You really don't need all that combat stuff," Medici said. Kenck took off his combat gear and carried it to the end room, then returned to the team room and sat across from Medici at a table with a red and white checkered tablecloth. Medici eyed Kenck over a mug of coffee. Kenck poured himself a cup.

"You'll probably be upset by what I'm going to do," Kenck said. He gazed out the teamroom door at what he knew must be Cambodia.

"Uh-huh," Medici said without emotion.

"Tom, you've got to realize that despite the excellent job you've done expanding Collection Team 5, administration of the network is now just too important to be handled out here in Ha Tien.

We need couriers to bring the reports directly to Saigon for analysis by the intelligence staff...."

"Especially the Cambodian Shop," Medici interjected, with a bitter half smile.

"Well, yes, I'll be the first to review the raw reports because of my contextual knowledge of the Cambodian situation, then pass on the *reliable* stuff to the staff and the joint command."

Reliable! Medici fumed. This fat little wimp had more temerity than he believed possible. He probably had already arranged at the staff Medici's relief from Ha Tien in order to speak in such certain terms. Medici was as hurt as he was angry. He had spent nine months risking his ass to get the Navy the best Cambodian intelligence. And now that the hard work was done, the staff pukes found it perfectly fine to cut his collection apparatus from under him at this turkey's urging.

Medici traced the cool steel of the Browning's hammer with his finger, then ran it along the washboard texture of the scored walnut grip. I should just shoot the fat little fucker right here, right through his tits, he thought. No, I'll get him out somewhere, then do it, so I can dispose of....

KAHWHUMP! The sound of the first round's impact reached his ears as he watched the second explode behind the Jeeps in the parking area. The canvas canopy blew off the major's Jeep. Shrapnel pitted the front wall of the team house and shards ripped through the screen door and plinked against the back wall of the team room.

"Hit the deck!" Medici yelled. Kenck was already on the floor, crawling butt-up into the corner between two plaster walls. He started to crawl to the hall, probably to get his flak jacket, but Medici flattened him and yelled, "Stay put." The third round KAHWHUMPED at the far door near Kenck's room and sprayed shrapnel into it and down the hall. Medici could smell burning palm thatch ignited by the red-hot shrapnel, even over the smell that came from Kenck's soiled pants.

The fourth and fifth rounds landed at the bottom of the hill in front of the small cemetery in which Em Chou was buried, among the four hooches occupied by Vietnamese who ran a bar for the river rats. They heard a woman wail from a hooch after the last round exploded.

The major and four enlisted men gathered in the team room, each alert, each carrying an M-16.

"Did anyone see where they came from, Major?" Medici asked.

"No. It was a quick hit-and-run, probably from the 'V' or right in town. Only five rounds, so they've already broken down the mortar tube and hidden. Did you see my damn Jeep?" he said in a high-pitched voice. He picked up the field phone to inform the District Chief.

Outside they watched familiar militiamen run to positions around the team house and downhill.

"They're our guys. Dai-Uy Hung's afraid there'll be a follow-up ground assault by sappers. These attacks are usually coordinated. He's going to perimeter the hill," the major said.

Kenck tried discreetly to examine his crotch and pant leg. He looked at Medici, found him watching, and ran down the hall to his room. In a flash he was back in clean pants, flak jacket, helmet and bandoleros, his CAR-15 locked and loaded.

"Stand easy, Lieutenant," Medici said. He pulled the clip and ejected the round from Kenck's rifle, then handed it back. Crestfallen, Kenck sat on the floor in the corner between the two plaster walls and lit a cigarette which shook in his hand. For the next three hours he stayed in the corner and chain-smoked in full combat dress.

61

Coup de Grace

For the turnover of Collection Team 5 to Kenck, Medici arranged a late afternoon meeting with his net handler Trung at the new Vietnamese Navy base. The base nested on the up-river end of Ha Tien Bay, close to the mangrove swamp that spread across the border into Cambodia. The base accepted day traffic of Vietnamese delivering food and providing services, so Trung, a vegetable and fruit merchant, would not blow his cover meeting them.

Medici and Kenck dropped from the patio wall onto the dirt path that led downhill. Medici watched Kenck gloating, waiting for the moment when he would break the Seafloat news. But a huge snake appeared in front of them and Kenck startled. Then in one smooth motion he brought the CAR-15 to his hip, released the safety and fired.

The cobra's caped head fell and rolled in the dust, cleanly severed from its body by the lucky shot. The body remained upright for a few seconds, swayed and fell across the path with a thump.

"You killed the cobra!"

"Yeah." Kenck smiled. "With one shot." He beamed at the new rifle.

"You bastard. You didn't have to kill him," Medici said.

Kenck squatted to pick up the head. "Maybe I can get this stuffed in Saigon...."

"Leave it there," Medici ordered. "Let's go," he said and pointed to the patrol boat waiting at the foot of the hill.

The PBR at the bottom of the hill loaded a pallet of parts delivered earlier by helo. Medici arranged with the coxswain to travel the two miles to the base on the boat to show Kenck the bay, town, and border.

As they got under way, Kenck sweated profusely. He had not removed the flak jacket, helmet, and bandeleros since the mortar attack on Phao Dai, plainly taking no chances. Medici, still in his shorts and thongs, fidgeted with the Browning tucked into his waistband.

Kenck popped open a Tab soda and sipped while Medici pointed out landmarks. He was not listening. He had more to tell Medici. He had saved the best for last.

"You know, Tom, with Collection Team 5 run from Saigon, we don't need your extraordinary talents in Ha Tien anymore." He interrupted Medici's description of Ha Tien's three-headed palm reported in *Ripley's Believe It or Not.*

Medici stopped and looked at Kenck. His eyes narrowed and bile boiled within him. Here it comes, he thought.

"You are without peer in our field organization. You shaped up this ramshackle network and brought us fresh, new, purely Navy Intelligence. Not many NILOs have that feather in their caps." Kenck cleared his throat. "But we need you to help us out in another area where our boys really need good intelligence, albeit tactical rather than strategic or political." He sipped some more soda.

"Captain Ross and I have agreed you should go down to Seafloat to help out the boat drivers. They never know where they'll get hit from next. You can find out, tell them, and reduce their casualties immensely. We'll transfer one of the other coastal NILOs up here to take care of liaison duties. The real work is done, though." He looked away from Medici, out over the river toward the mangroves near the base. The coxswain turned to approach the shallow water ramp at the base to unload his cargo.

"You son of a bitch!" Medici exploded. He reached over the crate and jerked Kenck off the gunwale by the bandolero. As he pulled Kenck toward him, his stomach muscles tightened and the waist of the shorts loosened. The Browning slid down the baggy leg, hit hard barrel-first on his left foot, and clattered to the deck.

Medici yelped, let go of the astonished Kenck, and bent to rub his foot, sputtering mad.

Kenck wasn't watching. He was mesmerized by a snaking rope of smoke that came out of the mangroves and flew, in slow motion it seemed, directly at him. He backed away from the smoke trail. The gunwale blocked his movement.

NILO Ha Tien

The coxswain saw the B-40 rocket headed for his boat. He gunned the twin diesels, and the Jacuzzi drive shot a rooster tail into the air when he wheeled sharply to starboard to escape the rocket. He almost made it. The rocket passed over the armored cockpit canopy and detonated on the searchlight stanchion above it. The explosion wasn't lethal, since the focused charge sprayed most of shrapnel out over the water, but everyone had minor shrapnel wounds, and the concussion broke the coxswain's and gunners' eardrums. The PBR sped directly toward the mangroves with its machine guns stuttering. It made two firing passes, then stood off while Vietnamese junks and PBRs from the base came to assist with mortars.

Medici peeked over the gunwale to see what was going on. The acceleration had thrown him to the deck, as he bent to rub his injured foot. The explosion left his ears ringing, and he had a couple of small shrapnel burns on his scalp and back. He held the Browning, but he didn't shoot at the mangrove with it, knowing it was a useless weapon in a firefight.

As the gunfire subsided, he looked around the boat for Kenck. He wasn't behind the crate or forward.

He asked the engineman who could still hear, "Where's LT. Kenck?"

"I don't fuckin' know, NILO. Last I saw him he was over on the starboard gunwale when the fuckin' 40 came in." The engineman fired a burst into the mangrove for good measure.

Medici smiled when it dawned on him what the effect of the emergency turn had been on Kenck. He told the crew to keep an eye out for Kenck in the water.

They idled back to the base after 20 minutes. Kenck was nowhere to be found. The commander had ordered the base to general quarters when the rocket attack had begun only yards from his shiny new Navy base. No one at the base had noticed anyone from the PBR.

Medici reported to Saigon that a search of the area turned up nothing, and that Kenck was missing in action. But when the tide went out, the water level fell in the estuary and a sharp-eyed Vietnamese seaman spotted two glossy black Corfam shoes poking from the water in front of the base.

389

They fished out Kenck's body. He hadn't a shrapnel wound on him, but his head was covered with gray muck from the river. The heavy flak jacket and bandeleros had sunk him straight into the bottom slime like an anchor. He had drowned in eight feet of water, unable to free himself of the gear.

62

Rootbeer

Kenck's death delayed Medici's transfer to Seafloat. The staff was more concerned with a proper replacement in the Cambodian Shop and continuity for Collection Team 5 than dealing with the disagreeable task of filling the Seafloat post. Medici's transfer was certain but would take effect only when Kenck's replacement had settled in the Cambodian Shop and had become familiar with Collection Team 5's sources and methods. The impending transfer hung like the sword of Damocles over the remaining eight weeks of Medici's tour.

After his outburst at the DIOCC meeting, Medici decided not to attend any more, and he simply conveyed reports through the Vietnamese NILO or Tom Roque, the team intelligence officer. The truth was he didn't give a damn. Increasingly he spent his days withdrawn, reading on the patio at Ha Tien, drinking beer and fantasizing about a coast watch operation on the languid Cambodian Pirate Islands. Out there he could finally catch some of the clever coastal infiltrators who had eluded capture since the overland Sihanoukville connection had been severed.

Toward this mission he brought down the portable SSB radio stored in the attic of an outbuilding, rigged it, and prepared to spend three weeks camped on Spyglass Hill on Hon Doc, the largest Cambodian Pirate Island, eating reconnaissance provisions and watching coastal traffic with binoculars to discern infiltration patterns. It would be safe out there, blue water, white beaches, swaying palms. No hassles, no trips to hostile mainland Cambodia or Saigon, protected from dangerous staff bullshit.

Medici feared the possibility of being overrun at Phao Dai, since the Navy river boats had moved to the new Vietnamese base. Early in his tour, they had practiced evacuation drills. They consisted of running down the hill under covering fire for transportation to the waiting LST. Now the LST and river boats were gone. 'I'm from the government and I'm here to help you.' So much for organized evacuation.

He replanned his own escape. He hoped he could commandeer at gunpoint a convenient fishing junk at the tip of Phao Dai and order it south to Singapore. A sailor, he had calculated that in either a southwest or northeast monsoon he would have a smooth beam reach down to Singapore in a sloop-rigged boat. Navigation would not be a problem as long as he steered a course high enough to hit the Malay peninsula, then run down to Singapore at its tip. As a surer alternative, he investigated impounding for his own use a suitable fishing boat under the pretext of its owner's gun smuggling. Singapore was far away. Returning to Vietnam, if it hadn't completely fallen when Ha Tien was overrun, would take months.

He slept fitfully. He often awoke trembling in the night, his bedding soaked with sweat. Then the fever would break and he would return to a restless sleep on a soggy mattress. He had intensely visual sexual dreams during which he felt he might explode from the tension. He had not been troubled this way before at Ha Tien.

Drinking no longer relaxed him. He would drink with others on the hill but could not get drunk. At Chau Doc one evening, visiting NILO Niles, he drank two Scotches with no effect—until he tried to play volleyball and felt his eyes bulge and his stomach swell. He had to stop and sit down because of dizziness and fatigue. He returned to Ha Tien the next day and with the sun blazing into the bathroom, he passed bluish gray stool and brown urine. He stayed dizzy and listless and couldn't sleep through the night.

Finally he asked the major, who acted as the team medical advisor, what might be wrong. The major had a hunch, but told Medici to call Jane, the Navy nurse at province medical team in Rach Gia, to describe the symptoms.

Medici felt nervous. Despite the risks he had taken with his life, an unknown medical problem unnerved him. He remembered his college roommate's father who was CIA chief of I Corps. Normally a robust man, he returned to the States for their graduation, a gaunt shadow of himself. He'd lost 20 pounds in six months, not unusual for Americans in Vietnam, he said. Medici stepped on the scale and found he was down to 128, about 25 pounds light. No wonder he couldn't sleep on his stomach anymore. The tips of his pelvis poked like Ping-Pong balls beneath his skin.

He rang up Jane on the field phone. A career Navy nurse, Jane had stayed at Ha Tien a few times. She was one of the guys.

"Hi, Jane," he shouted into the crackly field phone. "I think I need a medical consult."

"What is it, Tom? Too much Cambodian food?" She laughed.

"No. My—ah—stool is bluish gray. I'm not sleeping well at all, sweats and all that, and I'm dizzy and tired and listless…."

"Does your urine look like root beer?" she interrupted.

"Affirmative."

"I think it's hepatitis, Tom. Get on the next Medevac flight down here so we can do a blood test. It's the only way to tell for sure."

"Medevac! I'm not wounded. Can't I wait for the swing?"

"Negative! Get down here today. I'll call the Walrus and have him arrange a Medevac helo. Stay right there at Phao Dai and watch the helo pad for a red cross. See ya." She hung up.

Medici told the major. Jane had confirmed his suspicion.

"We probably should isolate you and your stuff. It's pretty contagious," he said. Medici nodded, the stuffing knocked out of him now that his illness had been diagnosed.

He went to his room and listlessly pulled on a jungle fatigue uniform. He didn't think he would bring the Browning, wouldn't need it for a blood test. Instead, from all his gear, without knowing why, he selected his dopp kit, the jade ring he had bought for his wife, and a new pair of thin prismatic binoculars he bought from the exchange mail-order catalogue. He sat and read quietly while waiting for the helo, finishing Eric Goldman's book *The Tragedy of Lyndon Johnson*.

63

Medevac

"Ha Tien, this is Red Rose Reprove, Dustoff chopper headed south across the dotted line with boocoo ARVN wounded. Understand you have a Medevac for us, over."

The radio operator answered, "That's affirmative Red Rose. One routine U.S. Medevac to province hospital at Rach Gia. Standing by."

"Roger, Ha Tien. We're inbound on vector 225 to your pad. See you there. Red Rose out."

Medici wanted to walk down the hill, but the major insisted on driving him. Medici didn't have the energy to resist. He thought it was funny how he lived with his symptoms before, but as soon as they were confirmed he felt really awful.

The Huey Lima with the big red cross came in fast and touched down quick, the pilots clearly pros. The major led Medici by the arm to the door that a medic swung open. Medici looked in. The cabin was jammed with moaning Vietnamese soldiers bleeding wetly into battle dressings. The scene was a panorama of protruding broken bones and yellow-white gristle. The smell was unique, partly exotic like nuoc mam, partly disgusting like urine and feces. The eyes of the seriously wounded men looked through him.

"I'm not going on this chopper. These guys are badly wounded," Medici shouted to the major over the helo's noise. He started to back away from the helo. The major held his arm.

"You're a Medevac, Tom. I can't let you stay. Standing orders on Dustoffs are to get them out as soon as possible. I could be court martialed," the major said.

Medici had never thought of the seriousness of being an official casualty. He had seen Medevacs a dozen times, but never thought about the technical consequences. He guessed the major was right. He nodded to him and climbed aboard, with a small wave. The medic forced a Vietnamese with a gaping leg wound, broken arm, and glazed eyes to slide over painfully on the canvas seat to make room for Medici. Medici reddened and perspired. He felt stupid sitting there without a visible wound, his AWOL bag between his legs as if he were going on holiday, human misery all around him.

No one spoke on the flight to Rach Gia. He had never sat quiet so long in a helo. All the while the Vietnamese moaned and oozed and bled. Pools of red and yellow human fluids slid across the diamond plate aluminum floor. Medici thought he might vomit, but held it back. He had never felt so depressed and sad in-country.

He tried to jump out when they landed at Rach Gia, but the medic ordered him out of the way so they could take the mortally wounded to the waiting ambulance. Medici felt diminished and trivial, a pawn in the technical endgame called Medevac.

In hospital they set him aside to treat the badly wounded first. When the doctors finished and sent the worst ones to surgery, they called to Medici where he read in a corner of the emergency room. Medici explained nurse Jane's diagnosis and said he needed a blood test. A doctor drew Medici's blood, then took a smear from his finger, explaining that hepatitis often masked symptoms of concurrent malaria. Great, Medici thought.

In 10 minutes they returned and told him he tested positive for infectious hepatitis, negative for malaria. They took him to a changing room, took his jungle fatigues, Cambodian beret and olive underwear and gave him ill-fitting blue hospital pajamas with ineradicable bloodstains on the chest. Medici filled with disgust. They assigned him a bed and told him to get in it and rest. He told them they didn't understand. He was NILO Ha Tien and had only come in for the test. He had to get back to Ha Tien to wind things up before he could rest. The doctor laughed.

"Son, you're as contagious as the clap right now. We can't send you back to Ha Tien. We'd be risking infection of your teammates. Lie back and enjoy it," the doctor said. "You're on your way home."

HL Serra

Printed in the United States
154590LV00002B/1/P